MYSTICISM AND DISSENT

MYSTICISM AND DISSENT

Socioreligious Thought in Qajar Iran

MANGOL BAYAT

Syracuse University Press 1982

Library of Congress Cataloging in Publication Data

Bayat, Mangol.
    Mysticism and dissent.

    Bibliography: p.
    Includes index.
    1. Shiites—Iran—History.   2. Islam and
politics—Iran. 3. Iran—Religion. 4. Iran—
History—Qajar dynasty, 1779–1925. I. Title.
BP192.7.I68B39   297′.1977′0955   82-5498
ISBN 0-8156-2260-0   AACR2

I dedicate this book to the memory of GUSTAVE E. VON GRUNEBAUM as a modest token of my deeply felt gratitude for his kind help, his encouragement, and the genuine interest he had in my studies. A number of us who were his students at the Near Eastern Center, UCLA, which he founded and directed until his untimely death in 1972, remember him as a highly inspiring teacher, critical yet open to criticism, imbued with humanist ideals which entailed a profound appreciation for Islam and Islamic civilization. His students, colleagues, and visiting fellow-scholars enjoyed the intellectually stimulating cosmopolitan ambiance he created at the Center where cultural differences enhanced rather than stifled free exchange of ideas and scholarly enquiry. My work bears the mark of the intellectual stimulus I received from him, even though my argument and conclusion might disagree with some of his general views of Islam and Islamic history. But there lies the greatness of his legacy: he inspired, he guided, and he opened up new perspectives which he himself did not explore but encouraged others to do.

MANGOL BAYAT received the Ph.D. in history from UCLA. She is a contributor to *Women in the Muslim World, Islam and Development,* and *Towards a Modern Iran.* Bayat taught at the University of Shiraz, Iran, and Harvard University.

Contents

Acknowledgments

Writing a book is a painful experience, indeed. It is a lonely, strenuous affair, breeding tension and anguish, if not despair. A few individuals greatly helped me with their moral and intellectual support. I am grateful to my husband, Thomas Philipp, for his love and shared professional interests. I wish to thank Ervand Abrahamian, Gene Garthwaite, Nikki Keddie, and Roy Mottahedeh for their friendship and scholarly help. I am indebted to Michele DeAngelis for her careful reading of chapter one and suggestions for improvement. I wish to express my appreciation for the valuable editing of Ms. Elizabeth Johns. Needless to say, I take full responsibility for any shortcomings.

Cambridge, Massachusetts   MB
Spring 1982

Introduction

THE 1978 REVOLUTION has pointed out one of the most fundamental weaknesses of Iranian political life in modern times—namely, the absence of a secular, nationalist ideology strong enough to sustain a war on two fronts: both against the absolutist regime of the Pahlavis, and against the predominant clerical presence in politics. Secular revolutionaries who participated in the major events of 1978–79 that led to the establishment of the Islamic Republic were unable to ride the tide of religious populism and were eventually engulfed by it. Both the weakness of the secular opposition and the contrasting strength of the religious leadership find their root in the tradition of Iranian socioreligious thought. To understand the current political and intellectual crisis in Iran, therefore, one has to study the tradition of dissent in Iranian history and its consequences at the turn of the century, when the reigning monarch of the ruling Qajar dynasty (1785–1925) was forced to grant a constitution to the nation.

If we were to study the concept of the Imamate in Shia Islam from a historical perspective, setting aside the all-important spiritual and theological significance that its believers later came to attach to it, we could define it as a necessary consequence or product of, rather than a cause for, social discontent and political dissent. The Shia, a political opposition group which came into being after the Prophet Muhammad's death in support of the claim to succession of Ali, his cousin and son-in-law, soon expanded its appeal to include several other groups of dissidents resisting the newly formed Islamic state. After 661 when, following the assassination of Ali, the Umayyad dynasty founded its rule, several protest movements were organized under the Shia banner. These movements were essentially politically oriented, aimed at achieving their respective leaders' political goals. Nevertheless, the messianic belief in a divinely appointed leader who would rise in defense of the oppressed against the oppressive rule of the "usurper," became a distinguishable feature of these movements. Increasing social discontent and political unrest reinforced the messianic impulse among certain segments of the Muslim community. The quest for a just social order and the aspiration for a world free from oppression transformed the political opposition into a sectarian religious movement, with serious doctrinal implications concerning the nature and function of the rightful leader referred to as the Imam.

By the mid-eighth century, a small but intellectually prominent group, later known as the Imami or Twelver Shia sect of Islam (which recognizes twelve Imams and to which the majority of the Iranians adhere), gave up armed struggle and declared the Imam's political function indefinitely postponed. The Imamate was then defined as the exclusive authoritative source of knowledge of the divine, the guide to the right path to God. The doctrine of the Occultation of the Iman (pronounced alive, ever present in this world, yet hidden from human view), promulgated in 873–74, further depoliticized the sect.

The current prominent role of the Shia clerical leaders in Iranian politics is all too often taken to be a traditional, doctrinally based, legitimate function. However, a careful reading of Shia and Iranian historical annals clearly shows that:

1. Contrary to commonly held views, Shia political dissent—that is, religious opposition to temporal power—was by far less important in the pre-twentieth century history of Iran than social and intellectual dissent. Western scholars of Shia political theories have often stressed the "illegitimacy" of all governments in times of Occultation and the political "vacuum" created as a result. In fact, there was no sudden vacuum, as the Imams while alive reportedly had renounced, albeit temporarily, political rule and had not required allegiance from their followers. Moreover, the doctrine of the Occultation allowed Shia thinkers to elaborate and systematize their dogma, divorced from any claim to political rule. Until the early sixteenth century, the Imami Shia sect existed primarily as an important progressive school of Islamic theology. Its official leaders, instead of transferring their allegiance to a political cause directed against the political establishment, coexisted peacefully and sometimes collaborated with the ruling government. Even when, in 1501, a newly founded dynasty, the Safavid, established the sect as the official state religion, high ranking religious leaders upheld the de facto depoliticization of Imami Shia sect. It was only toward the end of the nineteenth century that modern social forces and

concepts reactivated doctrinal considerations among certain, by no means all, circles of religious leaders, and transformed the official Shia stand from acquiescence to political activism.

2. Concern with dissident challenges from within the ranks of the religious institution, rather than a desire to check temporal author-- ity, is what lay behind the centralization of clerical power in the eighteenth century.

Until the turn of the present century, intellectuals in Iran, as in the Muslim world generally, were members of a class of clerics who wore the turban as a distinct sign of their learned status. Islam enforces the belief in the Koran, the divinely revealed book, as the source of all knowledge humans need to know. The learned members of society, *ulama*, were by definition men schooled in religious sciences. Theology, jurisprudence, philosophy, mysticism, Arabic language and grammar, and astronomy, among other disciplines, were all considered components of *ilm*, "knowledge of the divine." In fact, in Islamic centers of learning no attempt was made to distinguish sacred from profane knowledge.

Throughout the centuries, scientists, philosophers, mystics, and even speculative theologians rebelled against such a narrow definition of knowledge. They allowed themselves freedom from commonly enforced views, often through the application of various devices and means of Koranic interpretations. Here, then, the doctrine of the Imamate provided Shia thinkers in pre-Occultation times with a doctrinal basis for their divergence from majoritarian, or Sunni, views. For, implicit in the conception of the Imam as the infallible teacher whose primary task is to further perfect human knowledge of the divine as revealed in the Koran, is a belief in a progressive understanding of religion. Tension, however, arose as a result of the incompatibility of some views with aspects of the faith. It intensified in Iran in the sixteenth through the nineteenth centuries as a group of high ranking ulama, the *mujtahids*, who specialized in teaching and implementing the law, ruthlessly waged war against religious deviation. More inclined towards a legalistic approach to religion, seeking to dominate the intellectual scene in Iran, the mujtahids imposed strict adherence to religious law, of which they declared themselves the sole guardians. To do so more effectively, they came to restrict the speculative thought which had characterized the early formation of Shia Islam, claiming that in times of Occultation the further perfecting of Koranic revelation must be postponed till the return of the Imam.

3. Iranian thought was confined to religious modes of expression. Intellectual dissent thus took up the form of opposition to official

Shia views. Speculative thinkers developed the special discipline of theosophy, or philosophical theology, which blended philosophical, mystical, and Imami sectarian ideas. They were able to offer alternatives to the official religion. Despite the tensions that traditionally existed as a result of conflicting views, Shia centers of learning included most groups of thinkers: Sufi mystics, theosophers, speculative theologians. All were members in their own right of the broadly defined class of ulama. All equally contributed to the development of what is collectively known as Shia Islam, and which, in fact, embodies a variety of schools of thought. For, paradoxically, a certain measure of freedom was gained through the outward profession of orthodoxy. It is only when the authority of the mujtahids was directly challenged that persecution of thought occurred. More often than not, clerical politics rather than doctrinal disputes lay behind the civil strife that marred the social history of Iran in the past centuries. At stake was the ultimate issue of who was to assume the position of religious leadership.

Existing scholarship on the history of nineteenth century Iran generally has overstressed the political role of the ulama, deemed the leaders of the nation, in confronting the state. In the present study I argue that, for the greater part of the century, Shia religious policies were not national policies. Moreover, prominent clerics maintained harmonious relations with the then-ruling dynasty, the Qajar, which had not yet challenged clerical authority. Opposition to the power of high-ranking ulama came from within the ranks of the religious institution itself.

Nineteenth-century Iran witnessed the advent of a new era of religious renewal and political rethinking. Attempts were made to reformulate aspects of the Shia dogma and to question existing patterns of leadership, both religious and temporal. The Shaikhi school of theology founded by Ahmad Ahsai, its Kirman branch, the Babi religious revolt—all are important expressions of religious dissent within Shia Islam. Yet little is known about them, be it in the West or in Iran. While scholars of so-called Shia political theories tend to rely heavily on sources written by representatives of official ulama, scholars of Shia gnosis emphasize mystical and philosophical aspects, overlooking some very important social implications inherent in some of the trends. Thus, while the role of the ulama in Qajar Iran is studied almost exclusively in terms of the dynamics between the state and religion, proponents of Shia gnosis are viewed as essentially inward, concerned not so much with the necessity to reject temporal power as with the need to emphasize its unimportance. In the following chapters, I shall attempt to rectify such misconceptions and prove that (1) Shia thought is by far more complex and innovative than that offered by the ulama studied so far; and (2) Safavid and later theosophy laid the basis for nineteenth and early twentieth century socioreligious thought.

Naturally, there is an element of risk involved in such a historical approach to the study of Shia theosophy. More often than not, the theosophers indulged in an obscurantist style of writing, jealous as they were to safeguard their esoteric knowledge to the "chosen few," as well as to protect themselves from possible *takfir*, "declaring someone heretical," by orthodox ulama. *Taqiyya*, the time-honored practice of cautiously concealing one's true views from the public, was considered by the theosophers as the highest, most necessary virtue. Moreover, the social historian, eager to demonstrate that *métahistoire* was not necessarily the theosophers' sole concern, and that their metaphysics could carry, albeit implicitly, messages about this world, may fail duly to appreciate the essential spiritual quality of Shia theosophy, and reduce its spirituality to ideology. Indeed, the late Henry Corbin, the eminent French scholar of Islamic philosophy, repeatedly warned against the socialization of the spiritual, and against the predominance of social consciousness over theology. His numerous studies of Shia gnosis stressed the independence of divine truth from any determined social system. Yet, intellectual historians cannot fail to note the curious genealogy of ideas, in which a concept intended for one purpose may unwittingly serve quite another. The history of Iranian Shia ideas is no exception.

I propose to demonstrate that, contrary to the commonly held view, the new type of lay, modernist intellectuals that came into being in the second half of the nineteenth century, despite their adoption of Western concepts and political programs, were, in fact, carrying on the tradition of dissent in Shia Iran. The alienation lay intellectuals felt was from the traditional order dominated by the mujtahids, more than from the political power of an encroaching West and a despotic ruler. They assumed the avant-garde position of social critics. They found allies from among clerical dissidents, whom they converted to their secular cause. Using a rhetoric reminiscent of the theosophers', they expressed their concern with the need to see religion adapt itself to the reality of new social and cultural conditions. They wished to use Islam as a vehicle for change, and thus painstakingly attempted to accommodate foreign concepts to the traditional system. I shall then argue that the lay dissidents' ideas — constitutionalism, sovereignty of the people, liberal democracy, secularism—were more explosive than the

theosophers', since the social order that the official religion had dominated for so long was vitally threatened. Furthermore, unlike the
theosophers, lay intellectuals were waging a struggle on two fronts:
religious and political. For a nascent national consciousness led them
to combat the power of the Qajars, whom they accused of selling out
the nation to Western imperialist concerns. In their efforts to check the
shah's despotism, ironically, they were forced to seek the alliance of
some prominent religious leaders. In order to gain the latters' support,
they softened the bluntness of their secular, nationalist goals and spoke
the language of Islam, while pushing for adoption of a basically Western model of government.

Finally, I contend that, despite the vital role played by some high
ranking ulama in the Constitutional Revolution of 1906, the movement
marked the ascendency of the dissidents, both lay and clerical, who
then transformed their call for religious reforms into demands for the
secularization of important social institutions controlled by the ulama.
The secularization of the system of education was perhaps the most
lasting contribution of the Constitutionalists. As a result, the secularization of social thought in Iran effectively took place. Religious enforcement of certain types of intellectual taboos ceased, and modern
lay groups of lawyers, teachers, writers, and scientists came into being.
On the other hand, the "turbaned" class of ulama emerged as a distinct
class of theologians and religious guides, specialists in Islamic law and
the Traditions.

Nevertheless, as I point out, the essential tension that traditionally existed within Shia Islam remained unresolved. The spread of the
new learning and the establishment of modern social institutions were
not accompanied by doctrinal reforms. Paradoxically, modern social
forces and Western concepts achieved for official Shia Islam what the
traditional leadership had continually frowned upon, that is, direct
participation in temporal affairs. For the Constitution of 1906 granted a
council of five mujtahids the right to supervise all legislation. The role
of the ulama in Iranian politics in the early twentieth century, to a great
extent initiated and encouraged by the modernists themselves and
their natural clerical allies (the religious dissidents who then secularized their dissent and closely identified with the former group),
laid the basis for future conflicts between state and religion, a conflict
that had no real historical precedence.

The main theme of my work is dissent in Iranian thought. Thus,
in my analysis of some aspects of Shia theosophy, I focus on certain
ideas or general viewpoints which continually recur in the period I deal

with, and which I find important for the understanding of mid-nineteenth-century secularist thought. I indicate through these separate studies of Shia theosophy, Shaikhism, Babism, and secular nationalism, the progressive evolutionary transformation into sociopolitical concepts of some mystical and metaphysical ideas, reflecting their proponents' opposition to official Shia views. In the concluding chapter, I illustrate how religious dissent contributed to a major political event, the Revolution of 1906, considered by historians as a watershed in the history of modern Iran. This in no way means that I give priority to "unorthodox" over "orthodox" views, or that I choose to champion any particular religious cause or school over another. I merely intend to sort out and elucidate some ideas which lay behind some major events that shaped the history of Qajar Iran, and left their mark up to the present, as the recent Islamic Revolution has shown. In the epilogue I briefly explain how, deprived of a secular political forum independent from the state, and incapable of sustaining their ideological battle against the Pahlavis' absolute power without the support of the religious institution, lay Islamic ideologists of the 1970s had to repeat the 1906 experience. The alliance this time has proven to be much more costly.

MYSTICISM AND DISSENT

I

Shia and the Tradition of Dissent in Islamic Thought

I SLAM IS a monotheistic religion which recognizes no separation of
religious and temporal affairs. This statement, simplistic and com-
monplace as it may sound, underlines one of the most fundamental
problems that Muslims have had to confront in the course of their
social, political, and cultural development. It points to the dilemma
Muslim thinkers through the ages constantly faced. It explains the
tension, inconsistencies, and paradoxes that are inherent in some
aspects of Islamic thought, primarily due to the awkward and painstak-
ing attempt often made to reconcile basically incompatible views of
Islam. Above all, it provides an important clue to understanding the
differences of opinion over dogma which lay behind the founding of
the major sects and schools of speculative thought.

As the Prophet Muhammad, in the first half of the seventh
century, revealed the Koran and proclaimed Islam as the last and most
perfect of all divine revelations, superseding and hence abrogating all
preceding religions, and as he succeeded in establishing in his own
lifetime a religious community of which he was both the Prophet-
legislator and executor, the fusion of political and religious leadership
was irrevocably accomplished. The Koran, the eternal word of God
sent to instruct humanity, was declared to be the source of all knowledge, and its rulings, as taught and implemented by the Prophet,
encompassed all aspects of the life of the individual believer. To be a
Muslim meant to believe in the unity of God and in the prophethood of
Muhammad, and to abide by the latter's religious, moral, legal, and
political commands. As the infallible representative of God, he could
be neither questioned nor challenged.

1

Thus future Muslim states were provided with a theocratic model which was difficult to maintain, given the differences between their own sociopolitical and geographic conditions and those of the first religious community. The Koran does not provide any specific method of solving questions that Muhammad did not put to himself or that did not exist in his time. Furthermore, he left his own community with an immediate, formidable problem to solve, namely, that of succession, which had far-reaching repercussions on both the religious and sociopolitical development of the Islamic societies. For sociopolitical conflicts necessarily became religious conflicts, over not only the qualifications, attributes, and functions of the leader, but also over the dogma, the nature of faith and of *ilm*, "knowledge of the divine." Sects came into being, expressing clear social protest combined with new views of religion and religious issues.

The religio-ideological source, Islam, to which the sects appealed and to which they sought to remain faithful, is only one of the factors that determined the form they assumed and their patterns of thought and action. Social forces and the influx of foreign ideas from the conquered lands—Judeo-Christian, Hellenic and ancient Iranian—shaped the movements and influenced the formulation of their doctrines. All Muslim sects underwent unavoidable changes. However, all were entitled to invoke the name of the Prophet, except for the extreme cases with which the present chapter is not concerned. For, despite the fact that social forces and imported ideas were stronger than original Islam in shaping the course of development of the various sects, the prophetic ideal, as defined in the Koran and in the Traditions, (the records of Mohammad's deeds and sayings) constituted the main motif of the various sects and schools of Islamic thought.

THE POLITICAL DEVELOPMENT OF EARLY SHIA ISLAM

When the Prophet Muhammad died in A.D. 632, Abu Bakr, one of his closest and oldest companions was elected by the rest as Vicar of the Messenger of God, or Caliph, a choice which was accepted by the majority of Muslims and which seemed to rule out the concept of the hereditary right of succession. A small group, however, chose to rally around the person of Ali ibn Abu Talib, the Prophet's cousin and son-in-law, and support his claim to leadership of the community based on hereditary right. But Ali did not assume office until after the death of the third Caliph, Uthman, in 656, and even then his authority was seriously challenged by a powerful political opponent, Muawiya. The latter eventually succeeded in establishing his own dynasty, the Umayyad, after Ali was murdered in 661.

Almost a century of Umayyad rule, centered in Damascus, Syria, witnessed the consolidation of the Arab Muslim Empire which, by the middle of the seventh century, came to include territories formerly under Byzantine and Sassanian imperial rule. Arab hegemony over recent converts in the conquered lands was enforced. The growing discontent of the non-Arab Muslims, in addition to existing social and political tensions among Arab elements themselves, further encouraged sectarian disputes and rebellions.

The Shia movement, as the party of Ali came to be known, thus survived his death, rapidly expanding its appeal to include other groups of dissidents. Though Ali's older son Hasan soon retired from politics, his second son Husain, as well as other members of the Prophet's family, kept up the spirit of revolt against the political predominance of the Sunnis, the Muslim majority who abided by the Caliph's rule. These movements, carrying the Shia banner, were essentially politically oriented, aiming at achieving their respective leaders' political goal. Nevertheless, they soon acquired a religious undertone as the messianic concept of a divinely appointed leader, who would rise in defense of the right religion and of the oppressed against the oppressive rule of the usurper, found many adherents from among the discontented elements of the Muslim community. The quest for social justice, and the aspiration for a world free from oppression, brought about serious doctrinal differences with majoritarian Sunnis over the nature and function of the righteous leader, the Imam.

Husain's tragic death and the bloody massacre of his supporters at the hands of the Umayyad army in 680 at Kerbala did not put an end to the movement. On the contrary, it seemed to have radicalized the political dissent further by adding to it a new religious dimension. For the battle came to symbolize the necessary struggle between justice and tyranny, and the figure of Husain became the archetype of the martyr for the true faith. The persecuted Shia groups thus acquired from the start definite characteristic features—namely, the millennarian tradition (the belief that the evil world, so full of temptation and corruption, would come to an end one day and would be replaced by a better and purer world); the disposition to distinguish sharply between good and evil; a secretive mode of actions; and, finally, the charismatic appeal of the leader.

Who the actual leaders or Imams (as opposed to the Sunni title of Caliph) were during the Shia's turbulent history in the first two centuries of the Muslim era is still a debatable question. Not all Shia groups supported the claim of Ali's direct descendants through his wife, Fatima, the Prophet's daughter. Such movements periodically encountered military defeats. The Abbasids (ruling from 750 to 1258), who had carried the Shia banner while fighting the Umayyads, betrayed their supporters once in power. The majority of the Shia preferred active militant means to establish the reign of the just, asserting that the Imam had to proclaim publicly his leadership with the sword, waging holy war against the enemies of the true religion. However, Husain's son Zain al-Abidin (d. 714), his own son al-Baqir (d. 733), and the latter's son al-Sadiq (d. 765) avoided involvement in any political adventure.

Although Husain's descendants' policy of political acquiescence caused them to be overshadowed by rival claimants who kept up the original spirit of revolt, it ensured the survival of their respective claims in later times, for it was from within their moderate ranks that the leadership of what came to be known as Twelver or Imami Shia was to emerge. Jafar al-Sadiq, the important religious thinker who was to rank sixth in the Imami's line of succession, is generally credited with formulating the doctrine of the Imamate. His chief task was twofold: to save the basic ideal of Shia Islam and to purify it from extremist tendencies. Thus, he insisted that the Imam, who must be a descendant of the Prophet through Ali and Fatima, derives his authority not by political claims but by *nass* (designation by the preceding Imam) and through *ilm*, the "knowledge of the divine," he inherits from his predecessors once he is designated. Basing the claim on a Tradition attributed to the Prophet, "I am the city of knowledge and Ali is my gate," al-Sadiq defined the Imam as the exclusive authoritative source of knowledge in religious matters. Bearing in mind his family's past experiences, he differed sharply from both the extremist Shia and the Abbasids, who regarded the Imamate and the Caliphate as inseparable. Hence, he divorced religious authority from political rule until such time when God would decide otherwise. The political function of the Imam, to wage holy war for the establishment of justice and equity on earth, was declared postponed to an indefinite future. He consequently requested his followers not to challenge the authority of the Abbasids directly, and strongly advised them to practice *taqiyya* (dissimulation of their true beliefs). "Fear for your religion," he allegedly said, "and protect it with *taqiyya*, for there is no faith when there is no *taqiyya*."[1]

After the death of al-Sadiq, the activists from among his follow-ers chose his son Ismail, who had predeceased him, as their Imam, maintaining Ismail had not died and would reappear as soon as the time was ripe for his return. Others recognized Ismail's son Muham-mad. The former group composed a separate sect known as the Is-mailiyya. Little is known about the history of the movement until the ninth century, when it appeared as a secret revolutionary organization, with intensive missionary works led by preachers throughout the Muslim world. In Iran proper there were Ismaili strongholds in Rayy, an ancient town near modern Tehran, Khorasan, Fars, Sijistan, and Kirman. They were also to be found in the Indian subcontinent, in Yemen, North Africa, and in Syria and Mesopotamia. Toward the end of the ninth century, an Ismaili state named Qarmat was established in Bahrain on the Persian Gulf. It included Yemen and Oman, and was connected with Ismaili branches in southwest Iran, Syria and Iraq. Muhammad ibn Ismail was acknowledged as the Imam, declared in Occultation, but about to reappear to rule the world.

Another branch, which acquired the name of Fatimiyya, after the Prophet's daughter and wife of the first Imam, Ali, set its headquarters in North Africa. Though the group was not recognized by Ismailis in Iraq, Bahrain, and West Iran, the Fatimids' militant activities led to the conquest of Egypt in 969. Cairo was then founded as the capital of the Fatimid Ismaili state, which for two centuries was to challenge the Baghdad-based Sunni state.

The majority of the followers of al-Sadiq, on the other hand, paid allegiance to his other son, Musa al-Kazim (d. 799). They preferred the moderate trend initiated by al-Sadiq, and further shifted the central emphasis of their views from politics to theology. What the adherents of Imami Shia Islam lost in secular power and importance was made up in the sphere of doctrinal discourse. Throughout the formative period of the sect's history, in the eighth and ninth centuries, it existed as a separate school of theology and jurisprudence, comparable to its Sunni counterpart, from which it distinguished itself solely through its insis-tence on the recognition of the Imam as the rightful leader of the community.

Successive generations of moderate leaders further depoliticized this branch of Shia Islam. The Caliphate was persistently regarded in Shia literature as symbolic of oppression and injustice. Nevertheless, the believers were continually reminded that the time was not ripe for the establishment of the reign of the just, and that they had to live under existing temporal authority. Furthermore, prominent individual Shia scholars and jurists, some of whom were affluent members of the mercantile class of Baghdad, politically accommodated themselves to the unrighteous government. Far from shunning the Abbasid court, these influential leaders of the Shia community cultivated their ties with its officials. A good number of them even held government-appointed offices and practiced Sunni jurisprudence.[2]

This accommodation was reinforced when, in 873–4, as a result of the confusion created by the death of the eleventh Imam Hasan al-Askari (he apparently had no surviving son), and in response to threatening factionalism and the demand for political activism on the part of impatient followers and rivals, the twelfth Imam was declared in Occultation (alive, ever present, yet hidden from view).

It is interesting to note here that in the first stage of Occultation, known as the Lesser Occultation, whereby the Hidden Imam reportedly communicated through his agents, the Shia community fell even more under the control of the moderate scholars who, if they were not themselves members of the prosperous mercantile class, enjoyed its full support. The special deputyship of these agents, later defined and institutionalized by theologians, was at the time an expedient means to prove to the skeptics the existence of the twelfth Imam in hiding.

However, the deputyship was not successively held by four, and only four, particular individuals, as reported in the later works. Just as the Imams in their own lifetime did not enjoy the full support of the majority of the Shia, the agents seem to have had difficulties establishing their authority over the community at large. Several individuals simultaneously lay claim to the office. Some even went so far as to proclaim themselves the Hidden Imam, thus attracting a large following from among the disenchanted Shia who rejected the doctrine of Occultation. Disputes over the office of the deputy threatened the very foundation of the Imami Shia sect.

Consequently, aware of the challenges from within and without the community, and unable successfully to explain the prolonged absence of the Imam, Imami theologians proclaimed the Greater Occultation. The Hidden Imam was no longer in communication with anyone. His function was transformed into that of the eschatological figure of the universal savior who would appear at the end of time.[3]

The religious Traditions of the Twelver or Imami Shia sect, as it developed in the tenth century, recognize after al-Sadiq and Musa five more Imams: Ali al-Riza (d. 818); Muhammad al-Taqi (d. 835); Ali al-Hadi (d. 868); Hasan al-Askari (d. 873); and Muhammad al-Mahdi (in Occultation since 874). This sect proved itself to be the most discreet in its opposition to the state. Historical records clearly show that during the lifetime of the twelve Imams, with the exception of the eighth Imam, Riza, "there was no organized party of followers and no underground revolutionary activities with the aim of making them Caliphs."[4]

Imami Shia Islam revealed itself to be the religion of the initiated, the chosen few selected to become part of the inner circle of the living Imam, whose identity was concealed from the rest of the faithful, the commoners. Whether this inclination to secrecy was a direct result of persecution on the part of the state, in addition to the existence of rival pretenders to the Imamate, or whether it was from the start an innate characteristic of the sect, the fact remains that the Shia, in contrast to the Sunnis, developed an elitist conception of leadership. The practice of *taqiyya*, which supposedly the sixth Imam, Jafar al-Sadiq, had counseled his followers to adopt as a measure of protection against the repressive policies of the Sunnis toward them, increased the aura of mystery and impenetrable secrecy with which medieval Shia Islam wrapped itself. *Taqiyya* also came to denote an attitude of absolute respect for esoteric doctrines which only the qualified spiritual elite had the right to hear, as well as an acceptance of the alien condition of the minority who follow the spiritual cult of the Imam.[5]

DISSENT IN CLASSICAL ISLAMIC THOUGHT

Dynastic rule over the vast, multinational Islamic empire, first under the Umayyads (661–750), then under the Abbasids (750–1258), brought about a de facto separation of state and religion. There came into being a specific type of learned people, the ulama, who took up these tasks: commenting the Koran and exposing its meaning to the less learned; systematically sifting and compiling the Traditions which record the sayings and practice of the Prophet, as transmitted through the authoritative chains that could, ideally, be linked to his person or to a close companion; and formulating and implementing Islamic law based on the Koran, the Traditions, and the Prophet's own practice. The related sciences of Arabic language and grammar, and the art of gathering data for biographies of the Prophet and his companions, were also a necessary part of the ulama's activities. They came to hold an almost exclusive right over religious, juridic and educational institutions.

Put on the defensive with the growing onslaught of polemic arguments on dogma and faith from non-Muslims, and some Muslim rationalists, and despite their own predominant conviction that divine revelation is in no need of proof, the ulama attempted to explain points of religious belief rationally. Thus, the discipline of discursive or dialectical theology rapidly developed, giving rise to several competing theological schools. In the ninth century, one such school, the Mutazila, was the most intellectually effective in providing Islamic theology with a comprehensive, rational system. Itself influenced by Hellenic philosophy, it argued that nothing in the Koran is repellent to reason. Its rational argument went so far as to deny the commonly held belief of the Muslims that the holy book was eternal and uncreated. The Koran, it stated, is God's wishes as expressed through the Prophet. Such an extremist view only succeeded in provoking a strong reaction on the part of other schools of dialectical theology, such as the Ashari, named after its founder, who condemned the tendency to intellectualize and rationalize basic principles of faith. It emphatically affirmed the Koran's coeternity with God, uncreated and with no beginning; opposed faith to reason; and explained irrational aspects in terms of God's absoluteness and omnipotence.

Theological controversies continued unabated. However, despite their adoption of philosophical language with apparent logical and rational arguments in defense of their own religious stand, the dialectical specialists identified more closely with the traditionalist ulama, and equally stressed the primacy of the law. Thus the ulama specialists in the Traditions and jurisprudence emerged as the guardians of the law, and the protectors of the community of the believers against religious deviation. Conservative, law-minded ulama were bound to be challenged as the Islamic cultural horizon broadened and as Muslim intellectuals came into contact with and absorbed different ideas and views. A desire for freedom from commonly accepted dogmas among certain groups and individuals rapidly gave rise to more radical positions challenging orthodoxy as defined by law-minded ulama, either directly or indirectly.

Since Muslim speculative thought of all types — philosophical, mystic and sectarian — encountered the severe censorship of religious orthodoxy, which persistently maintained an intolerant and antagonistic attitude, it was of utmost importance for its exponents to prove themselves true Muslims. Hence, the essential feature that characterized all forms of dissent, whether sectarian or merely intellectual, was the unanimous acceptance of the Muslim prophecy as the last and most perfect, Muhammad being the Seal of all Prophets, and the Koran encompassing all knowledge in its entirety.

Despite the fundamental differences that set apart the mystics, the philosophers, and the Shia sects (and, within each grouping, the wide variety of opinions that separated one school or sect from another), there were undeniably striking similarities in ideas and approaches which allow the historian to draw some basic, even though general, conclusions regarding the nature of non-orthodox religious thought in the medieval period. Central in the dissidents' argument was a criticism of the law-minded ulama's restriction of the religious sciences to jurisprudence, the Traditions, and related studies. They stressed the need for an intellectual and/or spiritual interpretation of the Koran.

"We belong to God, and we go back to God" (Koran, sura 2:151). Muslims view the Creation as the descent of the Divine Will to the level of created beings, and the return as the ascent of created beings towards the Divine Will. The Revealed Books are the means for this cognizance. Philosophers, mystics and the various sects have attempted to interpret this fundamental Muslim view of the relationship of human beings to God in their own respective ways. Medieval philosophers, themselves disciples of the Greek and Hellenic schools, aimed at constructing a world view where all experiences and all values are brought together, and where the particular is seen as part of the general and a composite of the whole. They conceived the universe as eternal and timeless, originating from an absolutely transcendent One, the First Cause, whose attributes cannot be known. They thus rejected the commonly held religious view of the world as finite, historically bound with a beginning and an end, created by a Supreme Being known through the Being's attributes. They described the descent and the ascent of humans as a rational process, "reversing in our consciousness the descent from unity to multiplicity by reascending intellectually from multiplicity to ultimate unity."[6] Hence, they regarded the philosophic search as the truest way to God, the moral rules and religious doctrines by which ordinary people abide being imperfect in comparison. Furthermore, medieval philosophers distinguished the rational sciences, based on native human intellectual activities, from the transmitted sciences, based on the Traditions of the Prophet. They also contrasted philosophy, which transcends human diversity, to the religious laws and related sciences which are particular to each religious community.

Muslim philosophers in general, though perfectly aware of the incompatibility of philosophical and religious views, outwardly justified their activity as an attempt to defend the faith. However, some of them, such as al-Farabi (d. 950) in one of his most representative works, asserted that philosophy is "prior to religion in time" and that "religion is an imitation of philosophy in the restricted sense inasmuch as both comprise the same subjects and both give an account of the ultimate principles of the beings, or insofar as religion supplies an imaginative account of, and employs persuasion about, things of which philosophy possesses direct and demonstrative knowledge."[7] The philosophers drew a sharp line between knowledge based on the external appearance *(zahir)* of things, as emotionally and imaginatively perceived by ordinary people, and knowledge of "hidden secrets" *(batin)* rationally understood and demonstrated by a small elite. Religious law was revealed for the sake of the masses as "the saviour of the community from degeneration," since religious beliefs mold "the soul so that men will perform the directives of the Law out of inner compulsion and established habit from which it is hard to deviate."[8] In this sense the Prophet is depicted as a lawgiver whose revelation is essential to the proper functioning of society.

The philosophers believed that society, in its most perfect form, should be ruled by themselves, for only they could achieve the most complete happiness possible for humanity. In this sense, the philosopher, as teacher of the non-philosophic multitude, functions as a prophet. Yet, given the sociopolitical reality of their time, they were also aware of the futility of any attempt at realizing the ideal state. The perfect community, as they rationally understood it, remained a community "in speech," a Platonic virtuous city. They accepted life in an imperfect community, alienated and alienating, intellectually challenging yet socially persecuted, not renouncing kingship of the community, only concealing it. According to Muhsin Mahdi, "instead of manifest kingship, the philosopher assumes the role of a secret king, whether anyone acknowledges him as such or not, obeys him or not."[9]

The Sufis (a term used to mean Muslim mystics generally, be they Shia or Sunni) interpreted the Koranic verse regarding the ascent of the being in purely mystical terms, and declared the return to God could only be achieved through a spiritual experience and through the unveiling of the inner, or hidden, meaning of the scriptures by qualified initiates. The initiate experiences "divine illumination, immediate vision and knowledge of things unseen and unknown, when the veil of sense is suddenly lifted and the conscious self passes away in the overwhelming glory of the One True Light,"[10] and thus feels one with God.

Ibn Arabi (1164–1240), the Andalusian-born Arab mystic who was the first Muslim thinker to have developed the monist concept of unity of existence, asserted that union with God is not an eventual reaching or meeting God, but rather becoming aware of a relationship that has always existed. He took up the term of "Perfect Man," which appears in Manichean, neo-Platonist and Jewish mystical texts, to refer to such a person who awakens to the realization of this essential unity. Since the Perfect Man sees or reflects all the Divine Perfections, Ibn Arabi explained, the most perfect knowledge is accessible to him through mystical revelation or inspiration. Such a direct vision of Reality, of Universal Truth, qualifies the Perfect Man to act as the mediator between God and humans. Ibn Arabi, in fact, stressed the notion that the Perfect Man "is to God as the eye-pupil is to the eyes... and through him God beholds his creatures."[11] He unites the One and the Many, so that the Universe depends on him for its continued existence. Ibn Arabi and most Sunni Sufis believed that Perfect Men constituted a class of their own which comprised not only the Prophets from Adam to Muhammad, but also "the superlatively elect amongst the Sufis." They were arranged in a graduated hierarchy, with the leader, referred to as the Pole, at their head forming "a saintly board of administration by which the invisible government of the world is carried."[12]

Another mystic thinker, al-Gili (1366–1407), originally from Gilan, the Iranian province south of the Caspian, went so far as to surmise that all people are created potentially perfect but few are actually so — the prophets and the initiates. For Gili, the Prophet Muhammad is the absolutely Perfect Man, and in every age the Perfect Man is an outward manifestation of the essence of Muhammad, under a different guise or name.

The Sufis developed their own separate, highly centralized, hierarchically structured, and tightly knit organizations, headed by a spiritual leader who could show "the way to God." They conceived an esoteric world of hidden spiritual reality parallel to the external, visible world.

In similar fashion, the Shia asserted that the true function of scripture was to point to that "hidden" world, even while keeping it disguised in symbols, and they claimed that the ascent of humanity corresponds to the gradual "unveiling" of the Koranic inner truth. Like the Sufis, they believed that only qualified individuals could interpret the texts, but insisted that divine knowledge is directly transmitted through the Prophet's family lineage basing their claim on a Shia Tradition which attributed to Muhammad the saying, "I am the city of knowledge and Ali is its gate." They expanded the belief that God, after closing the prophetic cycle of revelations with Muhammad, initiated the opening of a new Imam cycle. Prophecy and the Imamate are, according to the Shia dogma, interdependent, inseparable, divinely ordained functions. Whereas the Sunnis believe that, after the Prophet, the Koran and the Prophet's recorded deeds and thoughts are God's proof, the Shia asserted that the Imam is God's proof. He is God's choice, infallible and sinless, the most perfect individual of his age. He has inherited the Prophet's cumulative knowledge and all his attributes, except divine inspiration without a mediator.[13] The Imam's function is said to lie in the spiritual interpretation and teaching of the Prophetic revelation.

The period from the mid-tenth to the mid-eleventh century was the Shia century par excellence. Enjoying the patronage of the Buyid family, who had seized de facto political power in Baghdad, Imami ulama such as Abu Sahl al-Naubakhti (d. 923), al-Kulaini (d. 940), al-Numani (d. 970–71), Ibn Babuya (d. 991–92), al-Mufid (d. 1022), al-Sharif al-Murtiza (d. 1044–45), and Shaikh al-Taifa Tusi (d. 1067), among others, systematically compiled Imami Traditions (the records of the Imams' deeds and sayings) which, in addition to the Prophet's Traditions, became standard sources for the creed. In pre-Safavid times, Imami Shia Islam thus existed primarily as an important school of Islamic theology with a distinct conception of religious leadership. The doctrine of Occultation allowed its exponents greater freedom further to elaborate and systematize the dogma, divorced from any individual claim to political rule. Like their Sunni counterparts, Imami theologians developed their own discipline of dialectical theology, which studied their doctrines from within a framework of a comprehensive rational system. More specifically influenced by the Mutazila school of Islamic thought (itself influenced by Hellenic thought), they were able to adopt rational arguments in defense of their doctrinal stands. Thus, they took up the Mutazila concept which states that God is just and wills what is most salutary and in the best interest of earthly creatures. Equally influenced by contemporary philosophical thought, Shia theologians accommodated the philosophers' (especially al-Farabi's) definition of an "imperfect community" one had to live in, in order to rationalize the indefinite postponement of the ideal rule on earth. They echoed the philosophers when proclaiming they were not renouncing the Imamate, only concealing it; for the Imam is Imam whether acknowledged as such or not, obeyed or not. Like other schools of Muslim speculative thought— philosophical, mystical and sectarian—which came into contact with and absorbed different ideas and views, Imami Shia challenged the intellectual supremacy of majoritarian Sunnism.

Hence, both the Sufis and the Shia relied on and further developed a method known as scriptural interpretation to provide themselves with religious legitimacy. Based on the belief that the holy texts possess both an exoteric *(zahir)* and esoteric *(batin)* meaning, the beginning of the method traces back to the Shia extremists of Iraq in the eighth century. The idea then emerged that, though the Prophet brought the Koran, it was the Imams who were charged with its interpretation. By the middle of the eighth century, the notion that in each generation there is a speaker to proclaim publicly the religious truth, and a silent interpreter to explain it to the adepts, grew in importance amongst Muslim speculative thinkers and socioreligious dissidents as a justification for the divergence of their opinions from the established norms.

The eduction of the esoteric from the exoteric text was an elitist practice enforcing: (1) the distinction between the mass of ordinary people and the select few; and (2) *taqiyya,* the absolute necessity to conceal the esoteric and protect it from the masses, lest it be misunderstood and put into evil use. As Hodgson puts it, scriptural interpretation was "symbolic or allegoristic in its method, sectarian in its aim, hierarchically imparted, and secret."[14] To ensure the safety of their secrets, Muslim speculative thinkers, including the philosophers, perfected the art of esoteric writing. This style was deliberately ambiguous and obscurantist, discussing traditional topics in what at first glance appears to be an orthodox fashion, offering proofs from the Koran and the Traditions, but with sudden unexpected breaks in the flow of ideas, when either a new subject is inserted or the old one is dealt with in an unorthodox way. Outward conformity was expertly used to camouflage the dissidents' radical parting from the theological norms.

It was the Ismailis who perfected the concept of esotericism and made it the central doctrine of their movement. Its exponents, influenced by the neo-Platonic ideal as much as the philosophers (with whom they shared an elitist view of knowledge as the privileged truth of the chosen few and inaccessible to the unworthy masses), developed a similar neo-Platonic cosmology where not only the Imams but also intellectuals like themselves played the role the philosopher alone had assumed. In fact, despite the crypto-Sufi-Shia tone permeating some of their writings, early Ismaili thought (as best displayed by the famous Brethren of Purity, as a group of tenth century active members of the sect came collectively to be known), is above all rational. Their aim was to offer to their adepts a compendium of all sciences known in their time, and of all human thought, be it divinely revealed or created. Like the philosophers, they conceived of an ideal city ruled by the learned and wise, where reason reigned supreme. Also like them, they distinguished the rational sciences from religion, reason from faith. However, since they chose to support the cause of a religious sect, they upheld the Koran as the source of all knowledge, its esoteric meaning having to be interpreted by the initiates. Similarly, writing at a time when Ismailism anticipated a total political victory, they were active in radical social protest and committed to the realization of the ideal society. Unlike the philosophers, they were prone to borrow and adapt the practical aspects of the Sufi organizations: the method of gradual initiation of the adepts to the various stages of knowledge; the hierarchical structure of the order; the secretive tone; and the absolute loyalty binding the members to one another and to their immediate superior officer.

All three major categories of Islamic speculative thought— philosophical, mystical, and sectarian — followed different paths, aimed at different goals, and essentially addressed themselves to different types of audiences. Nevertheless, they shared in common a mutually exclusive conception of themselves as the only true believers in possession of true knowledge, and they expressed a profound disillusion with the established orthodoxy. Moreover, implicit in their thought was the messianic expectation of the human leader, divinely or rationally guided, who would restore order and justice and establish the ideal rule of the Sage. However, whereas the philosophers, mystics, and Imami Shia generally remained aloof from social or political commitment of any kind, among the most radical Shia sects such an expectation prompted independent political activity against the existing regime, in the name of some claimant or another to the Imamate.

A possible consequence of the belief in knowledge as the exclusive property of the chosen ones, whose function is to complete the Prophetic mission, is the conviction that from their ranks would also come the ideal ruler, the deliverer from distress. Medieval Iranian history provides ample evidence of the threat heterodox movements brought to the sociocultural and even political establishment. The pre-Safavid period saw many "righteous" leaders carrying the banner of messianic Shia, and inciting the populace to revolt against the central authority.

The Nizari Ismaili movement of the eleventh century, known as the Order of the Assassins, is perhaps the most important case of such a politico-religious group which succeeded in establishing a state of its own. For a century and a half, Ismaili groups, clustered all over the Iranian highlands with their headquarters in the city-state of Alamut, lived as a society apart from the rest of the Muslims while continuously sending out their preachers to recruit new converts. Hierarchism and their secretive methods prepared disciplined cadres to support the politico-religious claims of their leaders. It is significant that, although the founder of the state, Hasan al-Sabbah (d. 1124), claimed to be only the representative of the Nizari Imam, later rulers went so far as to proclaim themselves to be the expected "Imam of the time" himself.

In 1164 Hasan II officially declared the advent of the Last Day, when all would be judged. Muslim law was declared no longer binding, for the inner secrets were revealed. As Hodgson put it, "It was the end of a religious era, and the beginning of a spiritual dispensation of moral, not physical, perfection.... The inner life of moral and mystical experience was the sole reality henceforth to be attended to."[15] Faithful Ismailis were pronounced spiritually perfect, enjoying eternal spiritual bliss, and their opponents denounced as spiritually lifeless. In its last phase of existence as a state, because of an internal decline and external political and military pressures, the Nizari officials once more declared their Imam concealed. After the fall of the state as a result of the Mongol invasion in the second half of the thirteenth century, the Ismaili sect turned inward, and managed to survive primarily as a kind of Sufi order.

TEMPORAL AUTHORITY IN IMAMI SHIA ISLAM

Scholars of so-called Shia political theories have continually emphasized the illegitimacy of all governments in times of Occultation, and the political vaccum created as a result. But in fact, no vacuum was created then, since the Imams while alive had given up, albeit temporarily, political rule, and had not required allegiance from their followers. The doctrine of Occultation further justified the postponement of the political function of the Imam. Shia scholars of the ninth century did not discuss in their writings the unrighteousness or righteousness of the government during the Occultation. Instead, they attempted to ward off criticism from militant extremists who were seeking direct political action to realize their ideal, from lukewarm Shias, as well as from non-Shia opponents who derided the whole concept of a leader who was absent yet present.[16] Shia theological works were written in vindication of their doctrines, especially that of the Imamate. Instead of transferring their allegiance to any political party or cause directed against an existing government, Imami Shia fully accepted their religious alienation in society. Their Imamate was the philosophers' "virtuous city." Moreover, while developing their own school of theology, Shia ulama continued to coexist peacefully, if not collaborate with, the Sunni state. Most of them practiced *taqiyya* to "encourage and even require Shias to accommodate themselves to the Sunni majorities" and to "minimize enmity that could originate from public statements about the Imamate doctrine that would be subjected to misunderstanding."[17] Thus, by divorcing religious affairs from government affairs, leading Shia ulama were in fact condoning the de facto secularization of politics. An Imami Shia political theory simply did not come into being in this period.

The fall of the Buyid state following the Seljuq conquest of Baghdad in 1055 did not bring about the defeat of Shia Islam. Though the anti-Shia policies of the Turkic state forced the temporary retreat of Shia ulama from the capital, and despite periodic anti-Shia riots, Shia centers flourished in Iraq, Iran, and elsewhere. They had their mosques, schools, and libraries. Eventually, prominent Shias assumed high ranking government posts, as their predecessors did in the Buyid and earlier periods. This expedient policy of peaceful coexistence with the illegitimate state, doctrinally rationalized by the concept of Occultation, allowed the Shia ulama freedom of action and political flexibility. The controversial case of Nasir al-Din Tusi (d. 1273), one of the most famous Shia thinkers of the late Seljuq and early Mongol period, offers a remarkable example of how the absence of political doctrine in Imami Shia Islam freed some of its adherents from lasting loyalty to any system.

Brought up in Khurasan as an Imami Shia, Tusi[18] was professionally inclined to the study of mathematics, astronomy, and philosophy. Throughout his adult life, he transferred his allegiance from one state to another as long as he could pursue his intellectual interests in peace. His most intellectually productive years were spent in the service of high-ranking officials of the Ismaili state of Alamut, to whom he initially dedicated a number of his most prominent works. Despite the seemingly favorable and encouraging intellectual environment provided by Tusi's Ismaili patrons, who held him in high esteem, he did not hesitate, whenever the occasion arose, to seek support elsewhere. Thus, he secretly wrote to the Abbasid Caliph asking for his patronage and for asylum in Baghdad, only to be betrayed by the Caliph's chief minister, Ibn al-Alqami (d. 1258), an Imami Shia leader who revealed Tusi's intentions to the Ismaili ruler.

In 1247 Tusi defected to the invading Mongols, whose chieftain, Hulagu, immediately adopted him as his adviser. Tusi's close collaboration with the then non-Muslim Mongol rulers is acknowledged by all historians, who hold him responsible for counseling Hulagu to destroy the Ismaili state, to lay siege to Baghdad and, following its fall, to have the last Abbasid Caliph killed, thus putting an end to a Muslim ruling institution which for centuries was recognized by the majority of the Muslims as the official state. Regardless of the true motive behind Tusi's controversial action, the fact remains that politically he gave no importance to theological or sectarian differences. He indiscriminately cultivated ties with Ismailis, Sunnis, non-Muslims, and Imami Shia, whose community he finally rejoined.

Leading Imami Shia theologians, including the above-mentioned Ibn al-Alqami, and the famous Hasan ibn Yusuf al-Muhaqqiq al-Hilli (d. 1277–78), played a similar important role in the fall of Baghdad and the triumph of the non-Muslim invading army. It is reported that certain Traditions were circulated at that time which might have encouraged the Shia to collaborate with Hulagu. One such Tradition allegedly claimed the advent of the Turk (sic) to power would usher in the Hidden Imam's victory.[19]

Tusi and other Shia ulama are credited in Shia annals with the rejuvenation of the Shia creed by helping create, through their close ties with the Mongol rulers, a necessary ambiance of religious tolerance, and attracting rich endowments for their institutions. In fact, their own personal gains by far outweighed those of the community at large. Tusi enjoyed Hulagu's full trust and esteem and was given high ranking administrative posts, as well as financial support for the library and observatory he had established in Maragha (in East Azerbaijan); others received generous stipends and endowments. However, Shia Islam remained a minority sect. Conflicts between Sunnis and Shia periodically erupted. The Mongol rulers merely played the role of intermediaries.

Temporal authority, in Imami Shia views, continued to be separate from religious authority. Theologians who acted as advisers and administrators to Mongol rulers developed a theory of kingship modeled after the ancient Iranian institution, in the same way Sunni ulama had under the Buyids and the Seljuqs.[20] In Imami Shia, as in Sunni Islam, temporal authority became an integral part of the Islamic social order, a necessity for the preservation and good functioning of the Muslim law. Historical reality took precedence over religious ideals in the few Imami Shia essays written on the subject of government.

In 1501 Shah Ismail Safavi, the founder of the new Safavid dynasty in Iran, proclaimed Shia Islam the official religion of the state. The conversion of the Iranians, which was enforced by the royal tribal army, was ruthless, bloody and swift. Shah Ismail, in order to establish the legal and theological foundations of the new sect, had to import Shia ulama from neighboring Shia centers in Iraq and Bahrain. They were received with great honor, and given both financial and political support to carry on their task. The *"taqiyya*-oriented" existence of Shia was rendered obsolete. Thus the leaders of the now-recognized creed were allowed fully to implement doctrines they and their predecessors had given theoretical consideration only.

A Shia political theory could have emerged at this time, had attempts been made to define the nature and function of the state in times of Occultation. Such doctrines could have dealt with the ever-increasing discrepancy between the ideal and historical reality. A reconsideration would have required the ulama to shift political positions, from mere acceptance to an actual doctrinal recognition of state authority, thus conferring legitimacy on temporal rule in times of Occultation. Steps in this direction were taken when the principles, which for centuries had motivated Imami leaders to postpone the realization of the Shia political ideal, were compromised as a result of the ulama's alliance with the Safavids.

Shah Ismail had come to power at the head of an extremist messianic revolutionary movement that supported his claim to divine authority. The historical background of the Sufi order he headed, his ability to fuse personal political ambitions with religious zeal to fight a holy war, the nature of his religious ideology—all bear characteristic features of the militant, basically heretical groups which moderate Imamis had until then relentlessly condemned. Majlisi, the leading seventeenth century theologian, went so far as to compare Shah Ismail's achievement in establishing Shia Islam as the state religion with the expected twelfth Imam's political function of fighting for the right religion.[21] Such a sanctification of a monarch's rule, however, did not lead to any doctrinal reconsideration of temporal power in times of Occultation. The legitimacy or illegitimacy of a government was not discussed. Theoretically, Safavid theologians upheld the early Imami belief that only the Imam, or his directly-appointed deputy, could assume political functions such as forming a government, declaring holy war, or leading Friday service.[22] In practice, they counseled the sovereign to rule justly and wisely, while simultaneously demanding the faithful to obey and serve the king, regardless of whether the latter was just or not.[23] Thus, no attention was given to the problem of reconciling Shia theory with political reality.

The ulama devoted their pens to religious polemics and the exposition of Shia doctrine. The theoretical separation of temporal power from divine authority, a necessary consequence of the doctrine of Occultation of the Imam, continued to provide a justification for the de facto secularization of the political institutions. Among some leading ulama, temporal power was consistently viewed with contempt and cooperation with the government shunned. Nevertheless, just as in earlier times Imami theologians collaborated with the state and often accepted government appointments, many ulama in Safavid and post-Safavid Iran were directly associated with the state. Mulla Taqi Majlisi (d. 1659–60) held a government-appointed position. His more famous son, Muhammad Baqir Majlisi, held three different positions simultaneously, including a post specially created for him as head of the ulama hierarchy.[24]

THE RISE OF THE MUJTAHID TO POWER

Kingly power dominated the clerical leadership for as long as the relationship between the state and the ulama was based on mutual cooperation. In the later Safavid period, when weaker personalities ascended the throne, a power struggle launched by influential members of the religious hierarchy ended with the emergence of two distinct centers of power, religious and temporal. At stake was the issue of the Imam's deputyship, and who was best qualified to hold the title. Early Safavid Shahs, basing their claim on their alleged descent from one of the Imams and carrying the banner of messianic Shia Islam, had self-righteously assumed it for themselves. But some high-ranking ulama challenged the monarchs' right to act as the source of religious authority, and succeeded in assuming the title collectively. They based their claim on a late ninth-century Tradition attributed to the Twelfth Imam, referring believers to the transmitters of his sayings, the ulama, for guidance over religious matters in his absence. Majlisi reportedly altered this Tradition to make the ulama, and not all believers as implied in the original text, answerable to the Imam, thus enforcing their own directives upon all.[25] Although this novel interpretation provided the ulama with a potential source of power in social and political affairs, it was not meant to challenge temporal authority. Nor did it indicate the ulama's wish to assume authority over temporal matters. It ensured the ulama's position as the legal custodians and spiritual leaders of the community. A religious institution distinct from the government, a historical necessity in pre-Safavid time, came into existence in Shia Iran.

Institutionalized Shia Islam produced an official hierarchy of religious leadership. While the Imamate increasingly became eschatological in nature, the jurists (specialists of Islamic law) gradually established control over religious affairs and personal legal matters. Like their Sunni counterparts, they devoted their studies to aspects of theology, law and jurisprudence, compiling and verifying the authenticity of the chains of transmission of Imami Traditions. Shia dialectical theology, again like its Sunni counterpart, and despite its attempt to understand religion rationally, basically stressed the primacy of religious law. Law-minded ulama formed the bulk of the religious establishment.

The Sunnis had based their legal practices on the concept of *ijma*, or consensus of the community (which was rapidly defined as the consensus of the ulama), resorting to analogical reasoning in matters not covered by the Koran or the recorded deeds and sayings of the Prophet. Shia theologians, writing in defense of their doctrine of the Imamate, asserted their own concept of authority based on divine right. In their view, only the Imam's opinion is infallible; hence, only he can instruct the believers about the religious duties God has imposed upon them in order for them to attain reward in this life and the next. Consequently, the Imam's opinion constitutes the sole source of the law. In his absence, his opinion must be discovered with absolute certainty before legal pronouncements are made. Once this opinion is determined, it becomes an authoritative source of the law. *Ijma* is used by the jurists to designate that opinion. Thus, in Imami jurisprudence, *ijma* is not a proof in itself but an evidence of the proof, since authority lies not in the person who reveals the Imam's utterance, but in the utterance itself. For an *ijma* to become an authoritative source of the law, agreement of all jurists is not required, as long as it reveals with certainty the Imam's opinion. Any method used to determine the correct opinion was considered equally valid.[26]

Though the practice of *ijtihad*, the endeavor to determine the Imam's true opinion, was limited in the tenth and eleventh centuries,[27] with time it gained increasing recognition. The religious dignitary who exercised it, the *mujtahid*, came to acquire the highest ranking position amongst the ulama. The qualities of infallibility and supreme authority, however, were still denied the office. It is worth noting here that, despite the jurists' argument to the contrary, the legal basis of Shia jurisprudence is no different from the Sunni's, at least in practice. For, in the last analysis, the method used to "discover with certainty" the Imam's opinion amounts to following the judgment of individual mujtahids who would prove arbitrarily that their opinion was the Imam's.

The position of the mujtahid, however, was to be contested from within the ranks of the religious organization itself, by members of the Akhbari school of theology. Founded by Shaikh Muhammad Sharif Astarabadi (d. 1624), it rejected the function of *ijtihad* as incompatible with the authority of the Imam. Like the view of earlier Shia jurists, it conceived the entire community as followers of the Imam's teachings, and declared the position of the mujtahid unnecessary. It denounced the practice of *ijma,* accused the mujtahids of practicing analogical reasoning like the Sunnis, and claimed that the Traditions of the Prophet and the Imams (or *akhbar,* hence the name of their school) provide sufficient guidance to understanding the Shia faith and doctrine.[28]

Contemporary scholars view the Akhbaris' literal acceptance of the holy texts as an indication of a traditionalist, inflexible attitude, "non-systematic and dominated by purely doctrinal considerations," that would not tolerate individual rational judgment. In contrast, the mujtahid stand (which came to be known as the Usuli* view) is depicted as ensuring "a living continuous leadership of the believers" and providing "flexibility regarding legal and especially political questions" which would make it possible for them to act as legislators for their followers.[29] Such an analysis needs rectification.

The bitter Akhbari-Usuli controversy that dominated Twelver Shia circles in the seventeenth, eighteenth and early nineteenth centuries must be viewed as a reaction to the power acquired by the mujtahids. Some leading Sufi masters and theosophers also strongly resented the mujtahids' dominance of the Shia intellectual scene, and objected to the limitations imposed by the official Usuli determination of Shia doctrines. Some of them echoed the Akhbaris in charging the mujtahids with literalism and a narrow-minded interpretation of the holy texts.[30] It is significant that the Akhbari school suffered final defeat at the end of the eighteenth century at the hand of Aqa

---

*The *usul* are the fundamental principles the jurists relied upon to derive the religious law from the compiled Traditions of the Prophet and the Imams.

Muhammad Baqir Bihbahani (d. 1780–91) and his son, Mulla Muham-mad Ali Bihbahani (d. 1801–02), who earned himself the title of Sufi-killer. Both religious leaders acquired reputations as the fiercest and most revengeful opponents of those who challenged Shia orthodoxy, as defined by the Safavid and post-Safavid mujtahids. It was not only a matter of doctrinal disputes, but also a struggle to consolidate the mujtahids' power that lay behind the ruthless elimination of any form of religious dissent. The controversy led to open scenes of violence in the streets of Najaf and Kerbala in Iraq, as well as in the major cities of Iran. Many leading Akhbaris were killed, and others were declared heretics.

The Usuli mujtahids ensured their direct influence upon their followers' conduct, and provided a basis for their power, by making *taqlid* (following the directives of one particular mujtahid whom the believer considered most worthy) incumbent upon the believers. Fol-lowing the ruling of a deceased one was forbidden. A mujtahid had to be learned in theology, grammar, Arabic, logic, and jurisprudence. He must have demonstrated his knowledge and established for himself a scholarly reputation through the number of licenses he held from reputable ulama, and through his teaching, lectures, and writings. Such qualifications, in addition to certain personal features (maturity, intelligence, being of the male sex, piety, justice, and legitimate birth), were necessary conditions to attain such a prestigious post. Because scholastic learning was inaccessible to the ordinary people, who were neither socially nor individually distinguished for such a career, the subordinate rank of *mulla,* or *akhund,* was available to them. Their function was to execute the mujtahid's orders, teach in the lower schools, and perform religious services. The position of mujtahid in-creasingly became either hereditary, and/or kept in the hands of an exclusive group of ulama who appointed their successors from among their favorite disciples.

By the nineteenth century, an official hierarchy of orthodox ulama had come into being, whose source of power was not to be found in the classical Shia doctrine as developed by generations of Imami theologians. The entire Shia community came to be regarded as consisting of two distinct groups: the small group of mujtahids acting as the guides, and the majority of their dutiful followers. Imami Shia produced its own class of law-minded ulama who, like their Sunni counterparts, declared themselves the guardians of the law, and the protectors of religion against the deviators. Consequently, Shia or-thodoxy succeeded in subduing, and even suppressing, the original spirit of speculative radicalism which characterized the early formation of the sect.

"The institution of the mujtahid," writes Hamid Algar, "had the practical merit of ensuring a continuous leadership of the community and of providing a source of immediate authority that was neither too great to offend the claims of Vilaya (belief in the Imam as leader of the community), nor too restricted to be without practical effect."[31] However, such a claim clearly reflects the mujtahids' own arbitrary judgment that only they could personify the religious leadership of the community. In fact, they did not hesitate to use coercive means to enforce their view and suppress any other that might contradict, and hence challenge, their position as the sole interpreters of the religious law, and as its protectors against any kind of innovation. Sheer force helped them to establish their power, and force also kept them in power. Algar's assertion that "the ulama were deemed the leaders of the nation, and it was natural for leadership to enforce its directives,"[32] is questionable. In the beginning of the nineteenth century the ulama's concern was not the nation. Their religious policy was not a national policy; nor was it meant to be. Similarly, the centralization of the religious hierarchy, which was essentially the result of Usuli religious policy was not aimed at "modernizing the national church."[33] To attribute to the ulama's activities any kind of nationalist, modernist ideology would be entirely misleading and anachronistic, to say the least. Furthermore, a concern with the religious deviators' threat to the ulama's authority, rather than their desire to check temporal power, lies behind the centralization of clerical power in modern Iran. The rise to power of the mujtahids occurred at a time when a corresponding center of state power did not exist.

The fall of the Safavid dynasty in 1722 with the Sunni Afghan tribe's invasion of Iran; the brief, militant reign of Nadir Asfhar (1736–47); following the death of the latter, a relatively long period of tribal wars; the advent to power in the late eighteenth century of the Turcoman Qajar tribe whose monarchs, though assuming the title of Shadow of God on Earth, neither sought religious sanction nor claimed descent from any Imami line—all these political events, in fact, helped clear the path for successive generations of ulama to consolidate their religious institutions further. Throughout the half-century-long temporal power struggle, the mujtahids kept aloof from the political scene. Following the defeat of the Safavids, they had taken headquarters in the Shia holy centers of Najaf and Kerbala in Ottoman-ruled Arab Iraq. Thus, by the time the Qajars established, in 1795, their absolute political control over the nation, a highly-centralized religious institution was emerging, owing its power, its organizational development, its affluence and prestige, to forces beyond their reach. The state was not yet in a position to challenge in any fashion the ulama's authority; nor did the enforcement of *taqlid* indicate as yet a clerical attempt to dominate the state. The tradition of keeping king-ship separate from religion was maintained.

Much has been written about the ulama's rise to political power in the nineteenth and early twentieth centuries, and about the predom-inant role they played in the major events which led to, and finally culminated in, the political defeat of the Qajars in 1905–11. The root of their power is indicated by their daily contacts with the people who felt alienated from the state and mistrustful of its officials, and who natur-ally turned to them for protection. Matters of family law, commercial deeds, education, religious festivities, birth, marriage, and death all required the ulama's offices. Close ties existed between them and the merchant class, as well as with the various craft guilds. Moreover, the fact that the seat of Twelver Shia Islam was outside Iranian territory gave the mujtahids political immunity. They enjoyed financial inde-pendence, with substantial incomes resulting from charity endow-ments, administration of individuals' estates, gifts in kind, and cash. They could mobilize their own private armies recruited from among the students of the religious schools and the *lutis* (street gangs), who, when not fighting (and sometimes while fighting for a cause) often reverted to acts of lawlessness. They used *takfir*, declaring an opponent heretical, as a formidable weapon against their enemies. These were important factors that contributed to the emergence of the mujtahids to the position of religious leadership.

The ulama in Iran, as elsewhere in the Middle East both in the modern and medieval periods, did not constitute a uniform, ideologi-cally cohesive, distinct class of their own with binding allegiances and loyalties. Their ranks were seriously divided by internal factions, di-vergences in religious outlook, and conflicts of interest that often shifted some ulama's concerns from purely religious to economic and political considerations. Even in the nineteenth century, when the mujtahids emerged as a viable and powerful group, the ulama formed a loosely-defined association with no clearly marked class delineation. Since education was almost exclusively religious, received in the *madrasas* (schools administered and taught by the ulama), where reli-gious studies formed the bulk of the curriculum, practically the entire educated class of the nation who had not joined the civil service, the military, or who were not engaged primarily in independent commercial enterprises, were considered ulama. These individuals wore the turban as a sign of distinction indicating their learned status. A number of them owned land and shared common interests with the landowning class as well as with the wealthy merchants. Some were related to the royalty or to the tribal chieftains. Many held government appointments, including the powerful position of *imam juma* (chief religious leader of a town or city), and received stipends from state officials, royal patrons, and wealthy individuals.

Similarly, the ulama included within their ranks philosophers and speculative theologians, mystics of all sorts who formed their own respective orders with separate hierarchical organizations. Deviators heading a variety of movements were more or less openly active. Dissatisfied elements from within these different groupings often built up intricate networks of communication and means to promote their views over rival ones. Such highly elaborate systems of expedient alliances, more or less short-lived, enjoyed the patronage of some powerful members of the ruling classes who shared common interests. The most virulent anti-mujtahid stand came from within the ranks of ulama, among those who defied official orthodoxy. Shia dissidents, periodically encountering the relentless hostility of the orthodox jurists, continuously rejected—albeit mostly in private, secluded circles —the authority of the religious establishment. Charging the law-minded ulama with anti-intellectualism, they maintained an attitude of resistance to religious conformism, and sought to widen their intellectual horizon. In fact, the most lasting and fiercest feuds, which divided the society into several enemy camps and often plunged whole regions into bloody civil strife, involved not the secular state and the ulama, but orthodox ulama and the religious dissidents, or two rival schools of theology. At stake was the ultimate issue of freedom of religious expression.

In pre-Pahlavi Iran, when religion permeated all aspects of national life—intellectual, political and even economic—nothing could be further from the truth than to claim that the mujtahids were the sole exponents of Islam, or that they represented the collective voice of religious conscience.

MYSTICISM AND DISSENT IN IMAMI SHIA THOUGHT

Shia Islam accepts the general Muslim view that Muhammad's revelation was final and complete, yet it allows for a further perfection in the
interpretation of the revelation in the work of the successive Imams. It
believes that the Imams in their lifetime progressively taught their
adepts its esoteric spiritual truth, and that, due to the Occultation of
the Twelfth Imam, the revelation of the esoteric truth will be completed
only with the manifestation of the Hidden Imam on the Day of Resurrection. Law-minded ulama declared the gate to the Imam's knowledge (that is, the search for a more perfect understanding of the
revelation) closed. Implied in such a conception is the conviction that
this ideal truth is beyond the reach of the believers in the present era of
Occultation. Through the centuries, orthodox Shia ulama devoted
their studies to aspects of theology, law, and jurisprudence, compiling
and verifying the authenticity of the chains of transmission of Imami
Tradition. Shia dialectical theology, like its Sunni counterpart, closely
followed the jurists' view. The jurists came to forbid, or at least to frown
upon, attempts made to reach the more esoteric knowledge of Imami
teachings.

Shia mystics and philosophers tried to transcend the legalistic
approach to religion, and to keep Shia spirituality alive. The question
of how much medieval Islamic philosophy, Sufism, and Ismailism
influenced the development of Twelver Shia thought is beyond the
scope of the present study. Suffice it to state here that major currents of
ideas freely flowed both ways.

Iranian Ismailism, reinvigorated by the Nizari activities both
before and after the establishment of its state in Alamut, was an
important source of inspiration. Some fundamental aspects of their
doctrine infiltrated Imami theosophy, chiefly through the works of
Nasir al-Din Tusi, the thirteenth century philosopher who, with the
Mongol invasion, returned to Twelver Shia Islam. For instance, he
emphasized the importance in each age of the authoritative religious
teachings of Imam or, in times of Occultation, of his *hujjat* (proof or
guarantor of the Imam). Similarly, other Ismaili tendencies found their
way into Imami speculative thought. One was to exalt the status of the
Imam over that of the Prophet (a view shared by other Shia extremists)
and to regard scriptural interpretation as equal if not more important
than revelation, since it is equally dependent on divine intervention
yet more complete. The time-honored practice of concealing one's true

beliefs, *taqiyya*, and the art of esoteric writing continued to be used by the dissidents as self-protective measures.

Shia mystics were convinced that the progressive unveiling of the hidden meaning of the holy texts by qualified individuals was not only possible, but actually imperative. Scriptural interpretation, the Imam's primary function, was given in his absence to exceptionally gifted men whose task was to initiate his adepts to the esoteric truth. Spiritual initiation developed into an intricate, highly esoteric process, and gave birth, amongst the various Sufi orders at least, to a hierarchy of the spiritual elite headed by a shaikh, whose function was to lead the way to God, *tariqa* (a term which also means Sufi order).

Such an initiation by an individual leader was regarded by the orthodox ulama as blasphemous, because it meant sharing with the Imam the role of initiator. In the pre-Safavid period, great Shia masters of mysticism, such as Nasafi in the thirteenth century and Haidar Amuli in the fourteenth, attempted to reconcile the orthodox ulama to Sufism on the one hand, and to rally to the Shia the non-Shia Sufi schools on the other. Amuli called on the former to accept the validity of the mystics' esoteric interpretation of the Imami teaching, and urged the latter to admit that the secret of all science and esoteric learning lies in the teachings of the Imams, and that without Shia Sufism could not exist.

Shah Nimatullah Vali's (d. 1431) Sufi order, which acquired a predominant place among Iranian Sufis, brought forth similar arguments. Though originally a Sunni order, the Nimati came to play an important though brief political role in the early Safavid period. It succeeded in attracting a large following. However, under the reign of Shah Abbas the First, chiefly as a result of political intrigues by the leader of the order against the ruling monarch, the order was severely persecuted and, towards the end of the Safavid time, practically extinguished. It was revived again in the eighteenth century, and once more posed a serious threat to the mujtahids. It refused to validate the mujtahids' function, and often claimed that the Sufis were the true Shia. Such beliefs, and the large following the Sufi order commanded throughout the country, once more aroused the orthodox ulama's hostility. Many leading figures of the order were cruelly put to death. The rivalry between the Nimatis and orthodox ulama nevertheless persisted through the nineteenth century, as the order witnessed an invigorating revival. The Iranian cities of Kirman, Shiraz, and Hamadan remained important centers of the order.

MULLA SADRA AND THE ISFAHAN SCHOOL OF SHIA THEOSOPHY

In the seventeenth century, there emerged in Isfahan an important school of Shia theosophy, which developed its own method combining philosophical, Sufi and theological approaches. Its outward aim was to reveal the secret truth hidden in the Imams' texts. Its basic sources were the same as the orthodox ulama's—namely, the Traditions attributed to the Imams, and systematically compiled in the authoritative works of Kulaini (d. 940), Babuya (d. 991), and Safavid theologian Muhammad Baqir Majlisi. Leading philosophers wrote their own commentaries to these works. Some even compiled numerous Traditions which Majlisi had allegedly overlooked.[34] What from the start differentiated the theosophers' approach from that of the orthodox ulama was that while the latter was dialectical, the former was essentially hermeneutic, or spiritually interpretive. Echoing the Akhbaris, they denounced the orthodox ulama's scholastic approach to the study of religion. In fact, as I have already stated above, a number of Isfahan theosophers, notably Muhsin Faiz Kashani (d. 1680) and Qazi Said Qumi (d. 1691), defended the Akhbari school in the controversial fight against the Usulis.

Sadruddin Muhammad ibn Ibrahim Shirazi, known as Mulla Sadra (1572–1641), the most brilliant member of the Isfahan school, attempted to construct a philosophical system that would satisfy both the philosophic and religious demands, and reconcile mysticism to pure philosophy. Having studied the entire philosophical, religious and mystical heritage of Islam, he consciously created a synthesis of the neo-Platonic tradition of al-Farabi, Ibn Sina, and his school; the Ishraqi or Oriental philosophy of Illumination of Suhravardi (d. 1191) and his followers; and the Sufi theosophy of Ibn Arabi and his disciples.

Early in his career, Mulla Sadra had openly expressed his belief in a pantheistic doctrine of existence, and had affirmed Suhravardi's unorthodox view, as taught by Sadra's master, Mir Damad (d. 1631), that essence is the primary reality, existence being a mere mental phenomenon. Just as, centuries earlier, Suhravardi had to expiate and suffer martyrdom at the hands of the Sunni ulama, and Mir Damad encountered censorship from Shia clerics, so was Sadra forced to escape religious persecution by taking refuge in a small village near Qum for a period of seven to fifteen years (depending on the source). Solitary confinement, he tells us in the introduction to his most famous work, made him realize how he had erred by relying too much on his intellectual powers and not submitting to God's will. Strenuous religious exercises and intense contemplation helped him discover new truths, and comprehend intuitively what he had previously learned rationally. Through such mystical experiences, he wrote, "I came to know divine secrets I had as yet not understood."[35] The descriptions he gives of the visions that periodically enlightened his knowledge are reminiscent of the experiences of other Muslim mystics: Suhravardi, Haydar Amuli, Mir Damad. [36]

Despite the technical Sufi language he used, Sadra never belonged to any order. Fazlur Rahman, in his recent study of Mulla Sadra, writes that the philosopher's intuitive perception is not to be confused with the Sufi's "purely experiential spiritual itinerary ... ending up in an ethico-ecstatic idea," and that his method is "out-and-out rational and philosophical." To Sadra, "mystic truth is essentially intellectual truth and mystic experience is a cognitive experience, but this intellectual truth and this cognitive content have to be lived through to be fully realized; if they are intellectually entertained as rational propositions, they lose their essential character—not as cognitions, but as verities."[37] Sadra, in fact, attacked the Sufis for their lack of interest in philosophical inquiry. He wrote a whole treatise refuting Sufi practices and beliefs.[38] He also took to task the narrow-mindedness, the ignorance, and the stifling attitude of those ulama committed to literal traditionalism and the exoteric teaching of religion, an attitude he condemned as a major obstacle to the development of true knowledge.

True knowledge, Sadra emphatically asserted, is neither jurisprudence, nor philology, nor grammar, nor medicine; for all are nothing but the external garbs of the Koranic science. True knowledge, that is, the esoteric knowledge of the Imam's teachings, is different in spirit, and is accessible only to the initiated, the chosen few who have to protect it, and hence, conceal it from the uninitiated.[39] As Rahman notes, there are weaknesses in Sadra's thought which are direct consequences of the philosopher's effort to reconcile religion and philosophy, or to combine two different traditions together.[40] However, Sadra had insisted on the respectability of his ideas within the system of Shia thought. The light of the Koranic revelation, he often stated, can shine only through the eye that can see it and reflect it. Philosophical contemplation is this eye, the theosopher the beholder. Divine truth and philosophic truth are identical and interdependent. To possess one without the other is like treading in darkness.[41]

Sadra bade his disciples to renounce material wealth and worldly ambitions, and to forbear following the rulings of the mujtahids. Knowledge, he explained, is "polluted" if it results from acceptance of a human master's opinion, that is, from conformism.[42]

Sadra reviewed his ideas, and structured his entire philosophical system on the basis of the doctrine of the primordiality of existence, which allowed essence no independent reality other than as part of existence. Suhravardi had developed the notion of reality as "one single continuum of light arranged hierarchically from the Absolute Light" (that is, God) downward to what Suhravardi called "accidental light." One animal can be more of an animal, and a person more of a person than another. Sadra took over this doctrine and applied it to his notion of the "unity of existence," a gnostic term he borrowed from Ibn Arabi. But he put existence into perpetual motion, claiming that existence cannot be static and that movement occurs in the very substance as well as in the qualities of things.

This movement in substance constitutes Sadra's unique contribution to Islamic thought. Its result, Rahman writes, is that "grades of being are no longer fixed and static, but ceaselessly move and achieve higher forms of existence in time." This movement from the less perfect to the more perfect is "unidirectional and irreversible, for existence never moves backward."[43] At the bottom of the scale of existence lies primary matter, and at the highest point is God. Existence moves continuously and successively through higher and higher forms of evolutionary modes of being. Thus, according to Sadra, existence has a natural impulsion toward taking ever-new forms. All bodies, be they celestial or material, are subject to this substantial change in their very being. This change takes place imperceptibly all the time. The movement culminates in the "perfect man."

Here Sadra, influenced by Ibn Arabi's Sufi notion of Perfect Man, the Pole of the universe whose existence sustains the universe, explains his own doctrine of the Perfect Man as the highest grade of being, who contains all the lower forms from which he himself emerged, and which he sustains. At this point the Perfect Man has become a member of the Divine Realm. He has perfected his moral and intellective powers. He is, in a sense, one with the Intelligences or the Attributes of God. Without his existence, the universe would be destroyed. Echoing Ibn Arabi, Sadra defined this last stage of human perfection in terms of self-realization and awareness of the existing relationship with the Divine Being. "Man can experience this change within himself if he examines his own consciousness with sufficient subtlety and acuteness and can see that the absolutely changing is the absolutely stable and can visualize the possibility of his finally transcending this spatio-temporal realm and becoming a member of the divine order, since all this change is rooted in and manifestation of that order itself."[44] The Perfect Men, to Sadra the Shia, were the Prophet, the twelve Imams, and following them, the specially gifted. The Perfect Man is the ruler of all the worlds, physical, psychic and intelligible. He may or may not be obeyed. If he is not, this does not detract from his perfection.

THE LEGACY OF SHIA THEOSOPHY

Mulla Sadra's vision was in sharp contrast to the pessimistic historical determinism of the Traditionalists, who viewed the history of the world and of the Shia community in the period of Occultation as going from bad to worse, until corruption and injustice reach their utmost limit with the advent of the imposter Dajjal (the anti-Christ figure in Islamic theology), an event which constitutes the first sign of the eventual manifestation of the Hidden Imam. Mulla Sadra and his fellow theosophers proposed a more humanist vision of the world in perpetual progressive evolution towards spiritual perfection, and a more positive faith in the ability of humans to perfect themselves. For the belief in the Perfect Man offers a promise of redemption in this dark age of Occultation. Similarly, the philosopher's insistence that the Koranic revelation has yet to be esoterically interpreted underlined his basic rejection of the traditionalist conception of knowledge as already given in its entirety, with nothing more to add to it until the advent of the Expected Imam. Such anthropocentrism was achieved, paradoxically (yet understandably) enough, from within an imamocentric system. Although the concept of the Perfect Man which Sadra conceived represented a concrete symbol of human creative power at its highest degree of self-realization, it did not project a truly modern humanist faith in the ability of humans to achieve progress through their own means rather than by an external transcendental force. Invoking the name of the Hidden Imam and relying on scriptural interpretation, Mulla Sadra and his fellow theosophers tried to establish the traditional roots of their progressive viewpoints, in a way very reminiscent of their predecessors, the philosophers, both Sunni and Shia, of the classical medieval period.

Like his medieval colleagues, Mulla Sadra faced the problem of having to reconcile faith to reason. He had to abide by the intellectual limits set up by his religious environment, yet pursue his natural inclination to philosophical inquiry. Unable to espouse openly some theologically controversial ideas without risking excommunication, he reverted to the practice of *taqiyya* and to a rather abusive use of esoteric writing destined for a very select private audience, while publicly claiming the legitimacy of his ideas. This cautious compromise allowed him a certain measure of freedom in developing truly unorthodox views about some basic theological principles, and, above all, conferred on a philosopher like himself an almost holy status, high above not only ordinary people, but also, and especially, above the mujtahids themselves. To be a philosopher and yet remain faithful necessitated choosing among the numerous philosophical and mystical concepts ones susceptible to adaptation. Mulla Sadra conformed by denying validity to the function of the Sufi shaikh, while accepting the concept of the Perfect Man as an idea; by rejecting Sufi practices as excessive and contrary to reason and faith, yet giving spiritual initiation and inspiration a status equal to intellectual analysis; and by using the Traditions as his sources and the Imams as his masters, though admitting that their esoteric teaching is accessible only to the adepts, who do not include the jurists.

Sadra, inspired by Mir Damad, who was himself influenced by Nasir al-Din Tusi, attempted to ensure the survival of philosophy in the Imami Shia world by further elaborating on this peculiar discipline of theological philosophy. Against those who sharply distinguished religion from the rational sciences, Sadra and his school of Shia thinkers defended the ultimate unity and validity of all intellectual inquiries, both Sufi and philosophical, as the true end of religion. Yet, like al-Kindi, the ninth-century Muslim philosopher who was the first to attempt such a reconciliation, and like most subsequent Muslim thinkers, who wished to abandon neither the philosophical system nor the revealed dogmas, Sadra juxtaposed two, and sometimes even three, different modes of expression without attempting to integrate them. At times a semi-mystic philosopher and at others a theologian, he did not succeed in being both at the same time.

Such was the legacy of Shia theosophy. The consequence of this self-perpetuating tension between free philosophical inquiry and religion was that the philosopher's creativity and rational investigation were constantly prevented from out-growing this dichotomy. Shia thinkers were thus inhibited from conceiving of new dimensions in understanding people and human socio-political problems based on concrete practical experiences of life.

In spite of the few, though important, instances of Sufi leaders' aspiring for political prominence (such as the Nimati order in the early Safavid period), by and large Shia theosophers adopted an attitude of detachment from their sociopolitical environment. Their intellectual concerns, primarily metaphysical and mystical, reinforced the traditional Imami Shia political alienation. Mulla Sadra, echoing early Shia thinkers, stressed the fact that the community (that is, the masses) was not yet prepared for, and hence not worthy of, receiving the perfected message of the Prophetic revelation. The time was not yet ripe for the manifestation of the Imam. Sadra upheld the Imami Shia view of the doctrine of Occultation to explain that the authority of the Imam's spiritual presence, which the world could never be deprived of, essentially aims at the other world, and not at any material power in this one. Temporal power, he argued in classical Imami fashion, is not a necessity. The Imam is Imam, that is, the supreme spiritual authority, whether visible or not, acknowledged as such or not. People may elect a temporal head or ruler, but not an Imam.[45] Another Safavid theosopher, Qazi Said Qumi, similarly insisted on the spiritual aspect of the Imam's leadership. The Prophet and the Imams, he stated, were "servants of God," and not political rulers. The Imams were not pretenders to the throne, competing with the Umayyads or the Abbasids. There is a definite, clear-cut difference between dynastic worldly power and the authority of the Imam.[46]

Although both Sadra and Qumi, while writing these comments, had in mind the Sunni Caliphate, which they wished to dismiss as a mere temporal position, in contrast to the divine spiritual function of the Imams, their view also reflected their political stand vis-à-vis the Safavid state on the one hand, and the official religious organization on the other. The theosophers, even more than the law-minded ulama, perpetuated the notion of the alienated condition of the "true Shia." Implicit in the philosophers' belief in the Perfect Man—a neo-Platonic philosopher-king idea, which was blended with the Sufi notion of the master-initiator of the esoteric truth—is the firm conviction that the philosophers' judgment ultimately supersedes that of the jurists, the exponents of the exoteric law, and that of the secular monarch. It is symbolic of their ideal society, the heavenly city where the sages reign, an ideal which clashed with, and in fact was rejected by, the political and religious establishment. Whereas the theosophers' hostility to the jurists was openly expressed in their writings, their rejection of secular power was much more subtle. They were not openly in revolt against it—far from it. Yet their aloof detachment, in addition to their belief in the Imam as the supreme authority, clearly reveals a strong and conscious refusal to accept any temporal power as binding.

The theosophers were highly critical of the scholastic tendency to limit the religious sciences, and knowledge in general, to rigid rules which only a handful of high-ranking ulama had the right to interpret, and which they protected against any kind of innovation. And yet, they persistently upheld the elitist conception of knowledge as a precious possession of the chosen few. They developed a self-assertive, conscious sense of independence vis-à-vis other social groups. Towards the masses, they displayed an attitude of open scorn, demanding surrender and obedience, very much in the tradition of most philosophers in the Muslim world throughout the ages. It was an attitude that reflected their perception of themselves as an intellectually-distinct category of special, superior beings. Their practice of *taqiyya* had the double merit of protecting them from persecution, as well as jealously safeguarding their "esoteric truth" from public exposure. They argued that traditional Shia theology lacked the dimension of spiritual experience, and that it had far too finite a view of the possibilities open to Shia doctrines. Yet, Shia Islam seemed to have emerged too esoteric from philosophical speculations and the esoteric possibilities were too absolute a reversal of conventional literalism. Like most Muslim thinkers of their own time and earlier, the theosophers wrote in Arabic, a language that was inaccessible to the masses, and even to the unqualified literate. Mulla Sadra's sole work written in Persian, *Sa Asl,* is so heavily arabicized that a reader with no knowledge of Arabic would have extreme difficulty understanding it.

Philosophers and mystics baffled the common reader with their private language, but far from being scientists, they were merely theologians defending preconceived positions. The circle of intellectuals in pre-modern Iran was artificially polarized into two theological camps. For the jurists and the theosophers did not constitute two separate classes of thinkers. From amongst the jurists there were a number of partisans of gnostic thought. Similarly, the theosophers were, more often than not, jurists themselves, at least by virtue of their training in the religious sciences, if not by profession. Seen from a sociopolitical perspective, the *urafa-fuqaha* (theosophers-jurists) controversies appear to have been more polemical battles over methodology, or intellectual disputes over esoteric doctrines which did not even concern, or relate to, the daily life of the ordinary, common believer. Beyond its polemical consequences, the excommunication of a philosopher rarely affected the life and work of the declared heretic, except possibly in terms of forced social isolation. Mulla Sadra was eventually received in his native town, Shiraz, with great respect and honor. He was allowed to teach in a newly established school. His students and disciples subsequently taught and spread his ideas, albeit in restricted circles.

It was only when theological differences of opinion also implied political differences, especially if the mujtahid's function in society was challenged, that the latter's hostility turned into active belligerence. Shia theosophy, inasmuch as it dealt with pure ideas without worldly consequences, was allowed to survive. The idea of the Perfect Man, as it was debated, developed, and refined by a restricted circle of philosophers through the centuries, remained alive. This survival should not be mistaken for freedom of thought per se for those who speculated with ideas. For it essentially reflected mere indifference on the part of the orthodox authorities. Persecution of thought occurred when its practical consequences and its political implications clashed with the influential organized religious authority, as it did in the case of the Usuli-Akhbari controversy. In the nineteenth century, movements of religious renewal were to challenge even more severely official Shia Islam.

2

The Radicalization of Dissent in Shia Thought: Early Shaikhism

M ULLA SADRA, the seventeenth-century thinker, provided speculative thought with a new impetus and vigor. Despite orthodox censorship, his ideas continued to influence Iranian thinkers who ventured into the hazardous realm of metaphysics and philosophy, studies traditionally considered to be the highest intellectual training. Successive generations of faithful, though restricted, circles of disciples preserved his works, studying them extensively. Sadra's pursuit of prophetic philosophy, or the esoteric ideal of the Revelation, dominated Iranian thought throughout the Qajar period. His ideas, and those of earlier philosophers and mystics as he synthesized and incorporated them into his system, provided the foundation for a new school of Imami Shia theology, Shaikhism. It was one that generated controversies which shook the intellectual, theological, and, eventually, the political circles in Iran.

The founder of the Shaikhi school, Shaikh Ahmad Ahsai, born in 1753, was the son of an Arab bedouin nomad who had converted to Shia Islam after settling in a small village near Ahsa in Bahrain. From early childhood, he revealed a natural disposition towards learning and mystical experiences. In his autobiography,[1] he recounts how he used to prefer solitude and meditation to the boisterous, fun-loving company of his peers, whose tempting music sessions he would sometimes attend with guilty feelings. He relates how, on visiting neighborhood historical sites, he would often cry over past glories and heroes long dead. Ahsa, once the flourishing center of the Ismaili state which Nasir Khosrow, the eleventh-century Ismaili thinker, visited and described with great admiration in his works, was then, Shaikh Ahmad tells us, intellectually barren and spiritually degenerate. Ignorance was widespread, and people could no longer distinguish evil from good. His insatiable thirst for knowledge was not satisfied with the mediocre teaching of his local masters. Frequent dreams, he writes, compensated this deficiency. For the Imams themselves regularly visited him in his dreams to instruct him and gradually reveal to him the scriptural interpretation of Koranic verses and the esoteric meaning of their Traditions.

Accounts of visionary experiences such as these are recurring themes in the history of Islamic Shia mysticism. As Corbin notes, one can detect in Ahsai's visions, and in those of his Shaikhi successors, motifs and symbols which conform to the archetypal forms of Shia mystical consciousness.[2] He would see strange things that would fill him with awe; he would visit the heavens, the invisible worlds; then he would wake up, completely certain of the proofs he had received from holy sources.

Following the first vision, Ahsai decisively rejected the study of grammar and philology in order to concentrate on theology proper. In 1772–73, at the age of twenty, he left his native land to settle in the Shia holy cities of Najaf and Kerbala in Iraq, although not permanently. A kind of physical, as well as mental, restlessness characterized his life, periodically pushing him to move from place to place. In 1807, he came to Iran, where for a period of approximately fifteen years he traveled extensively, spending a few years or a few months, depending on local circumstances, in Yazd, Isfahan, Mashhad, Qazvin, Kirmanshah, and Tehran. Throughout these years (but much less frequently while in Iran, Ahsai claims in his memoirs), he kept on seeing and hearing the Imams in his dreams. He would ask them questions or request clarification of obscure points of doctrine, and they would oblige. In his writings and public debates, Ahsai insisted that the source of all his knowledge was the Imams themselves, with whom he regularly communicated. "I do not say anything they would not say," he would reply to his critics. He also reported that he had received twelve separate licenses, one from each Imam.[3]

Ahsai's learning and his debating abilities attracted many admiring followers. In the beginning of his stay in Najaf and Kerbala, leading mujtahids awarded him licenses which entitled him to a position of teacher and spiritual guide. In Iran, he was often the guest of honor in the homes of prominent government and religious figures. Royal princes bestowed upon him financial and moral support, seeking his friendship and religious advice. Fathali Shah, the reigning monarch of the time, invited him to settle permanently in Tehran (an invitation he promptly declined). Ahsai nevertheless enjoyed the financial benefits of royal patronage, receiving land and stipends, along with the security such protection entailed.

Despite the immense popularity and the triumphant reception he received everywhere he went, or possibly because of it, Ahsai also attracted the hostility of some orthodox ulama in Iran, as well as in Iraq. Rumors were maliciously spread alleging his acceptance of vast sums of cash and properties from some Qajar princes, in return for which, it was said, he sold them tickets to paradise. Accounts of his dreams and visions were met with sarcasm and disbelief. His claim to know intuitively the authenticity of a Tradition was ridiculed, to the point that the shaikh himself came to realize the futility of his attempts to explain his spiritual experiences. There were too many "ignorant and jealous" people around, he complained in private.[4]

Eventually, however, more serious doctrinal challenges and refutations succeeded in undermining Ahsai's position in Shia circles. He often saw himself forced publicly to disavow some of his pronouncements and to profess orthodoxy, in order to clear his name from growing accusations of heresy. "Whatever I believe in," he would eloquently address his audience from the pulpit of a mosque, "is in accordance with the Shia creed." To quote A. L. M. Nicolas, "Never before was the law of taqiyya, which authorizes a man to conceal his beliefs when they are threatened, so completely, nor so blindly, nor so fruitlessly followed."[5] Hostility to the person and the ideas of Ahsai went on unabated. In Qazvin, where his controversial theory of the resurrection of the body was heatedly disputed, one of the influential ulama of the town, Mulla Muhammad Taqi Barghani, declared him an infidel. Mudarrisi writes that the ulama of Tehran and Kerbala followed suit.[6] But Corbin, citing Shaikhi sources, asserts that this accusation of heresy in Qazvin was a lone incident, the evildoing of four or five envious and ignorant mullas who were not even of the rank of mujtahid, and hence were not qualified to debate metaphysical issues.[7]

Whether this was a lone incident or a more widespread reaction, the fact remains that it was a symptom of a conflict, reflecting the tension created by the law-minded ulama's continuing hostility to theosophy. Many opponents identified the Shaikhi's position with that of the Akhbaris. And just as the Akhbari-Usuli controversy had split the Shia community into quarreling factions in the eighteenth and early nineteenth centuries, the so-called Shaikhi-Balasari* dispute became a global *cause célèbre* which aroused the never-dormant religious zeal of people of all classes in Iran and elsewhere in the Shia world.

After a lengthy stay in Iran, Ahsai went back to Kerbala. There, too, he found the ulama tense and resentful, and some involved in petty intrigues to discredit him. A few went so far as to denounce him to the Ottoman governor in Baghdad, pointing out passages in his works where he allegedly referred to the Sunni Caliphs in unflattering terms. Their hope was to obtain from the government authorities an official repudiation of the shaikh. In 1826, at the age of 75, Ahsai decided that Iraq was not an appropriate place to spend the rest of his life. He left for Mecca. However, he died before reaching it, a few miles outside Medina, where he was buried.

Sayyid Kazim Rashti, the shaikh's favorite disciple and most constant companion, emerged as the sole uncontested leader of the Shaikhis. He was born in Rasht, in the Iranian northern province of Gilan, into an Arab family of Sayyids (descendants of the Prophet) from Medina who had, two generations earlier, come to settle on the southern shore of the Caspian Sea. In his semi-autobiographical work,[8] Rashti describes his childhood inclination to solitary meditations, and the visionary dreams he had which initiated him to higher knowledge, accounts which are strikingly similar to Ahsai's and those of mystics. In one such dream at the age of fifteen, he reports, Fatima, the Prophet's daughter and wife of Ali, revealed to him the existence of Shaikh Ahmad, who was then residing in Yazd. Rashti then left his native town to join him. Thereupon, a lasting spiritual intimacy started between the two. They traveled together in Iran and in the Shia holy cities, the master initiating his disciple to the esoteric truth. Rashti's receptive eagerness, in addition to his total devotion to the person of the shaikh, was highly appreciated by the latter, who would often tell his entourage that no one understood him better than Kazim Rashti. Following the charges of heresy in Qazvin, and on the shaikh's advice, Rashti went back to Kerbala to settle permanently in Arab Iraq, taking only short trips to Arabia and rarely visiting his birthplace.

Most sources tend to agree that the Shaikhi controversy did not degenerate into violent opposition until after the death of Ahsai. The first two years of Rashti's leadership were relatively peaceful. How-

---

*The term Balasari came to refer to the Shaikhis' opponents, those who refused to abide by Ahsai's ruling that worshipping at the head *(balasar)* of an Imam's tomb was contrary to Shia principles.

ever, such peace could not have lasted long, as he continued to teach and preach his late master's doctrine. Although Rashti included amongst his followers a number of Qajar princes, the most important ones being Ibrahim Khan Zahir al-Daula Qajar, Governor of Kirman, and his son Hajj Karim Khan Kirmani, the future head of the largest Shaikhi branch in Iran, he certainly did not enjoy the widespread official protection and generous support that the royal patrons bestowed upon his predecessor. Rashti's sedentary life in Kerbala enabled him to establish for himself a vast network of followers, disciples and mercenary fighters, necessary for the spread and consolidation of his influence and prestige in the holy city. Kerbala, it is reported, was then self-governing, independent of the Ottoman authorities in Baghdad. The majority of the inhabitants were Iranians. Rashti and his chief rival, Sayyid Ibrahim Qazvini, competed for supremacy in local politics, each enjoying the armed support of one of the two leading factions of ruffians who controlled the streets. Rashti's involvement in local politics, activities which Ahsai had avoided, added fuel to his opponents' hostility. Rashti was often accused of spreading Ahsai's heresy. He would vehemently retort: " ... if I follow the same path ... why should they [the orthodox] scare me away? In my search for a guide, I had investigated his position and had seen nothing but a genuine quest for God's approval and for the straight path. I never saw him concerned in any fashion with worldly matters. . . . His truth was clear and evident to me. What reason do I have to part from his way?"[9] He insisted that his role, after having been the shaikh's follower, was now to guide the faithful to the truth. He defended Shaikhi views both in public and private debates, only succeeding in intensifying his opponents' campaign against the school.

By 1828, he was forced to practice *taqiyya*. At a public meeting, he had to account for the shaikh's ideas and terminology, despite his protest that the latter was never seriously challenged nor even questioned in his own lifetime, and that it would be futile to do so now. Following a lengthy, heated debated, he was compelled to submit a written confession: "Those words [the shaikh's controversial doctrines] if not commented upon, if not preceded or followed by anything . . . are heretical."[10] Rashti reportedly felt triumphantly safe, presuming that such a statement did not constitute a refutation of Shaikhi ideas, but rather affirmed their belief that esoteric truth is not accessible to the unqualified lay reader. But, as Nicolas rightly points out, the incident was, in fact, another revealing instance of the Shaikhis' blatant practice of *taqiyya*.[11]

Public demonstrations occurred frequently in the streets of Kerbala, denouncing Rashti as an infidel. His clerical opponents loudly demanded his expulsion from the holy city, and incited the populace to add their voices and efforts to the campaign against him. Repeatedly, self-professed Shaikhis were roughly harassed by their opponents. Letters written by leading jurists were sent all over the Shia world, proclaiming Rashti a heretic, and forbidding the faithful to read Shaikhi texts or to listen to Shaikhi speeches. Rashti would cautiously preach, stating his views in conformity with orthodoxy, outwardly repudiating some of the most controversial Shaikhi ideas. But it was to no avail: the opposition was merciless. Nicolas reports that attempts were twice made on his life. [12]

In January 1843 the dispute cooled considerably, with the raids on the Shia cities in Iraq by Sunni Ottoman forces (which caused widespread destruction and cost thousands of Shia—mainly Iranian—lives) and with the appointment of Sunni ulama to administer judicial affairs. Rashti had developed friendly relations with Nagib Pasha, the Ottoman governor of Baghdad. He had even attempted to mediate between the Ottoman forces and the Shia residents in Kerbala. During the raid, the house was not plundered, and the Sunni soldiers respectfully kept away from Shaikhi properties. Rashti himself died a year later, in January 1844, in Kerbala, where he was buried.

EARLY SHAIKHI DOCTRINES

For purposes of the present study, I shall first discuss the most important and controversial points of Shaikhi doctrine, and then concentrate on those issues that proved to be, at this early stage, of great sociopolitical significance to the history of Qajar Iran.

The Transmaterial World and Allegorical Interpretation of Shia Concepts

The entire Shaikhi system of thought rests on the basic Muslim theosophical conception of the universe as consisting of a structured hierarchy of worlds and interworlds of reality which correspond to the different levels of being — matter, soul, and intellect. In the twelfth century, Suhravardi, influenced by ancient Iranian thought which he interpreted in the light of neo-Platonic philosophy, had developed a scheme which put the world, the earthly realm of matter perceived through the senses, at the bottom of the scale. The interworld, or intermediary realm of the angels and of human souls — a world of "substances of light" perceived through the imaginative faculty — he placed in the middle. And at the highest level was the world of Pure Beings of Light, which have no material or physical body and are perceived through the intellect.

A century later, Ibn Arabi added a fourth realm, the sphere of the deity, and had elaborated on the concept of the intermediary world, the realm where the human soul imagines images which are as real as, if not more so, than the reality which is perceived through the senses. He depicted this interworld as an exact, ideal reflection of the physical world, a world of symbols or archetypal images of all earthly individuals and things, a transmaterial world that is "inaccessible to rational abstractions and to empirical materializations."[13]

Suhravardi reportedly experienced visionary dreams where Aristotle and Hermes, each in turn, enlightened him with their knowledge and helped him ascend to the intermediary world of light which, once reached, pushed the physical world back into darkness. Ibn Arabi similarly asserted that human dreams, meditations and visions take place in this intermediate world of "real reality," and that it is possible to accomplish such "visionary voyages" from the earthly world. Both Suhravardi and Ibn Arabi, and most subsequent theosophers, firmly believed that human consciousness awakens to this reality, which is the reality of the eternal celestial soul, through the individual's active imagination, the organ of visionary perception.[14]

Thus, neo-Platonic metaphysics, which developed on the basis of the Sufi theories of Suhravardi and Ibn Arabi, made it possible for seekers of "true knowledge," who wished to escape from the contingency of existence, to reach a higher form of existence nearer the Absolute. Such a view of the ascent to the Absolute or "return to God," whereby all alienation, all uncertainty is gradually removed, offered a hopeful conception of the individual's spiritual and intellectual abilities to transcend human nature and to conquer what are essentially physical limitations and liabilities. Moreover, this conception of an intermediary, transmaterial world helped the theosophers solve a number of problematic issues of religious dogma.

Orthodox theologians, for example, traditionally emphasized a belief in the physical resurrection of the body on the day of judgment and in the physical afterlife, thus accepting a literal understanding of

Koranic pronouncements on the subject. Majlisi, in his authoritative and comprehensive exposition of Imami Shia dogma, discussed at great length the issue of resurrection in a literal, physical sense.[15] Such an interpretation always produced a dilemma for the philosophers who wished to comprehend the metaphysical issues rationally. They ended up by refuting the doctrine of the physical resurrection, and asserting their own belief in the spiritual survival of the soul. Ibn Arabi, however, had the resurrection take place in this transmaterial world. In his view, it was a resurrection that was both physical (in the sense that it was the exact reflection of the earthly body) and spiritual, because the heavenly body is immaterial.[16]

Sadra further insisted that the world of images and its contents are real: a real body, a real paradise, a real hell with its fire, none of which are material. Faithful to his theory of substantive change, he explained how the human form goes through a continuous process of renewal. The body upon death sheds its impure matter, and acquires a refined spiritual body in the intermediary world, thus undergoing a minor resurrection. There it prepares itself for the final metamorphosis, or greater resurrection, to reach the realm of the intellect. Sadra, therefore, categorically denied the physical resurrection of the body in its earthly form. His doctrine of substantive change, which is conceived to be unidirectional and irreversible, would not allow it. Similarly, Sadra emphatically refuted the theologians' conception of a physical afterlife. The Koran, he wrote, "repeatedly tells us that the afterlife is a new creation, a new level of existence. This clearly means that we cannot look for a reappearance of earthly elemental bodies there."[17]

Ahsai, who was influenced by Sadra more than he wished to admit, accepted this conception of a hierarchical order of beings and realities, and used it to adapt many controversial theosophical ideas to the theological doctrine. He claimed that the transmaterial world, which he called *hurqalya*, can be perceived by the adept, the initiated. The degree of perception of things in *hurqalya* is directly proportionate to the degree of esoteric knowledge an individual possesses.

In order to accommodate his theosophical views to orthodox theology, Shaikh Ahmad drew a complicated and rather confusing scheme, whereby the human form is conceived as made of different layers of celestial and material substances, each corresponding to a different stage of its being. The scheme enabled him to accept, with minor differences, Sadra's argument that the progressive ascent of the human form—from the mineral, vegetable, and human stages to the final spiritual level of the pure intellect—is irreversible, and that there could be no physical resurrection.[18]

Closely linked to the issue of resurrection is the question of *maraj*, the Prophet's nocturnal ascent to Heaven. Orthodox theologians, true to their literalist interpretation of religion, postulate a belief in the physical *maraj*. Ahsai rejected this, and understood *maraj* to mean a spiritual experience symbolizing an ascent to the highest level of cognizance of the divine.

In accordance with his concept of the original spiritual substance of the human form, the shaikh also asserted that the Prophet and the Imans, upon death, left behind their earthly garb, which they had temporarily worn during their terrestrial sojourn to make themselves visible to humans. Thereafter, they reassumed their original refined, immaterial substance to enter the heavens. Their physical bodies decomposed, and the material components reverted to their respective elements.

This unorthodox interpretation rejected the official view that the bodies of the Prophet and the Imams were, by divine grace, exempted from physical decomposition. Furthermore, Ahsai's conviction that the Hidden Imam does not live, though invisibly, in this world, but rather in the transmaterial world, *hurqalya*, and that his manifestation will not occur in this world but, again, in *hurqalya*, was contrary to the most fundamental Imami Shia doctrine. Orthodox theologians insisted, and still insist, that the Imam is alive and ever present on earth, though concealed from human sight. Majlisi had argued that it was biologically possible for the Imam to live so long. He even maintained that the Imam had been seen occasionally, had performed miracles, and had taken part, unrecognized, in annual pilgrimage rituals in Mecca. Similarly, Majlisi confirmed the orthodox view of the Imam's return to this world at the end of time as marking the physical resurrection of humans in this world.[19]

Imamism

Of crucial importance to Ahsai's entire theosophical system is his conception of the nature, place and function of the Imams in the universe. Shaikhism, to use Corbin's definition, is essentially *"Imamisme spéculatif."*[20] It shares with the theosophical and theological schools the fundamental Shia idea of the Prophecy and the Imamate as being two separate stages of the Koranic revelation, one exoteric *(zahir)*, the other esoteric *(batin)*. Although the two stages were united in the person of the Prophet, the latter's mission was to reveal the exoteric meaning of the divine truth, thus leaving to the Imams the important task of gradually lifting the veil off the esoteric. Whereas the first stage ends with Muhammad, the second has its beginning with Ali. To quote Ibn Babuya, the tenth-century theologian: "The Imams are in authority. It is to them that Allah has ordained obedience, they are the witnesses for the people and they are the gates of Allah, the road to Him and the guides thereto, and the repositories of His knowledge and the interpreters of His revelations, and the pillars of His unity. They are immune from sins, and errors, they are those from whom Allah had removed all impurity and them absolutely pure; they are possessed of the [power of] miracles and of [irrefutable arguments]; they are for the protection of people of this earth just as the stars are for the inhabitants of the heavens."[21] He argued that the continued existence of the Imam, whether visible or concealed, is necessary because his nonexistence would deprive the earth of a witness from God. Hasan ibn Musa al-Naubakhti, another mid-tenth-century Imami scholar, similarly insisted that the "earth cannot be void of a Proof. If the Imamate disappeared even for a moment, the earth and its inhabitants would perish."[22] Ibn al-Mutahhar al-Hilli, writing in the thirteenth century, further reinforced this view of the Imamate as a universal authority in the things of religion and of the world.[23] However, at this point Shaikhism departs from orthodox Shia. For, although the theologians implicitly grant the Imams a status almost equal to the Prophet's, and see them as endowed with special divine grace, they do not recognize them as either independent or as divine beings. Ahsai, on the other hand, inspired by Sadra and his school of theosophy, drew a different conception of the Imams.

In Sadra's philosophical system, the being, after descending from the heavens into the abyss, returns to God. In its progressive ascent, it passes through three different stages of structured reality: the realm of matter, the realm of the soul, and finally, if it qualifies, back to the realm of pure intellect in the form of the Perfect Man who combines in himself all three realms[24] Whereas the human form in this world is material, in the other two worlds it is immaterial. The Perfect Beings are intermediate beings between the Necessary Being, God, and the contingent or earthy, world. Rahman quite rightly notes an ambiguity in Sadra's description of them as pure existence and absolute beings, and as part of God, since there must also be within them something of the worldly. He explains that it was necessary for Sadra, in order to maintain continuity in the chain of hierarchical beings, to put them at the highest point, next to God, who transcends all, ad infinitum. "Their position," Rahman writes, "seems to be the same as that of the Attributes of God who are also said by Sadra to be intermediate between the absolute being of God's Essence and the world of contingency." These intellects constitute a manifestation of God, and "God contemplates Himself through this manifestation. Intellects are, therefore, forms or images of God, from this point of view." And they, in turn, contemplate God through their contemplation of themselves, as the effects of God.[25] Thus, the Imam, the Perfect Man or the pure intellect, is truly the intermediary through whom, and only through whom, humans can reach and know God.[26]

Ahsai took over this hierarchical system, adding to it, like Ibn Arabi before him, a fourth stage. This was the realm of the deity, whence the Fourteen Very Pure—that is, the Prophet, Fatima and the twelve Imams—come and where they return. Aware of the theologians' uncompromising belief that there can be no separate immaterial substance besides God, and wishing to avoid criticism for attributing immateriality to other beings, Ahsai made use of Sadra's (which was originally Suhravardi's) notion of a scale of graded beings. He explained how beings, which are made of both spiritual matter (light) and elemental matter ("solidified light"), materially differ in degree. The Primordial Intellect (that is, each of the Fourteen Very Pure) is more immaterial than, say, a mineral, but less so than God. However, Ahsai's argument was too close to Sadra's to be accepted by the orthodox theologians. His notion of spiritual matter could, and did, sound like a euphemism for immateriality. Furthermore, the shaikh explicitly stated that the Imams possess a spiritually divine reality, and that their temporary human condition in this world is only accidental. In other words, the Imams are pre-existential divine beings. This view is consistent with his firm conviction that the "biological status" of all beings is pre-existentially determined, and that the animal condition of human beings, just like the Imam's human condition, is accidental since their essence belongs to the intermediate world of the soul.[27]

Ahsai further provoked shocked outcries from the orthodox ulama with unorthodox statements regarding the universal function of the Imams. They are "the cause of Creation," the cause of the existence of everything that is not God. They are "the place" of God's will, they fulfill God's wish. "If it were not for the Imams, God would not have created anything."[28] Such assertions, which abound in the shaikh's works, echo Nasir al-Din Tusi's views on the Imamate. In his Ismaili phase, Tusi had defined the Imam as the "Deified Perfect Man," "the Manifestation of the Primal Divine Volition on earth," "the cause and origin of the existence of all beings and creations," and "the Cause [while other beings are] the effects".[29]

Ahsai was consequently accused of actually professing faith in Ali, the first Imam, as the creator of the universe. To clarify his position and clear his name from such blasphemous charges, Ahsai argued that the Fourteen Very Pure, which are the Names and Attributes of the Divine, together constitute the eternal Muhammadan truth and through them, as God's agents, God's will manifests itself on earth. Hence, everything that exists, be it the intellect or the smallest particle of dust, exists as a result of this will and its agents. The entire world is the product of a voluntary act of the Imam, who derives his power and strength from God. Kazim Rashti further emphasized this point: "Perhaps everything that exists in this world, be it visible or invisible, is linked to the thought of the Imam. Should the Imam turn his attention away from it, the entire world would disappear. His thought is thus the cause of existence." By themselves, Ahsai cautiously explained, the Imams have no independent power. Just as a hot iron bar derives its heat from the fire but, once hot, generates heat continuously even if taken out of the fire, the Imams act freely because God has endowed them with such an attribute. In fact, "The Imams Very Pure possess all the Divine Attributes, and through them all acts of the Divine Being are manifested."[30] As Nicolas points out, Ahsai's argument meant to show that the act of creation cannot be attributed to the essence of God directly, but to the essence through the intermediary agency of the Imams. The Imams are, therefore, in the shaikh's view, not the architects of creation, but its contractors.[31]

Long is the list of Shaikhi deviations from orthodoxy. A number of them are deviations common to the philosophers and mystics, as epitomized in the works of Sadra. For instance, Ahsai's concept of the world as "eternal in time" yet "new in essence"[32] is reminiscent of Sadra's explanation of the world: eternal as a process, yet, because of the constant substantive movement of change, finite in content.[33] Both contradicted the theological view of the world as finite. Ahsai's justification for dropping God's attribute of justice *(adl)* as a fifth basic principle of Imami Shia—that to know God the One is to know all the attributes which are part of God, and that one cannot single out just one of them—echoes Sadra's assertion that God's attributes are identical with God's existence, and not additional to it.[34] It was, therefore, not without reason that both Ahsai and Rashti were accused of propagating Sufi and philosophical thought, which, in the orthodox theologians' opinion, was heretical. Ahsai vehemently denied any affiliation with Sadra's school, which he condemned for its Sufi and philosophical inclinations, and pretended that he himself relied only on the Imams' texts as sources. He even wrote several commentaries on the works of Sadra and his disciples to show the weaknesses inherent in their system. Although Ahsai outwardly condemned Sadra, in fact his writings owed much to the seventeenth-century philosopher. They were "two spirits of the same family of Shia gnosis,"[35] as Corbin puts it.

The Perfect Shia

Mystics believe that God cannot be known through discursive reasoning and can neither be known totally, for God can be known only through God. They affirmed that all existing beings nevertheless must have a direct "primordial knowledge" of God, "each according to his own measure," as Sadra puts it. For "a direct witnessing of God must be at the root of all knowledge, whether conscious or unconscious."[36] Ahsai similarly insisted that a purely spiritual, visionary perception of the Divine is the best way to knowledge, and thus rejected the mujtahids' use of discursive reasoning as a poor substitute for divine inspiration, a quality the orthodox theologians attributed to the Imams only. He questioned the validity of a mujtahid's authority, which he considered to be humanly fallible and hence not binding. He denounced *taqlid* (following a mujtahid's ruling) as contrary to the true faith of the Imams. He also accused the scholastic theologians of limiting their understanding of religion to legalistic aspects, and of overlooking the depth of its inner life.[37]

Ahsai based his harshest criticism against the Sufi orders on the ground that the individuals who assumed the spiritual leadership of the order not only competed with, but, in fact, usurped the Hidden Imam's position.[38] However, it is significant that he developed a similar concept of a hierarchical order of beings who act as intermediary agents between the Imam and the community of the faithful. He took over the traditional Sufi idea of Perfect Men whose existence sustain the world, and he mixed it with the Ismaili notion of *hujjat* (the Imam's guarantor, hence his agent). Referring to these agents as the "Perfect Shia," Ahsai considered them to be those rare, specially gifted beings whose conscious knowledge of the divine is immune from error by virtue of their close spiritual affinity to the Imam who initiates them to the unrevealed truth. They are capable of "seeing things in *hurqalya*" (the transmaterial world), to use the Shaikhis' favorite expression. They are the representatives of the Imam, and execute God's order as instructed by the Imam. They are therefore the gates to the Imam. From the earliest times in Islamic history, Ahsai claimed, there always existed such Perfect Shia, whose function was progressively to lift the veil off the esoteric truth, and thus enlighten their own restricted circle of adepts, just as the Imams did in their own lifetimes. Salman Farsi, the legendary, Iranian-born companion of the Prophet, who played a very central role in mystic literature, was chosen by the shaikh as the symbolic figure and initiator of this historically continuous chain of human agents. "To each age its own Salman the Pure," says a Tradition often quoted by the Shaikhis.[39] Only the Perfect Shia is worthy of the function of *ijtihad* (the endeavor to reach the Imam's correct opinion).

In an interesting essay written in an esoteric style, Rashti emphatically asserted that a qualified mujtahid, capable of "perfect *ijtihad*," is one endowed with a special "intellect," a "saintly power" that distinguishes him from ordinary beings. For he is the "Imam's deputy," "God's representative on earth," the "successor" of the Prophets and the Imams. The source of his knowledge is, in reality, divine, and not based on *taqlid*. "He is a learned man who asks no questions of anyone." Mujtahids who do not possess such qualifications, Rashti declared, are "corrupt imposters."[40]

Whether or not Shaikh Ahmad considered himself to be the Perfect Shia of his age was, and still is, a controversial question. Corbin, quoting from apologetic, self-protecting writings of some Kirmani Shaikhis, asserts that he did not.[41] Yet Ahsai's works are full of unmistakable references to his own special role as the initiator to esoteric divine truth. "Understand," he would tell his reader, "for truly I have thrown unto you a key of the keys to the Invisible World."[42] He would often state or imply that the source of his revelations was divine, that he was revealing things which were never before revealed. Or he would claim to be discussing subjects which no theologian or philosopher had ever dealt with; only the Imams and their adepts had. He would start his lectures proclaiming: "I have heard from Imam"; or "Last night, Imam told me." Kazim Rashti wrote in his *Dalil*: "Whatever he [the shaikh] said, he said it independently. Whatever he exposed is not to be found in any written book, nor reportedly attributed to anyone."[43]

Corbin comments that such a claim is peculiar to a distinct group of individuals in Iran known as the "Owaisis," who had no other master but the Invisible.[44] However, such pretensions do not constitute a strictly Iranian sociocultural trait. In early Shia circles, the title of *alim*, a person who possesses knowledge (pl. ulama, which later came generally to mean theologians), was given not only to the Prophet and the Imams, but also to their close associates, such as Salman, who were reputed to be exceptionally well-versed in religious knowledge. They all were believed to be in possession of the inner, unrevealed part of the Prophetic message, which was passed on from generation to generation of adepts. Their duty was progressively to complete the task of the Apostle of God. Early extremist Shia sects who deified Ali and some of the later Imams, also worshipped their associates—Salman in particular—as saints. Thus, to quote W. Iwanov," Alid knowledge had become a kind of Divine omniscience."[45]

Similarly, the Ismailis had developed the idea that in times of the Imam's Occultation, there are always some chosen individuals amongst his followers who know where he is and are in constant contact with him. "[The Imam] always has a Proof... who informs the followers, and reveals the truth to those who seek after it, being specially commissioned for this purpose by him."[46] Nasir al-Din Tusi, in his Ismaili phase, had further argued that the Perfect Teacher, in times of Occultation, is the supreme interpreter and guide of the community, acting as the sole living agent of the Imam. Such an intermediary agent, through whom the faithful could know the Imam, held the highest-ranking office in the Ismaili organization. This person was even believed to be endowed with an innate, superhuman knowledge of the Imam and all his mysteries. There was a firm conviction that the world could not be cut off from God's guidance. "It would be incompatible with His Justice ... if He would send an Apostle at one time, and none at another. He sends revelations to various people through prophets of uneven standing. ... Those saints who do not receive direct inspiration, nevertheless have it indirectly, knowing the scriptural interpretation of the Traditions and sacred book."[47]

Ahsai's successors' lavish, almost extravagant praise of him seems to confirm this Sufi-Ismaili tendency. Rashti referred to him as "the sign of God in the two [visible and invisible] worlds" and as "he reveals the way to the secret of the truth."[48] He described Ahsai's status as "a rank so high... and important, not accessible to any one, only to the one upon whom the Pure Friends [that is, the Imams] have bestowed their attention and special favor."[49] Furthermore, he explicitly stated that the divine truth is preached first by prophets, then Imams, and finally by those who possess true knowledge.[50]

Evolutionary Cycles of Revelations

In a strikingly unorthodox essay by Rashti,[51] the full impact of Sufi-Ismaili influence upon Shaikhi thought is highly noticeable. Rashti's main argument here closely follows the Ismaili idea that the revelation sent to Muhammad was to be progressively unveiled by the Imam of the time, and that the Imam's (or, when he is in Occultation, his representative's) authoritative teaching is as important as the Prophet's revelation, since it is equally dependent on divine intervention. Rashti further radicalized the idea of authoritative teaching. He distinguished what he termed the exoteric cycle of the Prophet and the Imams (which corresponds to the rule of the law as revealed in the seventh century, and which would last twelve hundred years) from the esoteric cycle of Perfect Men, whereby the hidden meanings of divine truth are progressively unveiled. Writing in the year 1257 of the Muslim calendar (1838–39 A.D.), he explained how religion and religious laws have to follow the progressive maturity of humanity.

In another essay written at about the same time, Rashti discussed the necessity for religious law to suit people's needs at different historical stages of their growth. He stated that humans at each stage had a divine law revealed to them, a law that fitted their condition and time best. From Abraham to Jesus, each revelation superseded and abrogated the preceding one, until Muhammad's prophecy. Rashti cautiously attested the Islamic belief that Muhammad's prophecy was the last of all prophecies, and that its law would never be abrogated. However, he carried his idea further, arguing that the Muslim revelation corresponded to the time of the child's (i.e., humanity's) birth into the world, whereas all previous ones corresponded to the stages of the child's growth in its mother's womb. As the newly born infant was still delicate in constitution, its nutritive diet was restricted to light, easily digestible meals. "Holy law and moral principles," he wrote, "are the nourishment of the spirit." It is, therefore, imperative that the laws be diverse; "sometimes earlier commands have to be cancelled," so that the child grows naturally in strength and ability.[52]

The issues of *bada* (change in God's commands) and *naskh* (abrogation) in religion have been debated at great length by Muslim theologians and philosophers throughout the centuries. There are a number of Koranic verses related to the idea that God's decision on these matters is pending, that a final judgment is still to come.[53] Similarly, the Prophet himself had abrogated some of his earlier commands and replaced them with new ones. This was interpreted by the Mutazilites, the medieval rationalist theologians, as fitting very naturally their doctrine of human free will and action, on the one hand, and their belief that the purpose of God's action is always the well-being of the Creation, on the other. Their Sunni opponents, the Asharites, who were more conservative and more literalist in their understanding of religion, considered those verses as part of God's absoluteness, believing that God can do whatever God likes. However, the medieval philosophers rejected the Mutazilites' view on the ground that "nothing higher acts for the sake of the lower, and that the perfection of the lower comes about as a by-product of the action of the higher. The purpose of God's action is, therefore, nothing but God himself."[54] Mulla Sadra, however, consistent with his theory of substantive change in the material bodies and the heavenly realm of the souls, declared that everything outside God's being is subject to change, including commands pertaining to affairs of the world of matter, which he differentiated from the unalterable, eternal Divine Will. The heavenly souls, according to Sadra, act as agents of change in the material world, by contacting the minds of the prophets or the Imams, the Perfect Men, and initiating them to "the new writing." For "commands in this world have to change according to times and climes through abrogation."[55] The Ismailis considered it possible for the Imam of the time to cancel the commandments of the law of the Prophet. In fact, they proclaimed that the "Imam is the ruler of the religion, and gives orders with regard to whatever he thinks is beneficial to the religious life or to the welfare of the people."[56] To the Imami Shia theologians, such thought naturally constituted sheer blasphemy. In their view, the Islamic law is God's last law, which has been further explained by the Prophet's legitimate successors, the Imams. In the time of the Occultation, a kind of accepted "status quo" prevails until the Imam's eventual manifestation. Even then, however, the Imam's task will not be to bring a new religion, or even abrogate some aspects of the law, but to restore the true religion to its rightful position, vindicate its true adherents, and destroy its enemies. Nasir al-Din Tusi himself, once he returned to the Imami Shia fold, confirmed the orthodox view that the Islamic law is valid to the end of time.[57]

That Rashti believed that Ahsai was the initiator of the new cycle of Perfect Shia, there is no doubt. He explicitly asserted that the shaikh has revealed secrets in order "for someone to spread those truths and manifest them." Furthermore, in a rather dubious (though quite revealing) statement, he explained that the "glorious name" of the Prophet has an earthly term, Muhammad, and a celestial one—Ahmad. Both are "the place of the manifestation of the Muhammadan Truth." But whereas the former term is the "place" for the first cycle, Ahmad is the "place" for the second.

At this point, Rashti cautiously refrained from explicitly identifying the Perfect Man of the new cycle. "If I were to explain the details of his place, of his time and age, of the good proportions of his body and limbs, I would do it with rational proofs and esoteric insight. But it would take too long. True, it would benefit all . . . but, verily, I have so little time at my disposal; my heart is so disturbed; I am encountering enmity and troubles . . . I therefore cannot for the moment further explain. If God allows me to live longer, and if He spares me those torments, I shall write an essay in which I will explain [who] heads the last hundred year cycle, in this year 1257 [1838–39 A.D.] of the Hijra [Muslim era]. I will explain his station, I will describe his attributes, and I will lift all doubts concerning him. Verily, he is the leader." And he solemnly proclaimed: "Verily, I have announced to you the news of him who is now with me, news of him who was before me."[58] By "who was before" him, Rashti, of course, meant Ahsai. However, the identity of the person meant by "who is now with me"—that is, his own designated successor—was destined to become a heated issue after his death, as we shall see in the following chapters.

THE SOCIAL SIGNIFICANCE OF SHAIKHISM

Henry Corbin, the scholar of Islamic philosophy and Sufism, eloquently argued that Ahsai and his successors were by no means deviators. They were, to quote him, "true adepts of the Perfect Shia Islam as taught by the Imams and their texts, a Shia which was either corrupted and/or neglected by the 'narrow-minded jurists,'" whose chief concern was to establish uniform orthodoxy. The Shaikis' self-appointed mission was to restore and develop *"l'enseignement intégral des Saints Imams"* ["fundamental teaching of the holy Imams"]. *"Integral,"* Corbin assures us, is not to be confused with conservatism, literalism or puritanic formalism, for it denotes rather a spiritual affinity with and deep understanding of Imami teachings, which the Shaikhis attempted to rediscover or reform. The Shaikhis' task was to develop a theosophy which, though superficially crossing the philosophy of Sadra, Sina and other philosophers, was solely based on the Imams' Traditions. Hence, Corbin emphatically states, Shaikhism represents a continuity in the Shia theosophical tradition, a "restoration but not an innovation."[59]

Doubtless, Ahsai and his disciple Rashti desired to see some basic Shia doctrines interpreted in the light of philosophical and Sufi notions of truth and reality, and thus enhance both the rational and the spiritual aspects inherent in Shia theology. They were in lineal descent from the theosophical tradition in Iranian Shia thought which through the centuries had kept up a persistent opposition to the dominant current of orthodoxy.

Ahsai's aim was obviously to reform some of the basic Shia principles. His concern was not only to reconcile philosophy to theology, as earlier Muslim thinkers had done before him, but essentially to rescue Shia Islam from what he called the narrow, literal interpretation officially allowed up to that point. However, whereas his predecessors, including Sadra, had mostly remained outside the inner circle of orthodox theologians, Ahsai and Rashti endeavored to penetrate the very heart of the official school system, and directly influence its traditional views. To do so effectively, they adopted the language of earlier theosophers. Just as the latter had deliberately complicated their style in order to cushion some of their unorthodox ideas, the Shaikhis tried to make their views look irreproachable by expressing them in the language and imagery of orthodoxy.

They upheld the traditional mystics' esoteric approach to knowledge, explaining that the Traditions are expressed in symbolic terms, with each symbol needing a scriptural interpretation. The question to be asked, Ahsai stated, is not whether a Tradition is authentic, but whether its substance, its meaning, is in accordance with the totality of the Imam's teachings.[60] Thus, the final judge is not a human being, a mujtahid, or a transmitter of a Tradition, but the Imam himself, "invisible yet present in the heart of his adepts." Ahsai claimed he could validate the content but not the chain of transmission of a Tradition. Rashti proudly stated that his master was endowed by the Imams with a special gift that enabled him to "pierce the darkness of ignorance," and bring to light "the truth."[61]

Implicit (and actually often explicitly stated as well) in such a belief was the Shaikhis' profound conviction that the orthodox ulama's understanding of the true faith was shallow and incomplete. It was precisely this conviction and its obvious consequences that irrevocably antagonized the mujtahids, who saw their very *raison d'être* once more, but more seriously, challenged from within their ranks.

Had the early Shaikhi leaders confined their ideas to a restricted, discreet circle of disciples, as Mulla Sadra had done centuries earlier, the orthodox ulama would not have gone beyond the banning of some of their works. But the patronage both Ahsai and Rashti enjoyed, especially amongst the Qajar royalty, in addition to the widespread popularity their teaching attracted in Najaf and Kerbala (the two holiest centers of orthodox Shia Islam), and elsewhere in Iraq and Iran, threatened the mujtahids' position of leadership. Hence, the relentless enmity and constant harassment the Shaikhis had to endure — a harassment which only succeeded in provoking in them a self-perception, which they shared with the early Shia, as wronged true believers. In the works of Ahsai, Rashti, and later, the leaders of the Kirmani branch, there are recurrent expressions of proud acceptance of their minority status. This apparently reinforced their self-proclaimed position as the true Shia, and confirmed their belief in a kind of general historical law that every great new prophet or Imam or adept is at first denied recognition. Kazim Rashti explicitly compared the Shaikhis' plight to that of the Prophet and Imam Ali.

At this point the historian would like to ask to what extent early Shaikhism constituted a threat to the socioreligious order in Iran. How much of this speculative thought was purely spiritual, and how much social? Are Shaikhi ideas to be studied in the context of "existential time" and not "chronological time," as Corbin suggested, and thus to be relegated to the "spiritual universe" for further metaphysical exploration by philosophers and mystics? Or are we to analyze them as the product of their historical period and socioreligious conditions?

Doubtless, the Shaikhi allegorical interpretation of basic Shia doctrines was supremely attractive to intellectuals of the time who opposed orthodox religious teachings, yet wished to remain loyal to their faith. Similarly, their conception that the religious law had to undergo constant adjustment to the times and conditions of a given society proved to be a useful means to justify the changes felt necessary by those who were committed to religious reforms.

Given the religious climate of their time, when orthodox theology officially dominated the scene so totally, and when the fear of *takfir* and persecution limited the pursuit of unorthodox thought, the Shaikhis' self-appointed task of reform, or—to use their favorite expression, to reveal the true teachings of the Imams—proved to be a hazardous mission. By daring to defy organized religion and its authority, no matter how cautiously, they trod a path that was bound to be as perilous as that traveled by the Sufi orders. In this sense, then, early Shaikhism had social-political as well as spiritual implications, for it reflected a rejection of the religious establishment. It also displayed the never-dormant resentment of the group of philosophers and mystics, and unorthodox thinkers in general towards the anti-intellectualism of the orthodox theologians. However, such an anti-establishment stand, such a challenge to orthodox anti-intellectualism, cannot be viewed as a new movement reflecting concern with rights of the individual. It was not new to the history of Islamic thought, nor were the proposed ideas original in any way. Here one would agree with Corbin's statement that the Shaikhis, like the Iranian theosophers of the last four centuries, though chronologically belonging to the modern age, are conceptually medieval. Their conception of religion and society basically reflects the tradition of dissent in Islam. Despite their progressive evolutionary view of a religious law that should follow human development, they do not project a sense of commitment to social and individual material progress. Moreover, their theory of knowledge in no way modifies the traditional perception of *ilm* (defined as knowledge of the divine) as the sole monopoly of a handful of extraordinary beings, the elite. In fact, they strongly upheld the idea of a double truth —one for the inner circle of adepts, the other for the public—and even raised the concept of *ilm* to loftier heights than had their predecessors. Their pretensions that they could actually communicate with the realm of the invisible, "to see things in *hurqalya*," lay greater claim to divine knowledge.

Nevertheless, inherent in the Shakhi view is the traditional messianic radicalism which characterized early Shia Islam, and led to, as it could again, political action. For Shaikhism rejects the orthodox, basically fatalistic vision of society, which sees the period of Occultation as one of decadence and corruption, and humans as primarily responsible for the disappearance of the Imam. In this view, society was doomed to decline and to follow a road paved with misery and despair, the hope implied in the messianic expectation in no way altering this fundamentally pessimistic vision. The Shaikhis' view (borrowed from the theosophers) is inherently more humanistic. They saw humans in a perpetual process of steady spiritual growth and perfection, with the final manifestation of the Imam representing a gift for their coming of age, rather than a redemption for long suffering. Implicit in such a progressive view is the conviction that human life is worthy of fulfillment in this world, and not only in the next, as the orthodox ulama's more literalist interpretation of the Imam's return take it to mean.

One cannot but notice the striking similarities between some of the more extremist Shaikhi thought and Nizari Ismailism. Like the Ismailis, the Shaikhis adopted the Sufi idea of a hierarchical structure of more or less perfect men destined to lead the community of faithful. Furthermore, the Shaikhis utilized the Ismaili concept of evolutionary cycles of progressive revelations. Behind Ahsai and Rashti's apparent acquiescence to their alien condition, which they understood to be necessary but temporary, and which they bore with a deep conviction that they were the Muslim elite, lay a high sense of mission reminiscent of the Ismailis' own activist spirit, which so markedly differentiated them from the moderate Twelver Shia branch. It was this missionary zeal that the rival successors to Rashti inherited and attempted, each in an individual way, to put into concrete practice.

With the death of Kazim Rashti, disputes over his succession on the one hand, and ideological controversies on the other, split the Shaikhi school. A moderate, though minor branch developed in Azerbaijan, headed by Shaikhi ulama in Tabriz. A main center of Shaikhism flourished in Kirman, drawing followers from all the major southern and central cities of Iran, including Tehran. It was led by Hajj Muhammad Karim Khan, a Qajar prince who strove to fulfill his political ambitions by religious means. Both the Azerbaijani and the Kirmani schools outwardly upheld an Imami Shia stand, while fighting orthodox elements from within the official system. However, it was with the Babi movement, headed by a merchant from Shiraz, Mirza Ali Muhammad, that a more militant, radical attempt was made to shake the foundation of the socioreligious order, by announcing the dawn of a new religious era.

3

The Socialization of Dissent in Shia Thought: Kirmani Shaikhism

THE MODERATE BRANCH of Shaikhis in Azerbaijan province was to play no important role in the religious controversies of the second half of the nineteenth century in Iran, except as fierce opponents of both Kirmani Shaikhism and Babism. Two prominent ulama of Tabriz lay simultaneous claims as Rashti's successors. One was Hajj Mirza Shafi Thiqat al-Islam Tabrizi (d. 1884), whose position was taken over by his son, Shaikh Musa Thiqat al-Islam. The second was Mulla Muhammad Mamaqani Hujjat al-Islam (d. 1851–52), who was also succeeded by his son, Mirza Muhammad Husain Hujjat al-Islam (d. 1885–86). Together with other Tabrizi Shaikhis, such as Hajj Mulla Mahmud Nizam al-Islam (d. 1856), the famous tutor of Nasir al-Din Shah, and Mirza Ali Asghar Shaikh al-Islam (d. 1848) and his son Mirza Abul Qasim Shaikh al-Islam, they greatly subdued the unorthodox tone of the school. Violent Shaikhi-Balasari riots in Tabriz, as well as the Kirmani Shaikhi and Babi controversies, forced them to retreat into orthodoxy. It was, therefore, as orthodox mujtahids that some of them attracted large followings from among government officials, local notables, and bazaar merchants.[1]

It was in the city of Kirman that Shaikhism continued to offer a challenging alternative to Shia orthodoxy. Though both the personality and the social background of its leader, Hajj Muhammad Karim Khan, account for the renewed vitality of the school (at least until it, too, was forced to retreat), the city's peculiar history and the religious composition of its inhabitants provided Shaikhism with a receptive environment.

THE SOCIORELIGIOUS CLIMATE IN KIRMAN

Kirman city, first built by the founder of the Sassanid dynasty, Ardishir I (d. 240), as a military garrison town, had become an urban center of some importance in both pre-Islamic and Islamic times. During the period of the Arab conquest and the Islamization of Iran, it remained, together with Yazd, a stronghold of Zoroastrianism, an ancient, pre-Islamic religion of Iran, even when, by the beginning of the eighth century, the bulk of the city's population had converted to Islam.

The mostly barren and desolate landscape of Kirman province, where a dry, rough climate and a scarcity of water account for the aridity of the soil and the lack of vegetation, was where a number of radical Muslim sects and Sufi orders chose to settle. Shah Nimatullah, the Sufi saint and founder of the order bearing his name, had taken up residence in Mahan in 1406 and remained until his death in 1431. The Mahan shrine then became a main center of pilgrimage for members of the order, who annually flocked into Kirman from other parts of Iran and the Middle East, and the Indian subcontinent. Extremist Shia sects, such as the Ahl al-haqq, had their own secluded communities. It is even reported that Mazdakism, the pre-Islamic reformist religious sect professing radical beliefs such as community property and social egalitarianism, was still practiced in remote villages. Similarly, from early times Ismailism was widespread in the province. Kirmani Ismailis maintained close ties with Fatimid Cairo, and, following the visit of Hasan al-Sabbah (the founder of the Ismaili state of Alamut) to the province, where he preached and recruited adepts for his cause, Kirman remained an important center of Nizari Ismailism.[2]

The history of Kirman in Qajar times was tumultuous. There was a constant struggle for power in the area among rival royal princes and governors, each supported by loyal or semi-loyal retinues of tribal chieftains, individual military commanders, and Sufi shaikhs. A striking feature of Kirmani political life was the more or less dominant role played by Sufi masters and sectarian leaders, whose worldly aspirations for influence and status went beyond doctrinal considerations.

The Nimati Sufi order, which had become socially and politically prominent in the early Safavid period before suffering a severe blow under Shah Abbas the Great, chiefly as a result of its own involvement in court intrigues, once more had to pay dearly for the active part it played in local politics. In the last decade of the eighteenth century, Kirman city had become a major battlefield for two rival contenders for absolute monarchy in Iran. The Zands, a powerful family from the province of Fars, had established their dynastic rule (1750–1795) in southern Iran with Shiraz as their capital. When the Qajars, a Turko-man tribe, conquered the northen provinces and moved southward, the Zands fiercely resisted surrender. However, the Zands were even-tually forced to flee Shiraz, march further south, and besiege Kirman city, where local notables, who supported the Qajars, attempted to prevent their entrance with no success. The leader of the Nimati order, a Qajar ally, was then declared a heretic by a mujtahid who had sided with the Zands, and stoned to death in 1791.[3]

With the establishment of the Qajar dynasty, the Nimati order closely associated with the ruling family, recruiting members from among prominent government officials and royalty. However, the rivalry existing within the ranks of its hierarchical leadership often gave rise to petty, cabal-type intrigues, which came to involve even its highest-ranking members, and which helped to fuel the fierce political competition among them.

The revolt of Aqa Khan Mahallati is another instance of a move-ment which combined political and religious motives. Aqa Khan was a direct descendant of the Nizari Ismaili rulers who, after the fall of the Alamut state in the thirteenth century, had lived, generation after generation, as Sufi masters and, by the eighteenth century, had be-come influential members of the Nimati order. Aqa Khan's grandfather was governor of Kirman until his death in 1791–92. A cousin inherited the position until the Qajar attack brought an end to it, for some of the Ismailis had fought on the Zand side. Aqa Khan himself was a son-in-law of Fathali Shah, the Qajar ruler who, in 1839, appointed him governor of the province. But upon the monarch's death, and due to the fact that he was loyal to the rival of the then chief minister in the Nimati order, Hajj Mirza Aqasi, Aqa Khan was dismissed from his post. Twice he attempted to regain the governorship by raising the standard of revolt against local authorities. However, a final crushing defeat in 1842 forced him to leave Iran and settle permanently in India. Ismailism colored with Sufism provided the revolt with a religious motif, and his claims to be the Imam, the Perfect Man, provided the rationale for Aqa Khan's ambition to autonomous rule.

Political claims to autonomous rule in the provinces were not always expressed in religious terms. In 1826–27, for instance, upon the death of the Governor of Kirman, Ibrahim Khan Zahir al-Daula Qajar, one of his sons, Abbas Quli Mirza, assumed office and almost im-mediately sent his troops to conquer Yazd, as a first step towards establishing his supremacy over all the country. His grand design, however, was fruitless: he failed to gain the support of his ministers and military commanders, and he was compelled to seek refuge in the Caspian province of Mazandaran. Local Kirmani chronicles offer numerous examples of other more or less short-lived revolts against the central government.

Despite the political turmoil, the city of Kirman itself offered a lively intellectual milieu for its circles of scholars, philosophers, and poets. Two important schools were founded in the first half of the nineteenth century: one by Zahir al-Daula during his twenty-two years of governorship; the other by a prominent religious leader, Sayyid Aqa Javad Shirazi (d. 1871), whose reputation as an accomplished scholar of religious studies and Persian poetry was well established. The most important Iranian philosopher of the time, Sabzavari, supposedly spent some time in the latter school. Leading Sufi masters held court in the city, and their order organized regular meetings to discuss lofty Sufi ideas at the same time as there were popular religious festivities and pilgrimages to the local holy shrines. Despite the orthodox ulama's constant threat of *takfir*, or accusations of heresy, speculative thought, both sectarian and theosophical, dominated the intellectual scene in Kirman, as elsewhere in Iran.

In the 1850s, Gobineau, a French diplomat-scholar, observed what he termed a "religious schism," or a doctrinal and ritual divergence from established orthodoxy. He noted, with some surprise, how Voltaire, the seventeenth-century French free thinker whose works had not been translated into Persian at that time, was held in high esteem by some Sufis, who had heard of his anti-clericalism.[5] However, a secular, or even an anti-religious world-view was not yet in the making, for religion still played a dominant role in Iranian life and thought. Writing in the late 1880s, E. G. Browne, the British scholar of Iranian history and literature, described, while in Kirman, meeting people "of every grade of society and every shade of piety and impiety . . . almost of every rank, from the Prince-Governor down to the mendicant dervish," and spending many evenings with the same variety of individuals "smoking opium and weaving metaphysics," reciting poems, and playing musical instruments. He remarked that the literary conversations he had with his acquaintances were all about religion and God. He testified eloquently, though not always admiringly, to the tendency among the Kirmanis (as well as among Iranians he encountered elsewhere) to express in religious terms their need for change, for intellectual and spiritual speculation, for moral commitment, and even for social entertainment.[6]

Kirman proved to be a fertile ground for Shaikhism and the religious and social upheavals it caused.

HAJJ MUHAMMAD KARIM KHAN KIRMANI, 1810–1871

Karim Khan was born in Kirman city in 1810, the oldest of Ibrahim Khan Zahir al-Daula's twenty sons and twenty-one daughters. His father was the wealthy Qajar prince, a cousin and stepson of Fathali Shah, who governed Kirman and Baluchistan for a period of twenty-two years until his death in 1826. He was a fervent admirer of Ahsai's thought and of theosophy in general. Upon the birth of his first child, he founded the famous Ibrahimiyya school, which he richly endowed to promote learning and create the right intellectual ambiance he wished for his children. In his short, highly stylized autobiography,[7] Karim Khan described his happy, carefree, sheltered childhood as the first-born and favorite child of his father. He boasted of having been "the most intelligent of them all," and said that "by the age of thirteen, fourteen, I had learned everything I had to learn from my masters. I was then their equal . . . sometimes my knowledge exceeded theirs."[8]

Shortly after his father's death, he met a disciple of Ahsai, who had come to stay in Kirman city for a year. This chance meeting proved to be a major turning point in his life. In his own words, Karim Khan saw himself developing a strong urge to become more acquainted with Ahsai's knowledge. A trip to Kerbala was then not easy to arrange, for, after the unsuccessful military revolt of his brother, Abbas Quli, he and the rest of Ibrahim Khan's children were kept under close surveillance and forbidden to leave the province by order of the new governor. Karim Khan nevertheless managed to escape.

He first went to Isfahan, where he met Ahsai's son. Upon his arrival in Kerbala, he was introduced to Kazim Rashti, with whom he rapidly established a master-disciple relationship. Karim Khan's visit lasted only eight months, for he was recalled back to his native town, apparently to settle disputes over the family estate. Four years later he returned to Kerbala to resume his "ecstatic" service and studies. It is reported that Karim Khan, the Qajar prince, enjoyed doing menial work for his master, such as cooking his meals. He also offered him his vast wealth and, when it was refused, paid him a religious tax amounting to one-fifth of his income. Sources friendly to the Kirmani Shaikhis describe Rashti's relationship to Karim Khan as being especially close, the disciple socially entertaining the master regularly in his home in Kerbala. However, competition for the leader's favoritism must have been fierce amongst the disciples. A Kirmani Shaikhi source, without actually admitting to the existence of such a rivalry, reports that two years after his return to Kerbala, Karim Khan had arranged a trip to Mecca together with Rashti. But, at the last moment, Rashti was "prevented" from leaving by "Iranian and Arab followers" in Kerbala. Thus, Karim Khan went on the pilgrimage alone and, shortly afterward, returned directly to Kirman.[9] Karim Khan himself stated in his autobiography that he had followed Rashti's specific instructions to go back to his native land, in order to "teach and guide the faithful" there.[10]

Karim Khan's social position in Kirman was that of a highly privileged grandee and an established religious leader. Himself a Qajar both on his father's side and his mother's, he married another Qajar, a granddaughter of Fathali Shah, who seemed to have enjoyed royal favors and was admitted to the inner circle of the court in Tehran. His wealth was considerable, for, in addition to the properties he inherited from his father, he derived a substantial income from the religious taxes his followers regularly paid him. His lifestyle was also that of an aristocrat. He was always treated with deference by his peers and numerous relatives, and was surrounded by a large entourage of respectful students and disciples. He never appeared in public without a suitable retinue of followers. Despite assertions by himself and by his biographers that he enjoyed a saintly, ascetic life, anyone reading through some of his essays would get a picture of a rather refined man with a taste for worldly pleasures. He wrote about the importance of women to the physical well-being of men, and defended the use of opium for the pleasant dreams and mild visions it induced. Essays on the importance of bathing and cleanliness, on the use of perfume, and on the necessity for a well-trimmed beard similarly display an aristocratic tendency to attach importance to physical appearance.

From the start, however, Karim Khan also geared his concerns towards loftier intellectual and religious pursuits. He acquired licenses from respectable mujtahids and from Kazim Rashti himself. Like most other mystics and like his Shaikhi predecessors, he lay claim to "special gifts" of the mind which set him apart from ordinary beings. In his autobiography, he recounted in detail dreams he supposedly had while in Kerbala and in Mecca which, again, bear striking resemblance to the visions which Muslim mystics throughout the ages had experienced. He described seeing the Imam in person, and seeing himself, in the midst of an assembly of angels, wearing a headgear and holding a cane, both belonging to the Prophet. In another dream, he saw himself in the midst of a crowd trying to get into a "strange machine" which led up to the heavens; and whereas others succeeded only in climbing up a few lower steps, he reached the top, thus finding himself in a position to maneuver the machine and guide all the passengers.[11] Karim Khan mesmerized himself with his own visions, and was firmly convinced that his was a special destiny. In his essays, he often asserted that all his instruction and guidance came directly from divine sources, and "confessed" that he did not follow the teachings of any living person. Expressing his dissatisfaction with existing works of theology, he set for himself the "holy task" of composing a *summa* based on the knowledge he "received" from God. "I have accumulated all [the knowledge] that the first and the last [masters] had accumulated as if I were one of them; nay, it is probable that I have accumulated even more, since I have in my possession, in addition to what they had, what I have personally accumulated. . . . I have turned over all issues, tested and verified everything, having no other purpose but to reveal truth as God has indicated it to me."[12] This high sense of mission, coupled with his self-righteous conviction that he had been chosen by God, dominated his thought and actions throughout his life. From the beginning of his career, he admonished his disciples to cease blindly following the ancients, who might have erred, and to shun the company and instruction of the unqualified. He exhorted them to refuse to conform.

A clash with the established ulama in Kirman was inevitable. Karim Khan found a most formidable opponent in the person of Sayyid Aqa Javad Shirazi, one of the most respected religious leaders in the city, and the founder of the school which competed for excellence with the Ibrahimiyya. Sayyid Aqa Javad, a son-in-law of Ibrahim Khan Zahir al-Daula and hence Karim Khan's brother-in-law, had succeeded in obtaining, in association with another mujtahid, complete administrative power over the late governor's estate, which included the Ibrahimiyya school and its rich endowment. Back from Kerbala and seeking to establish himself as the sole trustee of the estate, Karim Khan challenged Sayyid Aqa Javad's right to administer the endowments and accused him of embezzling funds. With the support of his own powerful family connections, he had the estate transferred to a new trust, over which he established his own absolute authority, delegating its administration to men loyal to him personally. However, Sayyid Aqa Javad refused to give up the directorship of the school, and an open clash between the two contenders, along with their respective students and partisans, turned the Ibrahimiyya into an embattled fortress. It is claimed that government officials were also involved in the fight, sending hired thugs to support their candidates. It was apparently one of these thugs who, together with his gang, finally succeeded in dragging Sayyid Aqa Javad's students out of their cells, beating them up, and ejecting them from the school premises. Karim Khan's triumph was complete as his rival's authority in the Ibrahimiyya was abolished, and Shaikhism was freely taught in its classrooms and mosque.[13]

Karim Khan, in his public speeches, writing, and teaching continually incited his audience to revolt against what he defined as archaic and erroneous understandings of the principles of religion. Upon Kazim Rashti's death in 1844, he proclaimed himself the new leader of the Shaikhi school and wrote a Shaikhi manifesto.[14] This pamphlet is one of the shortest, most precise and direct essays he had written.

Carrying on an early Shaikhi argument that there are four pillars of religion, consisting of (1) cognizance of God; (2) cognizance of the Prophet; (3) cognizance of the Imams; and (4) cognizance of the Shia, Karim Khan stated that just as one knows God through the Prophet, and the Prophet through the Imams, so one knows the Imams through those who are the true Shia. He declared obedience to the Shia ordinances regarding God, the Prophet, and the Imams to be obligatory, and that failing to do so was tantamount to heresy. Here Karim Khan stated in clear, unequivocal terms what Ahsai and Rashti, inspired by Ismaili and Imami Shia theosophy, had written about in esoteric style. He transformed the early Shaikhi conception of the Perfect Shia of the age into a concrete definition of the qualified religious leader of the community. Like them he contrasted the "true Shia" (that is, the chosen few in exclusive possession of knowledge of the divine) to the legalistic mujtahid specialist of "exoteric" aspects of religion. He firmly stated, like the Ismailis and some of the Sufis before him, that God in the period of Occultation, "does not leave the earth without a *padishah* [king], and never will."[15]

In this essay, Karim Khan devoted particular attention to developing the concept of the "fourth pillar." In each age, he wrote, God chooses some individuals from amongst the Shia, instructs them in the Imams' teachings, and sends them to act as the guides of ordinary people. Referring to these individuals as "God's governors," Karim Khan divided them into two distinct categories: (1) *nuqaba*, who, by permission of God, rule the country in absolute fashion, "nothing escaping their command," for they are the Imams' "aids," implementing their laws; and (2) the *nujaba*, who do not rule, yet are in possession of the Imams' knowledge, and whose task is to teach. These two categories, the author stated, function as rulers and instructors in this world. It is through them that the righteous are redeemed and the sinners damned; and it is they who, with the Imam's permission, decide who deserves to go to Hell and who to Paradise.

At this point, Karim Khan claimed that, though this "fourth pillar" of religion was previously hidden from and unknown to all, it had nevertheless always existed. In the present age, he went on, God has seen fit to "manifest and identify it," first through Ahmad Ahsai, who revealed it to humans, and then through Kazim Rashti. Those who have followed their instructions, Karim Khan asserted, have been saved, and those who have not are sinners. He concluded, "It must be known that after them [Ahsai and Rashti], God has not left the world void again, and He never shall until the manifestation of the Imam."[16] It was incumbent upon the faithful, therefore, to love this category of beings and their friends, and to hate their enemies: "For they have spread in the world nothing but the hidden truth of the Koran and the Traditions, and say nothing but what the people of Islam have reached agreement upon. . . . Thus, to oppose them is to oppose the Muslims' *ijma* [consensus], and that [is] heresy. . . . Similarly, to declare them enemies . . . is tantamount to heresy."[17]

While early Shaikhis were content with expressing their view of the Perfect Shia or "gate" to the Hidden Imam's knowledge simply as an idea, thus to provide legitimacy for their deviation from orthodoxy, Karim Khan aimed at actually establishing his own supreme religious authority. However, Shia jurisprudence grants no human being the right to claim absolute authority in times of Occultation, not even the mujtahids whose practice of *ijtihad* was defined as an endeavor to reach the correct opinion of the Imam. Though *taqlid* (following the rulings of a mujtahid in religious matters) was made incumbent upon all believers, the mujtahid's ruling was not viewed as binding. Nor was the individual bound to a single choice of religious leader. Moreover, in the year 940, orthodox Shia Islam had declared the "gate" to the Imam's knowledge closed in times of Occultation, and the Imam's exclusive function of further perfecting Muhammad's revelation through scriptural interpretation was indefinitely postponed.

The limitations on the mujtahids' function did not affect their influential position as the uncontested religious leaders of the community, which they consolidated in the beginning of the nineteenth century when they crushed the Akhbari opposition. As we shall see, Karim Khan's controversial Shaikhi stand threatened to revive the bitter Usuli-Akhbari dispute. Like the Akhbaris, he fiercely opposed the mujtahids' sociocultural power, which was based on their expertise in religious law, and he vehemently denounced their anti-intellectualism and literalist understanding of Shia texts. Like the Akhbaris, he rejected the enforcement of *taqlid*, a practice which provided the mujtahids' power with a social base. Rather, he insisted on the right to individual understanding of the holy texts. Karim Khan was, in fact, undertaking a power struggle directed against the collective mujtahids' leadership of the Shia institutional hierarchy.

In addition to his open defense of Shaikhi ideas, this remarkably frank exposition of the *rukn-i rabi* ("fourth pillar"), a term which earned the Kirmani Shaikhis the title of *rukniyya*, caused an uproar among orthodox ulama in Kirman and elsewhere. It led the Azerbaijani Shaikhis to accuse Karim Khan of inventing the "fourth pillar" and of distorting the teaching of Ahsai and Rashti. Personal harassment of Karim Khan and his followers intensified. His students frequently clashed with the orthodox students, both verbally and physically. Whenever he went to the mosque, he reportedly was surrounded immediately by soldiers, for rumors were spread throughout the country that he planned to overthrow the government in order to establish his own rule and change the religion. Stopping by Yazd on his way to Mashad, he encountered similar hostility among the local ulama, who tried to bar his entrance to the town. Though they failed to do so, they succeeded in keeping him away from their mosques and schools, forcing him to pray on Friday in an improvised tent. His Yazdi friends' attempt to organize a public debate was likewise met with contemptuous rejection. Karim Khan resorted to writing an essay "to clarify in simple, common language [Persian] my beliefs, and erase doubt," which he dedicated to the "masses of Shia all over."[18]

In this work, written in 1845 while he was still in Yazd, Karim Khan had already begun cautiously to express his ideas in orthodox fashion, to make them more respectable and to check the rumors his hostile opponents were spreading. He dissembled his fundamentally unorthodox thought behind an outward obedience to orthodoxy. He reassuringly proclaimed the Shaikhis' belief in Muhammad as the Seal of Prophets and in his physical ascension to heaven; in the Imams as the "noblest creatures of God" though not divine beings; in the return of the Hidden Imam on earth; in the physical resurrection; in Heaven and Hell; and in the right of the mujtahid to practice *ijtihad*. He even went so far as to assert that the dispute over the fourth pillar was purely a matter of semantics: "We mean the cognizance of the Shia. We mean those whose model we have to follow, that is, the mujtahids."[19] And he denied having any claim either to *ijtihad* or to leadership of any sort. Following this profession of orthodoxy, Karim Khan qualified his statements by adding that, just as it is a religious imperative to believe in those aspects of knowledge which have already been revealed, it is also an imperative to believe in the "new revelations of the present age, ... for in each age more is revealed to all."[20] He also specified that whereas obeying a mujtahid for the "external regulations" of religion is obligatory, when it comes to the principles of religion *(usul)*, obedience is not essential and is even forbidden, for "by *usul* we mean those matters [the four pillars] which the believer himself must understand through his own reason."[21] In accordance with the traditional Muslim theosophers' stand, Karim Khan restricted the function of the mujtahid to jurisprudence, and reserved the right to understand and reveal the inner truth to the "chosen ones." Like his predecessors, he assumed that such a clear-cut division of the religious functions would allow him freedom of interpretation in a field which he regarded as his own exclusive domain, and to which he denied the orthodox jurists any access.

Karim Khan stressed the fact that the Shaikhis' view was the same as the Imams', and opposition to it was tantamount to opposition to God and the Prophet. "We have done nothing but awaken the people from their sleep of ignorance," he wrote, "to show them the light of true Shia, to show them how to use their reason and judge which religious leader is worthy of following."[22] Following a lengthy, highly idealized biography of Ahsai aimed at clearing the shaikh's name from charges of heresy, he emphatically proclaimed: "The truth of the shaikh takes the place of the ulama's *ijma.* It is part of religion to have the right to know him. He was the leader. To refute him is to refute the Imams. His word has spread throughout the Shia world in the last thirty years; this is God's doing.... Other ulama cannot reach his level of learning and knowledge."[23] He deplored what he called the Shaikhi-Balasari "sectarianism" that was tearing the Shia community apart, and attributed it to "bad" ulama who, motivated by petty, personal issues rather than religious concern, were spreading false rumors and lies about the Shaikhis. Karim Khan lamented the fact that the "masses, their eyes glued to the mouth of the ulama ... and led astray...are now confused, fooled by them...and in doubt over who is right and who is wrong."[24] Consequently, the situation was such that the faithful must make a choice between one sect or the other, since, he wrote, a Shia has to have an official model to follow. To reject both was an act of heresy; but to accept both was one also. There was no in-between, no third alternative. In response to the ulama's excommunication of the Shaikhis, Karim Khan vehemently declared heretical "anyone who, knowing our beliefs, declares them heretical." Again and again, he condemned "those who oppose us" as "bad and enemies of religion," and he announced his readiness to repeat this statement publicly.[25]

The storms of controversy raged through the years, becoming increasingly violent, as Karim Khan further expanded Shaikhi thought. Often he saw himself compelled by circumstances to practice *taqiyya,* even though at times he publicly denied that this was what he was doing. In fact, however, he never failed to instruct his disciples on the necessary art of concealment of one's true beliefs. He reminded them that all the Imams used *taqiyya* to protect "the true religion" from its enemies, and thus revealed their knowledge only to a chosen few companions, and in some rare books. He insisted that in the present age of Occultation, the situation was even worse than in earlier times, and warned them against revealing all secrets. He explained that only some of those secrets could be entrusted to the initiated, and were not to be written down in any book, because it might fall into the hands of the enemy and the uninitiated. Should secrets be written down, he advised them again and again, the language should be neither precise nor clear, and was to be understood by the "people of learning" alone, thus to escape the attention of the ignorant masses. He highly recommended Arabic as the scientific language, in preference to Persian, the language of the masses. In the conclusion to one of his most important works, he actually ordered his disciples: "If God has willed the rule of the Hypocrites* over you, do not oppose them so that you do not cause any bloodshed, yours or your brothers'."[26]

As a result of this policy, Karim Khan's works do not offer any logical sequence of ideas, nor do they always present a consistent, coherent system to enable the reader to get a comprehensive view of his thought. Moreover, his tendencies to mix theosophy with social thought, metaphysics with the history of religion, and orthodox theology with speculative, radical notions of religion, make it difficult for

---

*In the Koran, this term is used to refer to enemies of the Prophet who pretended to convert to Islam. By derivation, it came to be used by self-proclaimed, righteous adherents of the "true" faith to refer to their opponents.

the analyst to know with certainty whether the author is mainly discussing spiritual issues or sociopolitical problems. Nevertheless, by pushing aside his tediously repetitive assurances of orthodox respectability, and especially by comparing pronouncements made in the earlier phase of his career to those made later on, one can derive a reasonably clear picture of his sociopolitical and religious views.

KARIM KHAN'S THOUGHT

On the whole, Karim Khan made no original contribution to the theosophical ideas expounded by Ahsai and Rashti. Despite some outbursts of orthodoxy, he merely reiterated early Shaikhi beliefs: that the resurrection is spiritual yet physical;[27] that the Prophet's ascension to heaven was a spiritual experience;[28] that the Hidden Imam exists in spirit in the transmaterial world of *hurqalya,* and is not physically hidden in this world;[29] that the Prophet and the Imams are divine beings, though dependent on God the Creator;[30] and that justice should be dropped as one of the five principles of Shia Islam, since it constitutes only one of God's attributes.[31] His conception of God was in accordance with traditional theosophy: that the Divine attributes are inherent in God's essence; and that God cannot be known by earthly beings, so that God has created the prophets—the intellects, or purest and highest form of being—through whom the Divine will is manifested to humans. His understanding of the four cosmic spheres is also consistent with traditional theosophy.

Similarly, his conception of the fall of created beings into the abyss, and their subsequent ascent to God—the more perfect being closest to God—closely follows that of the mystics. However, whereas the traditional theosophical view of the fall and ascent of beings is essentially spiritual, in the last analysis, Karim Khan's interpretation appears to acquire a chronological, historical dimension. He pictured a world of created beings in a perpetual, vertical, and irreversible ascension which began with the first prophet, Adam, and continued with successive divine revelations. Past ages are to be sought and can be seen below us, he wrote, and not next to us. Below us are the heavy ages of darkness and impurity, and higher up is the age of light and purity.[32] Karim Khan attributed this progressive ascent of created beings to God's concern for the well-being of earthly creatures, an idea which the Mutazilites and the Imami Shia had first propounded as being inherent in the divine attribute of justice, and which he carried through his entire scheme. However, whereas orthodox Imami scholars believed that what was "most salutary" for the believers' well-being was a central principle in explaining purely theological issues, Karim Khan, following the more radical Ismaili argument, made it the moving force behind the evolutionary changes that religion, and religious laws, necessarily go through. "God lay the foundation of progress,"[33] he asserted, by making humans perfectible, and hence able to advance their position from the lowest to the highest level of existence.[34]

Inspired by the works of Sadra, Ahsai, Rashti, the Ismailis, and through them by the vast spectrum of ideas with which the Islamic intellectual heritage provided him, Karim Khan sketched a cosmology and a religious structure which transformed the traditional view into a more progressive conception of human beings and the world. He manipulated the traditional theosophical doctrine of "relativity of being," which Sadra had perfected and which Ahsai had incorporated into his system of thought, further to socialize the mystical idea of a hierarchical structure of "more or less" perfect humans. In fact, the concept of the Perfect Man, or Perfect Shia, or Fourth Pillar, terms which Karim Khan more often than not used interchangeably, plays a central role in his socioreligious system. All his discussions of God, the Prophet, the Imams, divine revelations and of cosmology, served one purpose: to define and identify the sole legitimate leader of the community of faithful.

Progressive Evolution of Divine Revelations

People, Karim Khan wrote, change, and so does the world; hence, the conditions necessary for their well-being also change. For, after all, the created beings obey God and fulfill their obligations for the sake of their survival and self-improvement in this world. What is most salutary for humanity's well-being differs from one age to another, from one people to another. In every age, and for each group of people, a prophet is sent to show what is most salutary for them. The prophet's divine mission, suiting the new conditions of the specific time and place, supersedes the previous one. When and if, the author sternly warned, a people deliberately decide to reject that mission and, instead, abide by the old rulings, they condemn themselves to lead a "life behind their time," ill fitting their age.[35] Holy laws are comparable to the medical books that prescribe cures for human ills. "They diagnose the specifics of each act: which is evil, which is good; which is unjust, which is just; a lie or a truth." Since "what cures the disease of one age might not cure the disease of another," a new, living doctor is needed for every age to cure the sick.[36]

Reminiscent of Rashti's analysis is a favorite metaphor of Karim Khan's that compares the evolutionary development of revelations from imperfection to perfection to human growth from the embryonic stage to the age of full maturity. Each successive stage, he explained, receives a suitable, "nutritive," well-balanced diet. As the world progresses from one "messenger" to another, and as the ability of humans to understand increases, the revelations increase human knowledge accordingly. In each age, God grants the necessary and sufficient amount of knowledge to humanity. To each age its own measure, to each age its proper revelation.[37] Muhammad's prophecy corresponded to the time when the child, still in its mother's womb, was complete and about to be born. The Islamic law is, therefore, the last and most complete of all. However, Muhammad did not, and could not, reveal it in its entirety; humanity was not ready for it. "The Prophet brought the directives to the people of his age. As to the directives for the time after him, it was not up to him to bring them. For those later generations . . . successors were needed."[38] The actual birth occurred with Ali's Imamate; then, from one Imam to another, the infant grew in strength and age. At the time of the Occultation, the child was entrusted to the "ulama *zahiri*" (those learned in the external aspects of religion), who performed their function as elementary instructors adequately and dutifully. But by now, i.e., at the time Karim Khan wrote, the child was about to come of age; it was in need of new instruction, new teachers. "Old diets are no longer sufficient . . . the child is perishing from malnutrition."[39] Karim Khan announced that the time has come to prepare people for the most progressive stage, the utmost revelation of the esoteric truth. Humanity was getting stronger and more mature; hence, it deserved a new initiation. "The ulama of today cannot and should not teach the same elementary ABC again and again, as their predecessors had. [It] no longer serves any purpose."[40] Qualified teachers must take over the child's education, "whether the nannies [the jurists] like it or not. . . for they have been appointed by the parents [the Imams] themselves."[41]

The Evolutionary Concept of Ilm *("Knowledge of the Divine")*

Karim Khan professed his faith in the Koran as a miraculous and unsurpassed book encompassing all aspects of knowledge. He acknowledged it as the only valid source for philosophers and theologians, for people practicing any art or science. However, like the traditional theosophers, he also claimed that the esoteric meaning of the Koran is to be gradually revealed, since *ilm* is a perpetual, evolutionary process. Here in his writings, Karim Khan would carefully admit that *ilm* had already reached the stage of perfection with the Prophet, though it remained hidden; and he would reassure his reader that his conception of *ilm* as something that was evolutionary in no way constituted an innovation. It was the same religion, being gradually brought into the light for the first time. Similarly, Karim Khan argued that *ilm* is not acquired, but is given by God, at the time and place of God's choice, to the Perfect Beings. Echoing the philosophers, both Sunni and Shia, he stressed the fact that *ilm* is the highest divine attribute. It denotes an even greater perfection than miracles, a power with which only the prophets and the Imams are endowed. Whereas miracles are for the masses, who can only judge through what they actually see, *ilm* is for the "people with reason," for whom miracles without *ilm* cannot be attested. If there is *ilm*, there is no need for anything else to reach certitude; truth is in no need of miracles. Miracles are temporary, limited to the time of their occurrence; but *ilm* is everlasting, and enlightens more and more people as it spreads in time and space. Its advantages are greater. The world and the created beings, Karim Khan repeatedly claimed, cannot exist without *ilm*, as taught successively by the prophets, the Imams, and, in time of Occultation, by a living and present learned person. For naturally a teacher in Occultation or a dead master cannot teach.[42]

Having clearly established his notion of *ilm* as the knowledge of the divine which is progressively revealed through the ages to enlighten and guide humanity, Karim Khan set himself the task to disqualify the mujtahids from their position as religious leaders. He vehemently attacked the function of *ijtihad* as contrary to Shia principles, and accused the mujtahids of basing Shia jurisprudence on the Sunni practice of analogical reasoning and use of consensus. The consensus of fallible human beings, he protested, cannot be binding, since no one is legally compelled to abide by any particular mujtahid's ruling. It is important to note here that Karim Khan's stand against the practice of *ijtihad* (which reflects the views of the pre-Safavid Imami

Shia, as well as seventeenth- and eighteenth-century theosophers and Akhbaris) was aimed at discrediting the mujtahids' claim to religious authority, and thus at undermining their considerable power. In fact, he accused them of becoming a "government by force," having assumed authority illegally. Only God, he exclaimed, can appoint the leader of the community.[43] Those who call themselves ulama, he sarcastically wrote, are too often people with limited learning. They are wolves in disguise, seeking honors and privileges from secular rulers, leading hypocritical, immoral lives. They are the "sultan's functionaries," abusing their rank to take advantage of the persons and properties entrusted to them. They are incapable of waging successful war against the heresies flourishing in the country. A great number of them are possessed by the devil, hysterically denouncing their opponents as infidels, getting involved in fierce fist fights. "Our religion has fallen into the hands of Satan. ... In truth, religion is in need of a guardian to protect it from the evil of this group."[44] Karim Khan then sets up to identify the "guardian."

Rukn-i Rabi *(The Fourth Pillar)*

Ilm, Karim Khan stated, is the exclusive property of divinely inspired individuals endowed with a special imaginative perception allowing them to "see and hear things in *hurqalya,*" the transmaterial world. In the time of Occultation, they are the living witnesses, the "guarantors of God." In every age, God creates a pure creature to bear all the knowledge of Creation. He would be God's governor on earth "alive, present, and commander of his time," for past rules cannot fit the times a thousand years later. He would help "preserve the species" from corruption.[45] Although in some parts of his works Karim Khan was careful to say that this category of individuals is "hidden" from the eyes of people, in more candid paragraphs of the same works, he insisted that such a "governor" must be "seen and heard as the living Proof of God." Otherwise, he asked, "what difference is there between the Imam in Occultation and God who is beyond sight?" How could a Guarantor function in Occultation? If history and the Traditions were sufficient to guide people in this world, he argued, then the existence of the Prophet would have sufficed, and there would have been no need for the Imams, no purpose to their afflictions and pains.[46]

Karim Khan further explained that *ilm* reaches the common people through a chain of intermediaries who constitute a hierarchy of "more or less" Perfect Shia, each one representing the "gate" to a particular level of knowledge. These intermediaries are divided into two categories: (1) the *nuqaba*, "bearers of the Iman's *ilm*," who are themselves subdivided into those who possess "complete knowledge" and those with "partial knowledge"; and (2) the *nujaba*, the *nuqaba*'s representatives, who preach and call the Muslims to the right path, abiding by the *nuqaba*'s authoritative exposition of religion. The *nujaba* are also divided into two subgroups. They are all superior beings created to guide the people. Karim Khan acclaimed the *nuqaba* and the *nujaba* as the divine mediators between God and ordinary people, making it incumbent upon the faithful to abide by their rulings concerning "esoteric knowledge," just as it was incumbent upon them to obey the jurists in exoteric matters. In the event of conflict between them, he sternly advised his readers that the pronouncements of the *nuqaba* and the *nujaba* should be given preference over the jurists'. Karim Khan did not hesitate to assert clearly that the *nuqaba* and the *nujaba* were the successors of the Prophet in time of Occultation.[47]

At times, Karim Khan used the term Fourth Pillar to refer to the group in general, and at others to mean the head of the hierarchical structure. True to his conviction that only one person in any age is truly perfect, in most of his works he discussed the one Perfect Shia, the Salman of the time, the "gate to God on earth."[48] But by 1850–51, when the attacks against his ideas were becoming more virulent, he denied having posited the existence of a single such leader, and described the Fourth Pillar as a category of beings whose individual identities could not yet be revealed to humans, for time and circumstances did not allow it. He did not rule out the possibility that qualified initiates could know them directly.[49] And although, at times, Karim Khan confessed that the time to change the world had not yet come, and that the esoteric truth could not be divulged until the manifestation of the expected Imam, in his franker moments he openly claimed the opposite. He announced that "It is God's will that there be a teacher whose noble existence could infuse into the world the spirit of His inner teachings." Hence, in the thirteenth century of the Muslim era, God first manifested Shaikh Ahmad Ahsai, "the bearer of the secrets of the Imams the Pure," and then Kazim Rashti, to unfold slowly the esoteric meaning of the final revelation.[50] Karim Khan also explicitly stated, "I am the heir of his [Rashti's] knowledge," and added that just as the shaikh and the sayyid "were commissioned to reveal" what fitted the conditions of their respective times, and since "day by day, time progresses, and the people of today are more apt, I want to reveal more."[51] His works are full of passages praising himself. "God has given me an aptitude to explore and reveal religion He rarely gives to others." Referring to God's eternal "Book of knowledge," he would assert: "Know that whatever I write here is a dictation from that Book. The visible book I am writing with my hand is the copy of that Book written by God himself." Often he would tell his reader of his innate ability to see and hear things in *hurqalya,* the transmaterial world. [52]

Exoteric and Esoteric Governments

Karim Khan's attitude towards the government, too, was typically ambivalent. Although his discussion of the Fourth Pillar and the Perfect Shia was mainly in religious terms, and the chief target of his criticism was the religious establishment, his attacks were also aimed implicitly at the state as well. Consistent with his fundamental belief in the necessity for hierarchically structured authority, he condemned the idea of an equal sharing of power. Each age should be ruled by one and only one ruler, he explained, since in plurality there is dissent and corruption. He argued for the absolute need for one ruler, who would rule by divine right as God's representative. The ruler would act to bring harmony and accord among individuals living together in the same society, and to "lift dissension," since "dissension within the community is contrary to the Divine Will.... Dissension breeds corruption and self-destruction."[53]

At the same time, however, Karim Khan attempted to distinguish between what he termed the external government of the king, and the esoteric government of the religious leader. There could be no contradiction, no conflict between the one and the other, he hastened to admit, for the external world is obviously in need of an external king to rule over its subjects. He made a brief analysis of what constitutes a "good government," headed by the monarch and administered by appointed officials, who would take charge of the "four pillars of government": taxes, finances, defense, and justice, along with their respective hierarchies of subordinates. He concluded: "Hence, if in the visible world one cannot exist without a ruler, how can one find one's way to the invisible world without one?"[54]

Quoting verses from the Koran, Karim Khan interpreted them to mean that God created everything for the sake of the Perfect Beings, to be disposed of as they willed. He told his readers: "Do not believe that God addresses Himself to you," claiming God refers to the group of

Perfect Shia for whom the whole world was created, and adding, "all are sentenced to [follow] their command." His scheme amounted to a validation of the concept of the divine right of the rulers.

Karim Khan ended this highly controversial exposition by reverting to the earlier distinction he had made between external and the esoteric types of authority. "Just as in the external world," he wrote, "the king rules and the subjects obey, in the esoteric world, those for whom the sky and the earth are created must be obeyed."[5] The message was clear: it restated the traditional view of the temporal government as a necessary means to maintain social order, while expanding the notion of the right of the "chosen few" who possess divine *ilm* to supreme authority. Implicit in his argument was the claim that such a right could assert itself in this world, even while the Imam is in Occultation, and not only in the next.

Karim Khan's vehement attacks on the mujtahids went further than the theosophers' polemics against the jurists ever had; they even went beyond the policies of his Shaikhi predecessors. What he had done was to sketch, albeit in an esoteric fashion, a definite, hierarchical structure of leadership whereby the jurists and secular rulers, (the "external" officials) were given positions vital for the good functioning of society, but which were definitely and explicitly subordinate to the role of the true leader, the Perfect Shia or Fourth Pillar. Whereas the philosophers, Sufi masters, and Ahsai and Rashti themselves were content with mere speculative thought, Karim Khan was determined not only to plan a new socioreligious system, but also to see it implemented. In so doing, he would fulfill the centuries-old dream of the ancient Greek and Hellenized Muslim thinkers, of the Manicheans and Judeo-Christian mystics, and above all of the "true Shia" believers: to bring about the reign of the Sage, the Saint, the Qajar prince turned philosopher-king. However, powerful enemies, both religious and political, obstructed his plan.

Opposition

As exponents and guardians of the religious law, the mujtahids had collectively assumed a position of deputyship to the Hidden Iman. They would not tolerate any rival claim based on an alleged exclusive possession of knowledge of the divine. As already stated, classical Shia jurisprudence had declared the "gate" to such knowledge closed with the Occultation of the Imam. Similarly, Karim Khan's claim was seriously contested by Shaikhi leaders in Azerbaijan and, more importantly, by a rival contender for supreme authority. As we shall see in the following chapter, Mirza Ali Muhammad, a merchant from Shiraz, assumed the title of Bab, or "gate" to the Imam's knowledge, and declared himself the leader for whose advent Kazim Rashti had been a precursor, before he ultimately announced the dawn of a new religious era. Karim Khan and the Bab (as Mirza Ali Muhammad came to be known) held almost identical, radical theories of leadership, and both aimed at undermining the mujtahids' authority. However, when the Bab and his followers transformed doctrinal disputes into a movement of open revolt, Karim Khan, rather than joining their forces, chose to denounce the Bab as an imposter and, in consequence, subdue the tone of his own campaign for supreme leadership.

Because of the bewildering labyrinth of religious politics in nineteenth-century Iran, and the widespread practice of *taqiyya* and the art of esoteric writing, it is difficult for the historian to determine the exact nature and precise causes of the opposition which rose against Karim Khan and which so seriously divided Kirmani society into different religious camps. Information gathered from the few available sources at least seems to cast doubt that a concern for orthodoxy was what motivated Karim Khan's opponents.

A contemporary Bahai source claims that the chief subject of discord was the question of succession to Kazim Rashti, and alleges Sayyid Aqa Javad, a cousin of Mirza Ali Muhammad, had secretly converted to Babism.[56] No Muslim sources are available so far to prove this statement correct. However, the late Sayyid Muhammad Hashimi of Kirman, a modern Muslim historian-journalist, claimed that Sayyid Aqa Javad was responsible for releasing from prison a former Shaikhi follower of Karim Khan, a respected and learned man by the name of Mulla Muhammad Jafar, who had converted to Babism and was consequently denounced by his former master.[57] Another contemporary Muslim historian from Kirman, Bastani-Parizi, confirms Hashimi's statement that Sayyid Aqa Javad used his influence with the then Governor of Kirman to save Mulla Muhammad Jafar from the social and professional isolation (not prison, as Hashimi claims) imposed upon him as a result of Karim Khan's vengeful action. Sayyid Aqa Javad, according to Bastani-Parizi, had praised Mulla Jafar as a righteous religious leader, worthy of trust.[58] Given the merciless persecution the Babis, or any alleged Babi, suffered at the hands of the Muslims, one cannot help wondering how a religious leader of the stature of Sayyid Aqa Javad would bend his righteous principles to come to the rescue of a heretic, unless he himself had some kind of sympathy for the movement.

Furthermore, Bastani-Parizi states that the Bab had sent personal letters to Karim Khan and two other religious leaders, Aqa Ahmad, and Mulla Muhammad Jafar, requesting their support for his cause. Whereas the former publicly repudiated him, and the latter "kept silence," Aqa Ahmad cautiously answered: "The ulama of Kirman are not that influential," and advised him to "straighten out the situation in Isfahan and Tehran" and "we shall then follow."[59] Again, such a wait-and-see response to heresy on the part of a mujtahid displayed a tolerance that was highly untypical of the established orthodoxy. Was Aqa Ahmad also secretly sympathetic to Babism? Or were he and Aqa Javad merely adopting the traditional policy of befriending "the enemy of my enemy," at the risk of seriously compromising their reputation in times when to be seen with a Babi was cause enough for indictment?

Regardless of the religious coloring of his enemies' politics, Karim Khan encountered relentless opposition on three fronts: orthodox, Shaikhi (in Azerbaijan), and Babi. He directed his most openly vicious, polemical attacks against the Bab. He wrote several essays to refute the latter's claim to divine knowledge and to ridicule the *Bayan*, the Bab's "revealed book," for its blasphemous pretensions. "Our Prophet is the last prophet," he emphatically proclaimed, "and there will be no other after him, ever. Our Koran is God's and the Prophet's miracle. Anyone who pretends to be a new prophet bringing a new message is a heretic."[60] Using the two letters the Bab had allegedly written to him (one asking him to join the Babi revolt and declare holy war against the religious and secular establishment, the other asking him to mention the Bab's name in the Friday prayer) as evidence against him, the Shaikhi leader vowed to destroy the imposter. It was his sacred duty, he remarked, to obstruct his path. Karim Khan's fierce antagonism was obviously inspired by pure, self-promoting, competitive interests rather than shocked piety. He called the Bab "the gate to hell," and "the devil's disciple," charging he had abused and corrupted Ahsai's knowledge, and used it to achieve his own worldly ends. Karim Khan insisted that "the real Bab exists, a person who carries the Imam's light; God has commanded his existence," as the gate to the Imam's knowledge,[61] obviously meaning himself.

The Shaikhi leader lived to witness the crushing defeat of his hated rival in July 1850. When news of Mirza Ali Muhammad's death reached him, Karim Khan could not contain his jubilant relief. "Rejoice with the death of the Bab," he wrote gleefully. "His body was left for the vultures to devour to prove to all there is nothing divine about him. He has no tomb to be visited, no shrine. He did not die in prison...but [was] seen by all ... so that no one can claim he is in Occultation. Praised be God, there is no more need to mention his name."[62] Karim Khan's relief was short-lived, for the Bab's successors and followers carried on his challenge and sought by every means to undermine the Kirmani Shaikhi leadership.

Continued rumors that Karim Khan was preparing to establish an autonomous religious government, separate from both the religious and secular ruling establishment, reached the Shah's court in Tehran. Karim Khan was called to the capital and kept there under close surveillance for a period lasting a year and a half. Compelled to praise and pay allegiance to Nasir al-Din Shah, he defended the secular monarch's right to rule as a protector of religion against its enemies, and as a guardian preserving law and order among the faithful, who, left on their own, would tend to destroy each other and their society.[63] Additional opposition came from some orthodox ulama, who accused him of ordering his disciples to disregard the directives of the mujtahids; of claiming to be the Perfect Shia, the Fourth Pillar, even the Bab; of encouraging the expropriation of non-Shaikhi properties by the Shaikhis; and of espousing Akhbari ideas.

In addition to the orthodox ulama's hostility, the Babi revolt and its repercussions, as well as the endless political intrigues forced Karim Khan to adopt a subdued tone. By the early 1850s, his works reflected a defensive attitude. He denied all charges, protested his innocence, and, in turn, attacked his enemies, who, out of "sheer jealousy," he claimed, were determined to undermine his position by falsifying Shaikhi writings and distorting his pronouncements.

In an interesting and revealing essay addressed to his disciples[64] in which he assumed the stern, authoritarian tone of the master who sees himself in peril, he advised them to be prudent and passively accept the Shaikhi lot. He reprimanded them for their lack of respect to the mujtahids, and for spreading their belief that the Shaikhi leaders alone were the Fourth Pillars of their time. He declared this category of beings in Occultation. He forbade them to think of him as a man of status and authority: "I have often told you," he wrote, "and I am still telling you that, because of the knowledge God has bestowed on me, I have given up the Qajar garb. Curse upon those who would still treat me as one of them. Your behavior towards me should conform to the religious leaders' customs. ... Similarly, do not crowd any more the door of the mosques and school where I lecture. Do not follow me wherever I go, unless you have a specific question or issue you wish to discuss. . . . I have never liked such crowds. . . . Do not take refuge in my house. . . . Do not ask me to interfere on your behalf with the authorities. . . . Do not use titles while addressing me in public. . . . Do not try to protect me when enemies attack me behind my back."[65]

He counseled his followers to adopt the traditional Shia attitude of acquiescence towards the state, and to pay allegiance to whoever God has made king, and he severely rebuked them for participating in street fights. He told them not to add fuel to the fire, and not to oppose the mujtahids' instructions, even if they might run counter to their own beliefs. He begged them to stop discussing religious issues with others: "To each subject of conversation its proper place and its proper people."[66] Karim Khan concluded by expressing regret that he could not remedy his followers' situation, just as the Prophet was not able to remedy the situation of his community, nor were the Imams, nor the Shaikhs.

In all his works written in the 1850s and '60s, Karim Khan blatantly practiced *taqiyya*, to the point of totally refuting his earlier pronouncements and even denying having uttered them. Thus, he pretended that he considered the mujtahids to be among the category of Fourth Pillars, and that respect and obedience to them was incumbent upon the faithful. Vehemently denying any aspiration to power, he firmly stated Shaikhism is not Babism, and affirmed that the category of beings known as Fourth Pillars is definitely in Occultation. The effect was to reduce the whole Shaikhi controversy to mere differences over the understanding of some of the Traditions.[67]

Though he strongly denied practicing *taqiyya*, swearing he wrote what he truly thought, during the same period Karim Khan further developed his conception of religion as a medical cure requiring a living doctor to prescribe it for the patient, and he restated his conviction that there must always he a living Proof to act as the Guarantor of God on earth, and as the guide of the community. Repeating his earlier statements, in which he characterized the world as being in a perpetual process of change, with the divine rules and regulations changing accordingly, he insisted on the orthodoxy of his views by reminding his readers of the Prophet's abrogation of some of his earlier commands. He declared that the sum total of all the commands through the ages were contained in the Koran, and were being progressively revealed by God's representatives. Moreover, Karim Khan reaffirmed his belief that the mujtahids were not qualified for such a holy task, since their *ijtihad* was limited and limiting. He stated that God, in the absence of the Imam—who is "a spirit, an essence and not a body"—appoints a "successor to the Prophet's successor," whom he initiates and raises to a rank high above ordinary people. Each age, he wrote, including the present age, is given one and only one such Perfect Man, "a living intermediary," whether he is acknowledged as such or not.[68] In a final will, written shortly before his death, Karim Khan repeated his advice to his followers to practice *taqiyya* whenever necessary, and ordered them to abide by the rulings of the Perfect Shia.[69]

Shaikhi Conservatism

Like many other Muslim intellectual dissidents before him, Hajj Karim Khan revolted against the conception of knowledge as something already given in its entirety with the Koranic revelation, and instead promoted the belief that human understanding accumulates through the ages, as divine knowledge is constantly and progressively revealed by God through intermediaries. Humans, he wrote, are born with an innate craving for knowledge, similar to hunger and thirst; and it is to fulfill this need that God periodically sends prophets, Imams, and Fourth Pillars. "Only the sick and the perverse refuse to acknowledge this trait of human character."[70] With a much louder voice and a more imperative tone than anyone before him, the Shaikhi leader sought to infuse a nonconforming spirit into his disciples by inciting them to give up the passive and lazy attitude that shrugs off everything with an *"insha'allah"* ("God willing"), and to seek "true *ilm*" from a living master, "for that is the natural order of the world." He asked them to organize themselves and form a society of true believers, consisting of several small, tightly knit units of no more than five members each, to be headed by a leader. All would receive their *ilm* directly from authoritative sources, transmitted through a spiritually genealogic chain of believers. He explained, in a description reminiscent of the early Ismaili organizations, that an organized community is necessary since "a believer cannot go along God's path alone."[71] He often encouraged his followers to fight for their faith, and to be self-defensively on their guard. A "true believer" himself, he promised them that the "people of truth" would eventually triumph over their opponents. Fear not the "heretic majority," he would tell them reassuringly, for goodness though always numerically inferior to evil, is nearer to God: hadn't the Imams "always suffered defeat and martyrdom?"[72]

Despite his attempts to liberate divine knowledge from the static framework into which the jurists had been attempting to enclose it, Karim Khan's own conception of knowledge proved to be as narrow and as bound to cultural traditions as that of his opponents. For he basically reinforced, and in some cases revived, traditional Shia theosophical views: of knowledge as an omniscience in the exclusive possession of the few, who reveal its esoteric doctrines to the qualified adepts, the elite; and of the alienated condition of those few who follow the cult of the true leader. Like the theosophers and the early Shaikhis, he insisted on the superiority of inspiration philosophical inquiry over the theologians' legalistic approach to religion. Also like them, he sought a legitimate Islamic basis for his progressive view of people and society in a perpetual process of change, by reverting to the old practice of distinguishing the esoteric from the exoteric interpretation of the Koranic verses.

Karim Khan wished to inspire a renewal in religious understanding, freeing some of its doctrines from literal; orthodox interpretation, in order to make them more open to change. However, his reforms were basically aimed at promoting his own interests and his own status as the Fourth Pillar. He attacked the mujtahid's practice of *ijtihad* on the ground that it had no legitimate basis in Imami Shia; yet he lay claim to a divinely appointed position of leadership which was as difficult, if not more difficult, to justify doctrinally.

Despite his bold protest against orthodoxy, and despite his own heterodoxy, his socioreligious thought displayed a conservative outlook. For at the root of his structured, socioreligious system lies a firm belief in human inequality. Karim Khan espoused the traditional Muslim philosophers' view that some are born to rule, some to be ruled; some to be masters, others to be servants; that, in fact, all creatures of God have a definite place and rank in the cosmic hierarchy, and that it is contrary to the Divine Order to move upward, beyond one's assigned position on the scale of "graded beings."[73] Impatient with the orthodox ulama's acceptance of differences of opinion over minor religious issues, ultimately he wished to see established an absolute, unified system of thought which advocated absolutist solutions.

Karim Khan, the scholar who took so much pride in his knowledge, both scientific and religious, and devoted his leisure time to the study of astronomy, optics, chemistry and linguistics, no less than the orthodox ulama resisted the import of European ideas and scientific theories. At the time when only a handful of his compatriots were acquainted with Europe, its languages and civilization, and when the

ruling elite were barely beginning to realize the need for modernization, he vehemently criticized the central government's feeble attempts
at educational reform. He especially resented the establishment of Dar
al-Funun, a secular school teaching a modern curriculum, dismissing it
as a plot by incompetent Iranians and foreigners to corrupt the cream of
the Iranian youth. When he heard about some European scientific
views which ran counter to Islamic teachings, such as the existence of
vacuums or the heliocentricity of the universe, he did not hesitate to
reject them categorically, either as nonsensical and erroneously understood by ignorant travelers, or as being merely the "exoteric interpretation" of nonbelievers who did not possess the esoteric truth.[75]

Similarly, Karim Khan warned against the potential threat of
social and cultural contact with Europe. He deplored the eruption of a
"new malady" which, he declared, was rapidly reaching epidemic
proportions as a result of certain unhealthy wishes of pleasure-seeking
individuals, who refused to associate with the ulama, and would no
longer abide by their religious principles. The desire for anything
European, what he termed this "new malady," would only lead to the
national adoption of the infidels' evil customs, he warned repeatedly.
"Our mosques would turn into churches. Our women would be free to
go wherever they wish to, sit with whomever they wish, go out of the
house whenever they want. They [Europeans] have not yet established
complete sovereignty over our country, but they are already ordering
our women not to veil their faces. Would any Muslim accept that his
wife goes out in public, face all made up? Would any Muslim accept
that wine is freely sold in the bazaar to any man or woman ... that
women be drunk in public places? God forbid!"[75]

Karim Khan's attack on the new interest in secular reforms within
Iran was no less violent in tone. Describing its proponents as "ignorant, conceited youth who, when they hear the call of freedom, immediately make themselves look like Europeans, adopting European
customs and betraying Islam and Islamic values," he predicted, if they
succeeded, that "the ulama would have no power to speak." Muslim
children would be educated as Christians in European schools established all over the nation, and taught by Europeans using European
books. The reformers would allow the notables and the ulama to sit in
assemblies next to Zoroastrians, Jews and Armenians; hence, the religious minorities would become the masters, and the Muslims the
servants. Is this freedom? he asked. Sounding the alarm against "that
day when freedom has come, and no one fears Islam" and when, "By
God, thousands of Iranians would turn completely European," he

sternly pronounced heretical "anyone who befriends a European, for he would be considered a European himself ... and thus has apostasized and adopted the religion of the European."[76]

Thus, the Shaikhis, who, while confronting the orthodox jurists had proposed a far-reaching program of doctrinal reforms, emerged by the 1850s as staunch advocates of social and cultural isolation from the world of the "infidels." Karim Khan was perhaps one of the first clerics in Iran to sense the possible consequences of some of the ideas imported from the West—namely, that some ulama like himself stood to lose with the spread of new conceptions of knowledge, change, progress, secularism, and their like. His defensive attitude, itself a consequence of sociopolitical developments in the second half of the nineteenth century, was to prove fatal to the school's position as a champion of progressive Shia thought in Iran.

Socially isolated as a result of the controversies that his ideas gave rise to, defeated and embittered, Karim Khan spent his last years in secluded privacy on his estate in Langar, outside Kirman city, without the pomp and glamor to which he, the Qajar prince, had been accustomed. Under his leadership, Shaikhism had become an important and socially influential school of Shia theology, ranking among its followers princes, court dignitaries, and educated upper class men and women, as well as members of the upper class of ulama. But his ideas remained unrealized, his ambition unfulfilled. The radical transformation of Shaikhi ideas into a concrete program of action was instead undertaken by a merchant from a non-clerical, middle class background, who was successful in rallying to his cause capable leaders mostly from similar social backgrounds.

4

The Politicization of Dissent in Shia Thought: Babism

THE SHORT HISTORY (1844–50) of the Babi movement during the lifetime of its founder, Mirza Ali Muhammad known as the Bab, has received relatively scant attention from scholars of modern Iran. The ulama had condemned Babism as heresy and charged the Bab with apostasy. Consequently, sources available in Persian or Arabic are either hostile or apologetic, depending on the author's personal religious orientation. Moreover, distortions and selective omissions of facts and ideas are to be found in accounts written after the Bab's death in 1850 by followers of the two rival contenders for his succession: the Azalis (followers of Mirza Yahya Nuri Subh-i Azal), and the Bahais (followers of Mirza Husain Ali Nuri Bahaullah). Such conflicting and emotionally charged accounts render the historian's task especially difficult.

Mirza Ali Muhammad was born in Shiraz on October 20, 1819, into a family of merchants. An orphan since early childhood, he was raised by his maternal uncle, Hajj Mirza Sayyid Ali, and brought up to pursue the family's professional occupation. While in his teens, he was sent to Bushihr, the Persian Gulf port, to carry on his uncle's business there. Though he proved to be a capable merchant in his own right, both hostile and partisan sources describe the Shirazi youth as more inclined to solitary meditation. Whereas the famous Court chronicler, Lisan al-Mulk, depicts him as a mentally deranged Sufi, prone to ecstatic contemplation, who spent hours of hot summer days on the roof of the caravanserai where he lodged, sympathetic authors stress the spiritually creative nature of his solitary activities. Though the duration of his stay in Bushihr is not known exactly, with estimates ranging from one to five years depending on the source, all biographers agree that Mirza Ali Muhammad decided to give up a promising mercantile career to go to Kerbala, the center of Shia religious studies. There he met Kazim Rashti, whose lectures he attended. Here again biographers disagree on the length of his stay in the holy city and on whether he was a disciple of the Shaikhi leader. While Muslim sources insist he spent two years studying with Kazim Rashti, Babi writers, anxious to emphasize the uniqueness and independence of his thought, minimize his contact with Rashti, and reduce his actual sojourn in Kerbala to three months, claiming he spent a year in Najaf. Regardless of the conflicting statements, the influence of Shaikhi ideas is clearly discernable in the Bab's works. Moreover, there is absolutely no doubt that he had become a member of the Shaikhi circle in Kerbala, and had adopted Shaikhi practices of worship. In a number of his early works, he stated that he regarded himself as Rashti's disciple.

When Kazim Rashti died in 1844, Mirza Ali Muhammad was no longer in Kerbala, but back in Shiraz, ready to proclaim his own mission. The exact nature of this mission constitutes another subject of heated disputes among the few scholars who have worked on the early history of Babism. However, a careful study of all existing views, in addition to a thorough, chronological analysis of the Bab's writings, lead one to conclude that this mission was, from the start, aimed at revealing a new religion and not just reforming Shia Islam, but that he had adopted a cautious policy of issuing gradual proclamations. In his *Seven Proofs*, he openly admits to the fact that, in the beginning of his preaching, he spoke an orthodox language, referring to the Koran and to the Koranic law in order to avoid provoking an unncesssary shock among his potential followers. This would contradict Lisan al-Mulk's view (which was accepted by Gobineau, E. G. Browne, and A. L. M. Nicolas himself, before he revised his thinking) that Mirza Ali Muhammad had, in an opportunistic fashion, first declared himself to be the successor of Rashti, then the Bab or "gate" to the Imam's teaching, then the expected Imam, before finally proclaiming a new prophetic revelation. Instead, it seems, the young Shirazi actually was slowly laying the foundation for the ultimate unveiling of a new religion.

Most sources agree on the date Mirza Ali Muhammad supposedly received the "Divine Call": March 24, 1844[1], a date the Bab later chose to mark the beginning of the new Babi calendar. From the pulpit of the mosque near his home, he publicly pronounced that the gate (Bab) to the Imam's knowledge, which the orthodox ulama had declared shut in times of Occultation, was now open. While leading an intensive anti-ulama campaign, charging some of them with corruption and worldliness, he was secretly corresponding with adepts to explain the divine origin of his writings, at the same time counseling them discretion and prudence in spreading the word. He was also seeing a number of Shaikhis who, following Rashti's death, had rejected Karim Khan Kirmani's claims and came to meet him in Shiraz and pay allegiance to his cause. Among the first to convert were two Shaikhi disciples of Rashti: Mulla Husain Bushrui, a cleric and native of Khurasan whom he entitled Bab al-Bab ("Gate to the Gate"); and another cleric from Mazandaran, Mirza Muhammad Ali Barfurushi, later given the title of Quddus. Both proved to be his most zealous missionaries and most capable revolutionary leaders.

The Bab and his apostles decided it was of utmost importance to attract the attention, and possibly the patronage, of major religious and political personalities throughout the nation. Bushrui, who had previously demonstrated his great debating talent and persuasive abilities in defense of Shaikhi views while Rashti was alive, was chosen as the Bab's personal emissary to carry a letter to the Shah in Tehran and to contact government officials. Though Bushrui was not granted a royal audience, he succeeded in handling the Bab's dispatch to the then Chief Minister, Hajj Mirza Aqasi. Similarly, he found in the person of Manuchihr Khan, Mutamid al-Daula, governor of Isfahan, a powerful source of political support. He converted ulama, notables, and wealthy merchants in Isfahan, Tehran, Kashan and Khurasan, some of whom were to play a dominant role in the future events of the Babi movement. Among them were: Mulla Shaikh Ali and Mulla Sadiq, later known respectively as Azim and Muqaddas; Mirza Jani, the merchant of Kashan, who was to write the first important chronicle of the early Babi history; Mirza Husain Ali Nuri, the future Bahaullah, son of a rich and prominent Qajar civil servant; as well as Mirza Yahya Nuri, Husain Ali's half brother, who later was to assume the title of Subh-i Azal.

In Najaf and Kerbala, Babi missionary activities added fire to already-existing doctrinal disputes. Major Henry Rawlinson, the British political agent in Baghdad, in his diplomatic dispatches dated January and February 1845, correctly remarked: "I understand that considerable uneasiness is beginning to display itself in Kerbala and Najaf, in regard to the expected Manifestation of the Imam, and I am apprehensive that the measures now in progress will rather increase than allay the excitement."[2] Mulla Ali Bastami, a Babi convert sent by the Bab to preach in Iraq, was eventually arrested by the Ottoman authorities and sent to Istanbul by way of Baghdad. He was allegedly poisoned before reaching the Turkish capital, and his death thus provided the Babi cause with its first martyr.

It was also in Kerbala that Qurrat al-Ain (1814–52), the remarkable Babi woman convert whose story Lord Curzon describes as "the most affecting episode in modern history,"[3] began to attract wide public attention. A native of Qazvin, Zarrin-Taj, as she was then called, was the daughter of Hajj Mulla Salih, and niece of Hajj Mulla Muhammad Taqi, both men being prominent members of the local orthodox religious establishment and avowed enemies of Ahsai and Rashti. Though her husband, her uncle's son, also belonged to the orthodox circle, she chose to adhere to the Shaikhi school of theology introduced to her by another uncle, Mulla Muhammad Ali, a loyal Shaikhi, and she frequently corresponded with Sayyid Kazim, who had given her the title by which she became famous. Endowed with beauty, intelligence, and an indomitable power of will, she was well versed in the religious sciences, studies usually restricted to men, though it was not uncommon for daughters of ulama to receive a good education, and even become ulama themselves. She apparently used to astonish her entourage by boldly participating in learned discussions with the local notables and ulama, often demolishing their arguments to assert her own. From early adulthood, an aggressive, combative mood expressed her overt recognition of a woman's right to state her differences with traditional conventions. Thus, she ventured into a male-dominated realm, engaging in an activity that best suited her temper and native talents as well as provided her with an outlet for her rebellious restlessness. Pride, audacity, and fierce loyalty characterized her swift conversion to Babism and her subsequent activities as a dedicated missionary, and avant-garde leader of the movement.

Existing historical accounts of her life are too inadequate and inconsistent chronologically to draw a precise biographical sketch. Nicolas[4] and Jani[5] assert that Qurrat al-Ain was a regular student of Rashti while she was in Kerbala with her husband, and that she had then become acquainted with Shaikhi followers who were to become the Bab's faithful disciples. An Azali source[6] adds that in Kerbala she had also met Mirza Ali Muhammad, though it was back in Qazvin that she had heard of the "Call" and converted. Balyuzi, on the other hand, denies she ever met Rashti (having reached Kerbala shortly after the latter's death) or even the Bab; and he states that it was in the holy city that she heard of the Bab's claim through Mulla Ali Bastami.[7] Regardless of these discrepancies, most accounts of the Babi early history show her busy organizing public debates, corresponding and meeting with other major Babi leaders, and lecturing to vast crowds of men and women (separated from them by a curtain), whom she "bewitched" (to quote a hostile but admiring source) with the forcefulness of her personality and the eloquence of her rhetoric, thus successfully drawing new converts to her faith. All sources unanimously agree she proved to be a dominant figure in the movement—a brilliant commentator of the Bab's writings and doctrines, and skillful at convincing the skeptics of their validity by references to the Koran and the Traditions. Browne's tribute best summarizes a commonly held view: "The appearance of such a woman as Kurratu'l-Ayn is in any country and any age a rare phenomenon, but in such a country as Persia it is a prodigy, nay, almost a miracle. . . . She stands forth incomparable and immortal amidst her country women. Had the Babi religion no other claim to greatness, this were sufficient: that it produced a heroine like Kurratu'l-Ayn."[8]

In the fall of 1844, having sown the seed of his religious revolution in Shiraz, the Bab undertook a pilgrimage to Mecca, taking with him Quddus and his uncle. It appears that he had originally planned to fulfill Shia messianic prophecies in Kerbala, where he had summoned followers to join him. In fact, many had converged on the holy city in Iraq. Armed with weapons they had manufactured or purchased, they were ready to fight the last holy war which, in Shia Traditions, marks the manifestation of the expected Imam. However, for some reason the Bab changed his strategy. Hostile sources relate how, once in the holy Muslim city, Mirza Ali Muhammad stood by the sacred stone, the Kaba, center of the pilgrims' worship rituals, a sword in one hand and a Koran in the other, enacting the part of the expected Imam on the day of his manifestation as indicated in the Shia Traditions, thus crudely playing on the imagination of the credulous faithful. Babi sources do not deny the scene, though some challenge the sword and Koran part. The Bab himself explained this was the place where he publicly proclaimed "I am he whose advent you have been awaiting,"[9] and attempted to convince the pilgrims of the authenticity of his claim. Doubtless the Bab's intention then was to reserve his true doctrine to the chosen few adepts, and to speak the common orthodox language of the ordinary Shia believers, who would thus see in him the promised Imam, their conquering saint returning to plant the Shia banner over all the world and restore the reign of the true religion.

It is highly doubtful that the Bab's spectacular show in Mecca and Medina produced the desired result. On the other hand, his missionaries in Iraq and Iran achieved definite concrete gains for their master's cause. They had rapidly set up a network of couriers and preachers, carrying the Bab's messages and copies of his early writings to the various provinces, aiming at attracting converts, followers, and patrons to sponsor their cause. They campaigned vigorously in spite of the harassment and abuse, both verbal and physical, to which they were subjected by the outraged populace, led by both orthodox and Shaikhi ulama. Relentlessly and tirelessly, they organized public meetings where they spoke of the Bab and his message.

Back in Iran in the Spring of 1845, the Bab stopped in Bushihr, which he used as a temporary base to organize and direct the next phase of the movement. He had instructed his uncle to return to Shiraz via Iraq in order to preach his doctrine to the ulama of Baghdad and its neighboring towns, and, once in Shiraz, to arrange for a general convocation of all the believers. He had also asked his uncle to send for his missionaries scattered in the different provinces and have them converge on Shiraz.

When Muqaddas and Quddus arrived in Shiraz in the summer of 1845, they began preaching the new faith at the small neighborhood mosque where Mirza Ali Muhammad had first proclaimed his mission. From the pulpit, they mentioned the Bab's name in the call for prayer, which they directed towards the Bab's house, indicating it as the new *qibla* (point of direction for the Muslim prayer). Shiraz thus was to become the new Mecca. Muqaddas also addressed a sermon to the officials of the city, admonishing them to abide by the new rulings and warning them against "seizing what belongs to God."[10]

Public sentiment was aroused and both government and religious leaders were offended. Muqaddas, Quddus, and a third Babi were summoned to the Shiraz governor's residence, where they repeated their earlier statements, adding that not only were all worldly possessions the Bab's exclusive property, but also that only he could make political appointments. For such blasphemies, the three Babis were exposed to public ridicule, beaten up, and then expelled from the city. Soldiers were sent to Bushihr to bring the imposter back to Shiraz. Babi sources assert Mirza Ali Muhammad was already on his way to Shiraz when he met them.

According to hostile sources, the Bab was forced to recant at a public interrogation which was organized by the governor and the local religious leaders, where he was ridiculed, verbally abused, and sentenced to house arrest. A London *Times* correspondent confirmed that he "very wisely denied the charge of apostasy laid against him and thus escaped from punishment."[11] On the other hand, Babi accounts relate how, far from recanting, the Bab came out of his debate with the governor and the ulama in triumph. In reality, the young Shirazi both recanted and, in an esoteric fashion, remained true to his faith. In one of his writings,[12] he admitted he was "inspired" by God "with the word of negation" so that "my being was protected from the threat of death"; yet he described his "confession" as a necessary self-sacrifice for the cause, and compared himself to the third Imam, Husain, who suffered martyrdom for the sake of the Shia. He had outwitted his opponents, he added, for he had only denied being the Bab, the Imam's agent, which was true since he was really the Prophet of the Age, and not merely an intermediary. Nevertheless, in the same work Mirza Ali Muhammad both cried out for help "to conquer the enemy and defeat his evil," and cautioned his missionaries not to preach in his name for a while.

Thus, the ulama in Shiraz, dismissing the rebel as a lunatic of no further consequence, took no drastic measures to crush the movement beyond their harassment of suspected Babis. However, far from leading a discreet, quiet life as he was ordered, the Bab spent a period of fifteen months in intense activity, continuously converting and writing what he claimed to be divinely inspired tablets.

Three new converts of that period proved to be of great value to the cause. The first was Sayyid Yahya Darabi, son of Sayyid Jafar Darabi known as Kashfi, a famous and highly respected scholar of the time. Sayyid Yahya himself was a reputed young religious scholar of some influence in Muhammad Shah's court in Tehran. He was also a trusted companion of Tahmasp Mirza Muayyid al-Daula, a grandson of Fathali Shah and cousin of the reigning monarch. According to Nicolas, it was Tahmasp Mirza who had sent Yahya to Shiraz to gather information regarding the new heresy and report to the Court. However, the royal emissary, after extensive interviews with the Bab, converted and offered his services to the Babi cause. The second convert was Hajj Sayyid Javad Kerbalai, an influential Shaikhi who had enjoyed Rashti's confidence; the third was Mulla Muhammad Ali Hujjat al-Islam, a leading cleric of Zanjan.

Meetings were secretly organized to gather Babi disciples, and discuss the doctrine and future plans of action. Bushrui, the Bab al-Bab, emerged as the chief organizer and most important representative for the movement. Together with Quddus, Shaikh Azim, Muqaddas, and a few others who formed the nucleus of the Babi leadership, he founded a militia, aiming at one ultimate goal: the growth and spread of Babism all over the nation. All of the apostles of the Bab had their own affiliates and devoted followers who helped in the expansion of the Babi secret society. Kazem Beg, a contemporary observer who depicted Mirza Ali Muhammad as an ascetic Sufi inclined to meditation, a "dreamer" genuinely interested in religious and moral reforms, believed that the Bab was wrongly held responsible for many ideas which originated with his disciples—ambitious, scheming, unscrupulous militants who used him for their own political ends. Kazem Beg insists that, even if the Bab attended those meetings at all, it was reluctantly and only in order to provide the program with a spiritual and moral ideal.[13]

However, Mirza Ali Muhammad's works and personal correspondence lead one to conclude that, far from being a gifted but passive idealist, content with the moral and spiritual aspects of the movement he gave birth to, he took an active, leading part in the decision making and the planning of the revolt. In one of his earliest essays, *Qayyum al-Asma*, he specifically called for holy war as a necessary preparation for the advent of the expected Imam. "O armies of God!" he wrote, "when you wage war with the infidels, do not fear their numbers. . . . Slay those who have joined partners with God, and leave not a single one of the unbelievers alive upon earth, so that the earth and all that upon it may be purified for the Remnant of God, the expected One."[14] Similarly, in the Persian *Bayan*, his most important work, regarded as the new revealed book by his adepts, the Bab explicitly and unequivocally defined the position of his "Letters of the Living," as his apostles were called, as subordinate to and totally dependent on his will. Recognizing that they were especially blessed beings with access to the esoteric truth, he declared them to be his intermediary agents, who carried his commands to the rest of the believers, taught his doctrine, and provided ways and means to the end he alone, with God's permission, decided upon. In fact, in the Babi system of structured hierarchy which is discussed in the *Bayan*, there is only one source of authority, God's, as solely reflected in the Prophet of the Age.[15]

The names of the eighteen Letters of the Living (as the first disciples are called in Babi literature), vary from source to source. Bushrui, Barfurushi, Shaikh Azim and Muqaddas appear in most; Qurrat al-Ain is listed in some but not in others. Bahais include Yahya Darabi, while Azalis and early Babis mention Subh-i Azal. If the names of all are not known unquestionably, it is nevertheless certain that the apostles were active in recruiting new members in Azerbaijan, Khurasan, Iraq, Mazandaran, Kirman and Tehran, remaining constantly in touch with the Bab, to whom they regularly reported.

It was at this early stage of the movement that the Bab sought Hajj Karim Khan Kirmani's alliance, which he judged of utmost importance to his and his aides' plans. Quddus and Muqaddas, who had spent nearly a month in Yazd, preaching and debating with the local ulama, until an angry mob attacked them and expelled them from the city, arrived in Kirman carrying two letters to the Shaikhi leader. Addressing him in flattering terms, the Bab asked his rival to join forces and help spread the new cause. However, the Shaikhi leader publicly refuted and humiliated the Babi emissaries and demanded their expulsion from the province.

In Shiraz, relentless harassment on the part of the ulama and the populace, in addition to the outbreak of a cholera epidemic, forced Mirza Ali Muhammad to leave his native town. In September 1846, he headed towards Isfahan, where the governor, advised of his arrival, arranged for his safe entrance into the city and had him stay in the house of a local religious leader. It is difficult to know precisely the personal motives behind Manuchihr Khan's decision to protect the Bab. A Christian Georgian by birth, he was captured by Iranian royal troops as a young child, converted to Islam, castrated, and then given employment in the Shah's harem. He rapidly rose to higher government positions, as he proved to be an able military commander and talented administrator. He was certainly not inclined to philosophical speculation or religious meditation. By temperament he was a man of action, a ruthless officer who would crush tribal and urban popular uprisings with merciless swiftness, and an ambitious manipulator of his useful contacts in the Court to achieve his own ends. He must have seen in the Bab and his cause a means to further this end, for, not only did he give full protection to the refugee from Shiraz, but he allegedly offered his military services to conquer Iran and the lands "beyond Iran's frontiers," and convert all the kings and rulers of the world. The Bab reportedly declined his services, but accepted the governor's generous bequest of his personal fortune, which was immense.

Following a heated debate in an assembly of local notables and ulama, public hostility to the Bab forced the governor officially to expel the heretic from Isfahan, only to have him sneak back into the city in the darkness of the night, and lodge him in one of his private villas. The following months proved to be the most peaceful and relatively free period in the Bab's life since the time he publicly proclaimed his mission. The interval ended with Manuchihr Khan's death and the subsequent successful attempt of his nephew to lay hands on the entire estate, and with the eventual discovery of the Bab's refuge. The Shah, notified of his presence in Isfahan, sent for him to be brought to the capital.[16]

At this point in the history of the Babi movement, it is not clear whether the Shah and his minister, Hajj Mirza Aqasi (a member of the Nimatullahi Sufi order who had some influence upon the monarch's religious policies) were actually ill-disposed towards the young Shirazi's opposition to the religious establishment and his reformist spirit. They might have contemplated the possibility of using the movement as a means to undermine the orthodox ulama's position. Similarly, it is possible that, at that early stage, the Bab himself was outwardly cautious in his behavior towards the state, wishing to gain its support against the ulama. In fact, the Bab, looked forward to a promised royal audience to explain directly to the Shah the main purpose of his mission. As a writer recently remarked, "The Bab, clearly, did not conceive of his message as limited to Iran, or the Shia, or even the Muslim world, but envisioned a universal role for himself, complementary to that of Muhammad and the Imams."[17] For this highly ambitious scheme, he needed the political and military support of a monarch who would wage war on his behalf. Thus, he reportedly promised Muhammad Shah political power over foreign rulers and sovereignty over distant lands, should he pay allegiance to him. His hopes were not fulfilled, however; a last-minute decision of Mirza Aqasi prevented the Bab from entering Tehran. Instead, orders were given to his escorts to take him to prison in Maku, a remote, small town in Azerbaijan near the Russo-Turkish frontier. Aqasi's reversal of position, and the Shah's cool, evasive response to the Bab's letters asking for an explanation for the sudden change of plans provoked his angry resentment. It was then that, giving up the idea of a fruitful alliance with the state, the Babis' attitude changed to open belligerence.

Though Bahai sources take great pains to portray the Bab and his chief disciples as peace-loving individuals, the victims of their opponents' aggressiveness, the tone of the Babis' letters from that time shows the opposite. The Bab's supporters in Qazvin, Tehran, and Zanjan attempted to rescue him from the guards escorting him to Maku. Passing by Qazvin, he wrote to a resident Shaikhi, a former disciple of Rashti, "He whose virtues the late Sayyid unceasingly extolled, and to the approach of whose Revelation he continuously alluded, is now revealed. I am that promised one. Arise and deliver Me from the hand of the oppressor."[18] It was also on his way to prison that the Bab, stopping over Kashan for two nights, met Mirza Jani, the wealthy merchant-convert and the author of *Nuqtat al-kaf,* the earliest-known Babi historical source that depicts Babism as a militant anti-state, anti-ulama movement of revolt. When he reached Zanjan, the Bab tried to enlist the support of one of the leading military officials in town, to no avail.[19] However, he conferred with Muhammad Ali Hujjat al-Islam, to instruct him on his future plans of action.[20] Hujjat al-Islam was to lead a bloody rebellion against the local and central government authorities.

Early Babi accounts stress the overpowering fascination which the Bab aroused in the people with whom he came into contact during that journey. Shortly before its end, it is reported, the chief guard of his escort, Muhammad Bag, converted. The excitement of the populace wherever he went was such that orders were given to the group to avoid stopping in towns where disturbances might get out of control. Numerous miraculous incidents were attributed to him. True or false, they seem to have played on the popular imagination. By the time the Bab approached Tabriz, rumors, traveling faster than he did, had already reached the ears of the inhabitants. Thus, the Bab made a spectacular, almost triumphant entry into the northern city, where he remained for forty days before being sent to prison in Maku. His request to stay in Tabriz was rejected by the local military commander, who feared the effect of his presence in this relatively important Iranian city, seat of the crown prince.

The *Bayan* and the *Book of Seven Proofs,* important works he wrote while held captive in Maku, express the Bab's bitter resentment of his forced isolation in such a desolate place, "high on a mountain where the inhabitants . . . so ignorant and crude . . . do not even deserve to be mentioned."[21] He repeatedly wrote letters to Muhammad Shah warning him of the evil consequences of this injustice. "I am one of the sustaining pillars of the Primal word of God. Whosoever hath recognized Me, hath known all that is true and right, and hath attained all that is good and seemly; and whosoever hath failed to recognize Me, hath turned away from all that is true and right and hath succumbed to everything evil and unseemly. . . . I am the Primal Point from which have been generated all created things. . . . Make amends for thy shortcomings and failure . . . thy royal court hath become, until the Day of Resurrection, the object of the wrath of God."[22] Receiving no reply from the Shah, the Bab's anger and frustration increased the vengeful tone of his letters.* "If thou rejoicest in my imprisonment, woe then unto thee for the grievous torment will soon overtake thee,"[23] he wrote, threatening hell and fire should the Shah persist in ignoring his revelation. Again and again, he lay claim to supreme authority and accused the monarch of usurping sovereignty. "Verily, behold my habitation ... a lofty mountain wherein no one dwelleth. Woe betide thou that wrongfully do injustice to people, unjustly and deceitfully usurp the property of the believers in violation of His lucid Book; whereas I, who, in very truth, am the rightful sovereign of all men, designated by the true, the undeniable Leader, would never infringe on the integrity of the substance of the people. ... Rather would I consort with them as one of themselves and I would be their witness."[24]

In the same letters the Bab argued vehemently in his own defense, denying any political involvement and protesting he had no worldly ambition. "I swear by God! I seek no earthly goods from thee. ...Indeed, to possess anything of this world or of the next world would ... be tantamount to open blasphemy"; "I have no desire to seize thy property, nor do I wish to occupy thy position." However, the Bab was, indeed, claiming temporal as well as religious power, as we shall presently see; further, he had introduced himself to the Shah as the sole legitimate heir to Manuchihr Khan's fortune, requesting the monarch to intervene on his behalf with the late governor's nephew.

Despite his complaints, the Bab's imprisonment in Maku was by no means rigorously enforced. He was permitted to see and converse with his devoted followers, who flocked to Maku from all over Iran. Maku had, in fact, become the center of pilgrimage for new converts. The Bab also continued his correspondence with his apostles, sending them copies of his recent writings and instructing them with his new commands. The network of couriers was so effective, with the communication between the leader and his disciples scattered in the different provinces producing such desired results in spreading the Bab's message, that Aqasi, the Minister, felt compelled to order the prison warden to put an immediate stop to this correspondence. It was of no avail. Consequently, nine months after his arrival in Maku, orders came from the capital for the Bab's transfer to a more secluded fortress in Chihriq, outside the town of Urumiyya, where, it was hoped, he

---

*The archaic English in these quotations reflects the anonymous translator's attempt to convey the ornate style of the original Persian text.

would be more cut off from his followers and admirers. Apparently even this measure failed to break down the communication amongst the Babis; they reverted to intricate, secretive, but successful means of exchanging messages with the prisoner. The Bab continued to welcome and address masses of devotees. A Russian eyewitness account relates how "The concourse of people was so great that, the court not being spacious enough to contain all the audience, the greater number remained in the streets listening attentively to the verses of the new Koran."[25] The crowd did not necessarily consist only of Babis. Most probably a large number among them were mere spectators, sheer curiosity attracting them to the spot. Nevertheless, the potential for their changing from spectators to zealous partisans must have worried the authorities. An official interrogation was then decided upon.

A Shaikhi (and therefore hostile) account of the Bab's interrogation, which was held in Tabriz in the summer of 1848 and presided over by local Shaikhi ulama, confirms one's sense of the imminent threat which must have been felt by the concerned officials. The author relates that, when the Bab was first brought to a local public bath in Urumiyya, an overly excited crowd bought the water he used. He vividly describes how masses of people met him upon his arrival in Tabriz, wondering whether his claim was, after all, legitimate. The writer recounts how, on the day of the debate, they anxiously waited outside the building where it was held, expecting him to come out victorious over his opponents' objections, and how they were all, regardless of their social standing, ready to pay allegiance to him should he succeed. "A strange mood took over the city,"[26] the Shaikhi author concluded. When the Bab finally emerged from the building in apparent defeat, "many of the converts lost their faith,"[27] as Balyuzi himself admits.

Early Babi, Bahai, and hostile sources vary in their account of this famous interrogation in Tabriz. The first two insist that the Bab went through the whole ordeal with dignity, radiating confidence, cleverly and eloquently outwitting his opponents; they maintain that the examination was a farce, the sentence a foregone conclusion. However, whereas Mirza Jani's history depicted the crown prince, the future Nasir al-Din Shah, as one of the chief villains, abusing and taking malicious pleasure in provoking the Bab before ordering the bastinado be given to him, Bahai texts put the entire blame for the "farce" on the ulama themselves. Hostile sources, on the other hand, pictured the scene as one where the examiners were in full command of the situation, amusing themselves at the sight of an embarrassed, ignorant, and foolish young man who failed his test, and was thus reduced to recanting before being beaten in public. Regardless of the discrepancies, all the accounts clearly indicate that the examiners were merely interested in refuting the Bab's claims to be the expected Imam by pointing at (1) his allegedly deficient knowledge of Arabic, theology, and philosophy, and of basic sciences such as medicine and astronomy; and (2) his inability to perform miracles.

These accusations were undoubtedly well founded; so were the claims that the Bab performed poorly in the tests. Indeed, the Bab himself alluded to his deficient knowledge in the worldly sciences. Apologetic references abound in his works denying he ever had a formal education and boasting of the divine origin of his knowledge. He emphatically dismissed his mistakes in Arabic grammar as unimportant, since God's book is in no need of grammarians' rules; and he sternly admonished those who dared ask him irrelevant and fruitless questions on "inferior" subject matter, ranking far below his dignity as God's prophet, exclaiming, "How could anyone ask the merchant of rubies the price of straw?"[28] Echoing Muslim philosophers, Ismaili thinkers, and the Shaikhis, he argued that miracles are meant to convince the ignorant masses, and that learned men are in no need of them. He strongly refuted the orthodox view that Muhammad performed them, and asserted that the Prophet's ascension to Heaven was a spiritual experience and not a physical one.[29] Just as the Koran was the sole proof of Muhammad's Prophecy, he explained, so the *Bayan* constituted the undeniable sign of his own prophecy, adding: "My Revelation is indeed far more bewildering than that of Muhammad, the Apostle of God. . . . Behold, how strange that a person brought up amongst the people of Persia should be empowered by God to proclaim such irrefutable utterances as to silence every man of learning, or be enabled to spontaneously reveal verses far more rapidly than anyone could possibly set down in writing."[30]

The available proceedings of the Tabriz interrogation clearly indicate that both the clerical and state officials present in the assembly not only failed to grasp the grave sociopolitical implications of the Bab's doctrine, but also dismissed its potential political threat. After sentencing him to what appears to have been a mild punishment, they sent him back to prison and thus, unwittingly, gave his apostles and the entire Babi movement the occasion to raise the standard of revolt.

DOCTRINE

The reader of some works of early Babi history and doctrine is left with the impression that when the Bab was finally condemned to death it was simply because his religious views were considered heretical by the orthodox establishment. However the writings of the Bab himself provide enough crucial evidence to show that, in the last analysis, the case against him and his followers was, indeed, political.

I do not propose in the present work to give a comprehensive, chronological exposé of the Babi doctrine. I shall confine my discussion to those aspects of the new religion as it appeared in its final form by 1848, free from some of the Bab's earlier, cautious attempts to express his views in traditional Imami Shia terms. I shall prove that Babism was not just a call for spiritual and moral reforms, but essentially a serious movement aiming at establishing a new sociopolitical order. A superficial reading of the Persian *Bayan*, the Babi holy book, definitely leads to the conclusion that the Bab's concern was mainly to undertake a revolution in the Ismaili tradition. He set out to interpret Shia concepts and principles in order to "purify" them from the "gross," "literal," and "ignorant" meanings the ulama allegedly attributed to them, and thus demonstrate the "legitimacy" of his work. As Nicolas correctly noted, Mirza Ali Muhammad used the title of Bab chiefly to indicate that the gate to divine knowledge, which orthodox ulama in the tenth century had declared closed throughout the period of Occultation, always had been and still was open, and thereby link his ideas to the Shia tradition. Thus, he conceived of his mission as nothing less than a completion of Muhammad's own.[31]

In plain, precise, unambiguous language, the Bab, inspired by traditional Shia and Shaikhi theosophy, developed a concrete socioreligious system entirely based on the concept of unity of the divine. He believed that there is one eternal God who is pure Essence, a hidden treasure who willed cognizance. Since essence cannot be known, the Divine Will manifested itself through the ages in the persons of the various prophets. It was for the sake of these prophets, as the manifestations of Divine Will, that the universe and human beings were created. Through this Will all things were created, and towards this Will all return. To contemplate the Manifestation is to contemplate the Divine Will, for the former reflects the latter as the mirror reflects the sun.[32] Hence, to abide by the manifested truth is to abide by the divine truth. All prophetic revelations are one, though appearing in different aspects in different times. In fact, not only was the Muhammadan truth the same as other, previously revealed truths, but essentially Muhammad was Jesus, who was Moses, who was Abraham, who was Adam, each embodying all. They all constitute one divine spirit, returning in different guise.[33] Similarly, all the saints are one. Mary and the twelve Apostles in the time of Jesus, Fatima and the twelve Imams in the Koranic era—regardless of their different names, they were all bearers of the same truth.[34]

So far, the Bab's argument closely follows that of Shia theosophy. His conception of prophets and saints merely repeats the Shia mystical view of the Muhammadan Reality, which returns in different times under different guise in the person of the Perfect Man of the age.[35] At this point, Mirza Ali Muhammad, borrowing from the Ismaili concept of the progressive unveiling of the esoteric truth, asserted that each manifestation supersedes the preceding one, for its return takes place at a superior stage in human development.[36] Consequently, he added, each new divine book, every new divine law, because it is more perfect, abrogates the previous ones. Again following the theosophers' argument, the Bab explained that this did not mean that succeeding prophets were superior to their predecessors, since that would contradict the whole concept of unity. Rather, all prophets and all revelations reflect the different stages of understanding of one *ilm*, or divine knowledge. Through each Manifestation, the Divine Will chooses to reveal truth in direct proportion to the existing human ability to comprehend it and act in accordance. As humanity progresses and matures, so does the teaching.[37]

Also reminiscent of the Ismailis, and contrary to orthodox Muslim belief, was the Bab's repeated and emphatic assertion that divine manifestations have no end. God is eternal; God creates manifestations in order to be known and to reveal divine knowledge; there can be no limit to the possibilities of God's ever being known. Hence, creation has no beginning and no end, and just as God, and God's Will, have no beginning and no end, so God's manifestation through the prophets has no end. The sun of prophecy rises and sets in eternity, as God reveals the new law whenever the need arises.[38] Following Mulla Sadra's view of substantive change, the Bab went so far as to state that, within the eternal divine unity, there is constant renewal—new conditions, new creation, new order, while divergences and contradictions are merely illusory.[39]

Thus, Mirza Ali Muhammad lay the basis for his own claim as the Prophet or Manifestation of the Age. To attest the unity of God, he declared, was to attest his own Manifestation for he embodied the Muhammadan truth.[40] He was the Primal Point of the *Bayan*, as Muhammad was the Primal Point of the Koran. In fact, he was both, since the *Bayan*'s revelation was identical to, yet superseded, the Koranic revelation.[41] He was the return of Muhammad, just as the latter was the return of Jesus.[42] He was the Savior, as well as the Imam expected by the Shia, since in spirit he was one with all. Here the Bab categorically rejected the literal interpretation of Occultation, as the theosophers had before him, denying the possibility of the physical return of a thousand-year-old man in the form of a thirty- or forty-year-old one. Instead, he announced the return of the Imams in the persons of his own Letters of the Living, without, however, mentioning which Babi was the "return" of which Imam.[43]

The Bab did not accept the Shia view of the Day of Resurrection as the day, following the return of the Imam, on which the dead would be resurrected to face their final judgment, the good to be rewarded with Paradise, while the bad were to be punished with Hell. The Bab, echoing the Ismailis of Alamut, defined it instead as the actual era of a given revelation, when those who follow the path of the preceding prophet ultimately demonstrate their faithfulness by accepting the new revelation, and thus spiritually lead a heavenly life, while those who do not suffer the spiritual agony of Hell. He firmly denied the corporal resurrection of the dead, and stated that each living believer in spirit "resurrects" all the deceased believers, at the same time as each living non-believer "resurrects" the dead non-believers.[44] *Barzakh*, or the intermediary realm where, after death, the soul goes to await the Last Judgment, is nothing but the time period separating one Manifestation from another; and the realm of the divine is not, as some imagine, the summit of all heavens, but the actual place of the Manifestation. In the present, the "seat" of the divine was first in Shiraz, then in Maku, always following the Point of Manifestation.[45] It is only through the Point that one can know and "see" God. Paradise, he argued, is in this world, which is the origin and the end of all worlds. Human beings cannot experience from this world life in the afterworld. One enters Paradise on earth through faith in the *Bayan* and the Point, while Hell is the consequence of the rejection of faith.[46]

Hence, his own revelation, the Bab wrote, marked the day of resurrection of the Koran and the Muslims, just as Muhammad's corresponded with the day of resurrection of the Christians and Jesus's with that of the Jews, since each revelation prepares for the advent of the subsequent one. Thus, he warned, those Muslims who failed to acknowledge him and his mission, proved themselves to be irreligious and non-Muslims.[47] It is to himself that the Koran refers the faithful.[48] The Bab, therefore, pronounced all previously revealed books abrogated, and that Shiraz was the new Mecca, while all Muslim and Shia centers of pilgrimage were annulled.[49]

THE BABI SOCIOECONOMIC SYSTEM

In 1939 the Russian historian, Mikhail Ivanov,[50] studied the Babi movement as a democratic struggle against the existing feudal socioeconomic structure and Western imperialism. In his view, the Bab had promised his followers a new order based on equality, and an end to Western intervention in national economic activities. Attractive as it may sound, such an analysis overlooks two important facts: (1) that the entire Babi system rests on the theosophical concept of "graded beings," by tradition a mystical idea which the Babis (like the Ismailis and to a certain extent the Shaikhis before them) had applied to society, and which overrules any notion of equality in the democratic sense; and (2) as much as the Bab was concerned with the details of land ownership and fiscal issues, nowhere did he show an interest in, least of all promise, a new economic order. Rather, his views reflected in striking fashion the original, egalitarian spirit of the early Muslim community in the Prophet's lifetime and at the time of the early Muslim conquests, expressing a similar concern for the welfare of the believers. The Bab, in fact, reinforced the prevailing system of economic activities, merely shifting titles of land ownership, and, more importantly, legalizing trade transactions with non-Babis from foreign lands.[51] A careful reading of the *Bayan* confirms these remarks.

Consistent with his basic view of unity, Mirza Ali Muhammad declared that all created beings and things belong exclusively to God, for God is the Creator, and thereby the sole owner of heaven and earth. Since God, the Bab argued, created all and everything for the sake of the prophet, who is the Manifestation of God, and whose existence sustains the universe, the Manifestation is thereby the "master of all things." As a divine being, the one who manifests God's Will ranks higher than all reigning monarchs, all ulama, above all the wealthy and the mighty.[52]

In his community of believers, members are hierarchically ordered, each one assigned a place according to his or her degree of faith and intellectual abilities. At the top of the structure, the Point of the *Bayan* reigns supreme; utmost obedience to his commands is demanded from all his followers, and, indeed, from all human beings who might eventually see the light. All must behave in conformity with the rulings of his book, for he is the only source of divine knowledge. The "people of the *Bayan*," as the Bab referred to his followers, must understand that whatever they possess, be it spiritual or material, is bestowed upon them by the loving Point.[53] Since the esoteric divine truth cannot be comprehended by ordinary human beings, a hierarchy of agents, the Letters of the Living, act as intermediaries, to teach and to execute orders given by the Point. They themselves are not equal in rank, yet all are superior to the ordinary believers, since they are blessed creatures who "see the esoteric of the esoteric," and hence are closer to the Divine. Just as in the "Koranic cycle" the successive Imams guided the believers to God's path, and in their absence the ulama fulfilled this function, so in the present Manifestation the Letters, abiding by the Point's commands, lead the way. To act for their sake is to act for the sake of the Point, that is, for the sake of God. The Bab insisted that the Letters, though not fully acknowledged by the majority of the Muslim population, who continued to worship the "Letters of the previous Koranic manifestation" (the Imams), were in spirit identical to those "Koranic Letters." It is through them that the true believer must now follow God's orders.[54]

Though the Bab made it incumbent upon wealthy Babis to help the poor, and give away the surplus of what they owned, after deducting what they needed for themselves and their dependents,[55] he by no means intended the faithful to live strict, austere lives, nor did he condemn individual wealth. On the contrary, the *Bayan* explicitly allows those who can afford it to make use of precious gems and luxury items for their clothing and housing. It warns against vain pride in material possessions, for "the greater God's gifts, the more humble and more modest" should the owner be; yet it sanctions wealth and the "possession of all good things God has created," if the individual is faithful.[56] Similarly, it legalizes interest on money, declaring it to be "good" if it is profitable to all parties concerned, and thus puts an end to the Islamic ban on usury.[57] The *Bayan* also provides detailed instructions regarding individual taxes. Thus, if it can be afforded, each individual believer is ordered to purchase three diamonds, four topazes, six emeralds, and six rubies, and then to offer them to the Point, if manifested, or if not, to the Letters or "he whom God shall manifest." In addition, the owner of anything that has a value of 100 miscals of gold must give the value of nineteen miscals to the Point and his Letters, or to their respective heirs should they die. Out of 6005 miscals of gold and silver owned by an individual, 95 are the exclusive share of the Point, if alive, or of his Letters if not. All lands of great value and all palaces must "return to God," for God is the sole owner of such properties.[58] The Bab also declared it lawful to expropriate the land of unbelievers, who could reclaim their property only if and when they convert. Of the confiscated land, the most valuable becomes the exclusive possession of the Point for as long as he lives. After his death, it should either be put in trust and administered by merchants until the advent of the "new manifestation," or sold and its proceedings distributed to merchants for investment. The trustees would then be entitled to ten percent of the profit. Of the rest of the confiscated properties, the Letters of the Living receive one-fifth of its value for their missionary expenses. "Conquerors of the land," meaning Babi fighters, are given, by permission of their leaders, a share of the remaining fund in direct proportion to their rank and merit. The poor, the orphaned, and widows are to be provided for as well.[59] The Bab promised his faithful material prosperity. "God," he wrote in the *Bayan*, "has so many goods that if all men were to follow His path to help Him, no one would be left in need."[60]

The Bab reserved for the "people of the *Bayan*" exclusive rights over five important provinces of Iran: Fars, the "two Iraqs" (Arab and Iranian), Azerbaijan, Khurasan, and Mazandaran. No non-believers were to live within their borders. Only Christian traders were to be tolerated, since their profession was beneficial to the community.[61] The Bab understood that his wish to see the land of the *Bayan*, of people believing in "the one and indivisible religion of God," expand its frontiers might take a long time; yet he expressed a strong conviction in its possibility. "God hath indeed pledged to establish ... sovereignty throughout all countries and over the people that dwell therein."[62] There is in the *Bayan* an implicit assumption that Iran would eventually adopt Babism as the state religion.

Mirza Ali Muhammad incited his followers to conquest. Though he counseled them to avoid violence and seek peaceful means to make converts, such as satisfying the desire of some people for worldly goods, he also explicitly condoned coercive measures and holy war to force unbelievers to follow the right path: "There is no other means for the salvation of the entire world." He called for "powerful men," "lords of power," sultans, to wage war and spread the faith as they could. He sternly admonished Muhammad Shah to "lay aside, one and all, your dominion which belongeth unto God" and "subdue, with the truth ... the countries," even mentioning India and Turkey as places to begin with.[63]

Strictly from the doctrinal point of view, Babism aimed at establishing a theocracy, a reign of the "saints" on earth, in the tradition of Shia messianic thought. Judging from the *Bayan*, the most concrete, most coherent and most practical of all Babi works, Mirza Ali Muhammad was primarily interested in the triumph of his faith, and not so much in any explicit project of social and political reform. His concern for a just distribution of communal wealth based on individual merit merely reflects a religious leader's moral obligation to care for the well-being of his followers, and not, as already pointed out, to promote an egalitarian order. In fact, the Bab, and, as we shall presently see, his leaders, were fully aware of the poor as a potential force, an underprivileged class providing a social base for their cause, at the same time as they were to be kept at a distance from the esoteric aspect of the movement, being regarded as unfit to comprehend it.

Nevertheless, the Shaikhi idea of the Perfect Shia, i.e., a single, individual bearer of the Imam's knowledge, which the Bab so radically transformed into the doctrine of "He whom God manifests," with absolute power to rule, provided a foundation for inevitable sociopolitical changes. Just as the Ismailis of Alamut had done centuries earlier, Mirza Ali Muhammad stressed the unquestionable and irrefutable authority of the "Point of the *Bayan*" in abrogating the Islamic law and establishing his own, which he declared binding until the next manifestation. Inherent in such an emphasis was an utmost concern with the concrete, immediate reality of this world in the present moment. The past and the future, which hold such a dominant place in Shia traditions, were dismissed as less important: the former because it represents a less perfect stage of the manifestation of the Divine Will, and the latter because it cannot be known. It was this worldliness, so characteristic of the Babi doctrine despite the overall religious tone which permeates it, that proved it to be so supremely attractive to many converts. It strongly implied what some prior Muslim theosophers, including the Shaikhis, had esoterically hinted at: that the relationship of humans to the conditions of their existence is complex and subject to change; that a distinction must be made between conditions that are unchangeable and those that one can alter; and above all, that religious evolution has to accompany human social and intellectual evolution.

Despite the undeniable predominance of religious motives over social and political considerations, the reforming spirit inherent in the new creed cannot be overlooked. Through the mystico-religious labyrinth of his writings, the Bab's reforms stand out with noticeable clarity. He addressed the low legal and social status of women by limiting the number of wives a man could lawfully take to two (instead of the four allowed by Islamic law), with the second to be taken only on prior consent of the first wife and only in the event of her sterility; and in a radical departure from Islam, he gave the same right to women married to men proven impotent. Though he did not fully emancipate women, he allowed the sexes to socialize with some freedom, provided the reason was serious and not frivolous. Similarly, and paralleling the then growing nationalist tendencies in the country, were some of the Bab's religious policies: the substitution of Iranian centers of pilgrimage for Arab ones; the adoption of Nauruz, the ancient holiday celebrating the spring equinox, which Iranians had observed since pre-Islamic times, as the first day of the new Babi calendar; and the use of the Persian *Bayan,* rather than any of the Bab's other works written in Arabic, as the new holy book. And while the Bab's promises to the poor and his concern with their getting a share of God's abundant goods reflected a moral concern with the well-being of the faithful, rather than a desire to establish a new economic order; and though these promises were essentially steps to win over the support of the economically underprivileged, unaccompanied by any concrete overall economic policy; the populist aspects of his message, as written down in the *Bayan* and preached by his missionaries, still implied a commitment to change in the poor's favor.

Implicit in the Babi view of theocracy is a strong laicization trend. In the Babi system, the merchant class emerges as the most privileged, its interests secured and even sanctioned. In the tightly knit society the Bab envisioned, where the faithful were commanded to lead a secluded life within walls erected to separate them from the world of non-believers, only preachers and merchants were to be allowed freedom of movement to travel wherever it was necessary for their profession. More importantly, the merchants were to be fully entrusted, in times when he was not manifested, with the Point's funds, which would be managed at their discretion. They were thus given an essential economic function held by the ulama in Twelver Shia society. For, in fact, what the Bab had done was to eliminate entirely the all-powerful class of religious leaders. By declaring *ijtihad* illegal, since only the Point could be the source of knowledge, and by forbidding congregational prayer and asking the believer to worship individually, he rendered obsolete two important religious positions: that of the mujtahid and the imam juma. Though most of his Letters were trained in religious sciences, they did not constitute a clerical oligarchy, nor did they form a social class of their own.

Moreover, by interpreting allegorically religious concepts such as resurrection, the Day of Judgment, Heaven and Hell (and despite the mystical and metaphysical origin of most, if not all, of his ideas), the Bab directed the hopes and thoughts of his disciples to this world, and not the next (the "unseen," the "invisible"). Thus, by shifting people's interest from the traditional Shia eschatological other-worldliness to this world; by transforming their quiescent attitude of hopeful expectation of the Imam's return into a radical activist commitment to better their lives now; and by pushing them to realize their aspirations and desires, Babism could, and did, lead to a revolutionary social movement irreconcilably hostile to the established political and religious order.

In 1866 Kazem Beg noted down three types of Babi converts: the "blind adoring" member of the working poor or peasant class; the political "agitator"; and the "evilly-disposed" sectarian.[64] Commenting on this classification, Browne defined the three categories in more sympathetic terms as: pious faithful, genuinely convinced the Bab was the expected Imam himself; "progressive reformers"; and Sufis who regarded Babism "as a systematized and organized Sufism," a teaching that could cultivate "the divine spark latent in man."[65]

In the often confusing and contradictory historical accounts, one fact stands out clearly: throughout his short career, Mirza Ali Muhammad cautiously and expediently identified himself successively as the Bab to the Imam's knowledge, then as the Imam himself, and finally as the new Prophet of the Age. All sources indicate that he and his leaders felt the need, at least in the beginning, continuously to assure their followers of the respectability and "orthodoxy" of their thought. Obviously, then, the credulous amongst the converts, eager to realize in their own lifetimes the long-cherished Shia dream to see the Imam, took him to be just that. The more theosophically minded enthusiasts, both Shaikhi and Sufi, accepted him as their new esoteric master, while the revolutionarily inclined were attracted by the reforms they hoped the new faith would bring about. Given the universally acknowledged poetic and mystical appeal of the Bab, his writings, and his apostles, the genuineness of sentiment of most Babi converts—who, no matter what their initial motivation was, so heartedly sacrificed their lives for the cause—is beyond doubt. One cannot and should not underrate the magic power of the spoken word as an effective means to arouse the populace, and even sophisticated intellectuals. Most sources note the persuasive force of the Babi preachers, and their ability to stir the religious and spiritual emotions of their readers or listeners. In fact, it was this "miraculous" power of the word, enabling him to compose "incomparable" verses, that the Bab claimed as his sole but firm proof of prophethood.

THE LETTERS OF THE LIVING

Despite the powerful, charismatic appeal the Bab exercised over the converts, and despite his ability to guide and coordinate his apostles' actions from the isolated fortress where he was held captive, the Babi revolt would not have assumed the dimension it had, were it not for the leadership of his Letters of the Living. Undoubtedly it was through their action that what began as an essentially religious movement of protest, albeit with strong sociopolitical implications, was transformed into a revolt aimed at overthrowing both the clerical and state establishment. It was their individual personalities and views that shaped the historical events of 1848–52, marking the first phase of the Babi episode. It was also they who were chiefly responsible for politicizing some of the extremist ideas implicit in the Bab's works, thus further provoking their opponents' attempts to discredit Babism as an "immoral" and "anarchic" heresy. Finally, it was Qurrat al-Ain, Bushrui, Barfurushi, Mirza Ali Muhammad Zanjani, Yahya Darabi, and their like, who, either from sheer self-interest or genuine concern, or both, succeeded in releasing some of the prevailing social tensions and sought to polarize dissent at all levels.

In Kerbala, where she took up residence in the house of the late Kazim Rashti, Qurrat al-Ain quickly aroused the hostility of the local Ottoman Sunni authorities and of the resident Shia ulama. As a recent study has shown, of all the Letters of the Living it was she who first "saw the implications of the Bab's claims and ideas and found them consonant with her own attitudes."[66] She thus initiated a radical departure from traditional, cautious modes of religious expression and behavior. She "revealed" her "true identity" as the "return" or the Manifestation of Fatima, the Prophet's daughter and wife of Ali. There is no doubt that the young Babi woman was merely reiterating the Bab's own announcement that the Letters of the Living were the "return," "the place of manifestation" of the Fourteen Very Pure of the

Koranic Cycle. The Bab's view, based on the Sufi and theosophical idea of the spiritual "irradiation" of the Muhammadan Reality, manifesting itself at all times in different guises, is not to be confused with the concept of transmigration or metempsychosis, which is considered heretical by Muslims. Yet Qurrat al-Ain's opponents, and even some of her own Babi companions who were not yet initiated to the esoteric doctrine, took her statement to mean transmigration. Furthermore, again anticipating the Bab's pronouncement that faith "purifies," (renders a person or a possession or an object lawful),[67] she proudly declared "pure" all "impure" objects if submitted to her gaze.

Alarmed and angered by such extremist utterances, some of her fellow Babis wrote to the Bab complaining of her extravagant pretensions. In reply, the Bab rebuked them and asked them to "accept without questions whatever she might pronounce, for they were not in a position to understand and appreciate her station."[68] In addition, he conferred upon Qurrat al-Ain the new title of Tahira ("the Pure").

Because accounts of Babi events are so scarce, and existing ones so inconsistent, it is difficult to determine the exact nature and content of Qurrat al-Ain's controversial behavior and lectures, or that of the Babis in general. Doubtless she made use of the idea of "return" to impress her audience and provide her leadership with an aura of legitimacy in Muslim terms. In Shia society, where women, like Muslim women everywhere, are considered inferior to men, Fatima ranks high in the pious esteem of the faithful, as a holy figure in her own right. Qurrat al-Ain was waging a personal war to free herself from conventions she abhorred, and to attain public recognition in a position to which she aspired for and which Muslim conventions denied her. Feeling at odds with her society, she perforce had to attack it and abandon the more prudent ways of her fellow Babi leaders. Nevertheless, beyond her personal interest one can detect a no less firm determination to reform what she generally viewed as archaic religious values and norms. Often acting independently of the Bab, she shocked not only pious Muslims, be they Sunni or Shia, Shaikhi or Balasari, but also fellow Babis. She adopted unconventional behavior, and radically defied socioreligious norms. In Baghdad, where she went after her controversial stay in Kerbala, she appeared unveiled in the presence of men, and even announced "the suspension of all religious obligations." She was contemptuous of her fellow Babis' practice of *taqiyya*, which she claimed was motivated by fear. Reportedly she went so far as to proclaim herself freed by God from sins and errors.[69] According to Jani, the chief Mufti of Baghdad, on hearing her claims, nearly sentenced her to death, but instead resolved to have Ottoman officials expel her from Ottoman territories. Thus, Qurrat al-Ain, together with a group of Babis, returned to Iran via Kirmanshah and Hamadan, where she relentlessly preached her faith and converted admirers, until her relatives in Qazvin forced her to come back to her native town. There several attempts were made to reconcile her with her husband, but without success. She firmly rejected him as a man unworthy of her. "He, in that he rejects God's religion, is impure, while I am Pure: between us there can be naught in common."[70] The Bab was later to pronounce that a marriage between a believer and a nonbeliever was invalid, proclaiming that nonbelievers forfeit all their rights, including those over a believing spouse, "since everything belongs to God who disposes of them as He wishes."[71]

Kept captive in her own house and closely watched by her relatives, the indomitable Babi woman continued unabatedly to preach and convert, regularly corresponding with the Bab and his apostles. When Mulla Muhammad Taqi, her uncle and father-in-law, was stabbed to death, the Babis were held responsible for the crime and Qurrat al-Ain was accused of masterminding it. The self-confessed murderer, identifying himself as a devoted Shaikhi who could no longer tolerate his victim's repeated denunciation of Ahsai and Rashti, denied that the Babis were his accomplices. Yet he turned out to be a Babi convert. Similarly, the *Tarikh-i jadid*, the Bahai account of early Babi history, basing its report on the *Nuqtat-al kaf*, explicitly states that the Bab, passing by Qazvin on his way to prison in Maku, had written to Mulla Muhammad Taqi asking for his help, and that, on hearing of the Mulla's disdainful response and "unseemly remarks," had crossly replied, "Was there no one to smite him on the mouth?" The author, commenting on the murder, added, "Wherefore the Lord brought it to pass that he [Mulla Muhammad Taqi] was smitten in the mouth... that he might no more speak insolently of the Saints of religion."[72] It is difficult to determine whether the vengeful tone was merely rhetorical, or whether it implied an active Babi involvement in the assassination. Be that as it may, a public outcry demanding the death sentence for all heretics, and the execution of four local Babis, endangered Qurrat al-Ain's life in Qazvin. With the help of devoted followers, she secretly left town and headed towards Tehran. Her husband then divorced her. Mirza Husain Ali Nuri had sent some of his men to rescue her, and he met her and her escorts in some village south of Tehran, assuming total charge of her traveling expenses. Meanwhile, Mulla Husain Bushrui had been carrying on an intensive missionary campaign in his native province, reportedly gaining the support of two leading ulama of Naishapur. After a brief stay in prison for his heretical activities, he headed towards Badasht, a village at the Khurasan border, where Qurrat al-Ain, Barfurushi, Mirza Husain Ali Nuri, and other Babis had decided to hold a convention. The Bab had ordered the meeting, which was held in June 1848.

As Mirza Jani's fancy but accurate pun on the name of the village indicates (Badasht: the Plain of Innovation), this notorious assembly of leading Babis, which went down in Muslim annals as an orgy of sins and heresy, marked a turning point in Babi history. For it was in this meeting that the full innovative implications of the movement were revealed to the masses, and that some of the extremist Letters of the Living sought to actualize the theosophical ideas inherent in Babism. Bahai sources generally speak of it as an important council convened by Mirza Husain Ali Nuri to "settle a vital and cardinal issue: was this persuasion of theirs just an offshoot of Islam, or was it an independent Faith?" These sources suppress the content of some of the leaders' speeches which were considered extremist by Babi purists, Bahais, and Muslims alike. Doubtless, the meeting was held to divulge some of the main non-Islamic aspects of the doctrine; to declare the Koran officially abrogated and replaced by the *Bayan;* and to determine plans of future action. Also, the possibility of helping the Bab escape from prison was discussed.[73] Though one can easily dismiss the Muslim historians' accusations of lawlessness and sinful deeds as exaggerated distortions of actual facts, early Babi sources themselves confirm to a large extent the radical tendencies openly expressed during those days by Qurrat al-Ain and Barfurushi. The *Nuqtat al-kaf,* written before the Azali-Bahai split occurred, by one of the first converts at a time when the Babis were in open revolt against the religious establishment and thus did not resort to *taqiyya,* gives the most detailed account so far available of this important event.[74]

All sources agree on one fact: the dominant role played by Qurrat al-Ain in this gathering. She reportedly pushed her companions to lift the veil of secrecy, break all ties with Islam, and proclaim the new religious era. Though the identity of the main speaker who delivered the innovative speech, as it was reported by Jani, is difficult to conjecture, with Qurrat al-Ain and Barfurushi being the two main contenders, one can detect the woman's spiritual touch both in its form and content. For the ideas exposed that evening conform to her own as she revealed them before and after that gathering. Moreover, her views and Barfurushi's were much alike, so the question of identity remains inconsequential. In fact, it was in Badasht that the two met, and reportedly began a relationship referred to in the *Nuqtat-al kaf* as "the conjunction of the sun and the moon,"[75] and hailed by the Babis assembled then.

The audience, composed of some eighty Babis as well as curious peasants from Badasht and the neighboring villages, was told that God's ordinances were to be gradually revealed to the masses by "chosen superior beings," "the elect of the world." They were warned that they might feel reluctant to hear "the truth," and might wish to curse its exponents as "ignorant," since "unenlightened" masses never fail to do so when they hear it for the first time. But, they were told, the "Sun of Truth is always rising," whether in a veiled or unveiled fashion. The doctrine of unity was then explained in terms of the unification of all previously revealed religions into one, and the abrogation of all preceding laws on the day of the manifestation of the expected Savior. Unity was also explained as meaning that all goods belong to the one who manifests God's will: that all men and all women belong to him; and he gives and takes whatever pleases him to and from whoever pleases him. Hence, he can unite or separate wives and husbands, just as any master has authority over his servants and maids. Subsequently, the abrogation of the Koran was boldly proclaimed, and Muslim law was pronounced necessary only till the time when the Divine Manifestation in the person of the Bab had been universally acknowledged. The stricken audience was also advised to follow their individual consciences, to learn to distinguish evil from good on their own, and to feel free for the moment either to abide by the Muslim law or to reject it. In a dramatic gesture that seemingly symbolized the end of the Muslim era and of her own subjugation, Qurrat al-Ain then removed her veil and revealed herself to the eyes of the masses.[76]

Qurrat al-Ain's behavior, in addition to the lawlessness that evidently prevailed in the assembly following the speech, proved too overwhelming for a number of Babis present. Shocked and shaken beyond belief, many fled the scene where chaos and confusion reigned as devout Muslims attacked the heretics. The meeting broke up in disorder.

By emphasizing particular aspects of the doctrine they found most appealing, the Babi leaders revealed their individual character traits and wishes. For Qurrat al-Ain, a woman of great vision and intellectual abilities, who resented the traditional milieu in which she was unable to move at will, Babism provided a unique chance to achieve her emancipation. She took advantage of the movement to free herself from the bonds Islam imposed upon her. Her rejection of the veil symbolized her defiant attitude towards the traditional social customs pertaining to women. To Quddus, Bab al-Bab, and other leaders who were to play dominant roles in the insurrections, both during and after the Bab's time, Babism offered the opportunity and the justification for a revolt against the establishment, and a means to gain power. The forced isolation of the Bab allowed them to assume positions of leadership over the masses of recruits, and even enabled them to create a kind of hierarchical order whereby those on the top took supreme control and wrapped themselves in a quasi-divine aura.

At this point in its narration, *Nuqtat al-kaf's* references to the leaders indicate a hierarchical distinction had already been made. Barfurushi and Qurrat al-Ain definitely emerge as supreme leaders, while Bushrui, the original right hand of the Bab, who had bestowed on him the rank of Bab al-Bab, is slightly demoted. Though Jani promotes Bushrui to the title of Bab, instead of Bab al-Bab (Mirza Ali Muhammad by then was referred to as the Point of the *Bayan*), he is definitely given a lower status than Barfurushi, who reportedly also assumed the title he is known with, Quddus, in that meeting. It was also in Badasht, according to Jani, that Barfurushi declared himself the expected Savior, and his followers, after an initial hesitation, acknowledged him as such. Whether he was usurping the Bab's position by advancing a rival claim, or whether he wished to assume leadership in the latter's absence, is difficult to determine. However, later on in Mazandaran not only did Barfurushi advance even more extravagant claims, but many Babis regarded him as superior in rank to the Bab himself.[77]

Here, then, some of the Babis' ideas ran counter to original Babism. Though the Bab considered each of his Letters of the Living as the "return" or Manifestation of the Imams, never did he grant them a rank equal to his own. Nor did he intend any to be regarded as the expected Savior or the manifestation of Muhammad himself, since he reserved both claims to himself alone. As already stated, the Bab categorically and unequivocally defined his apostles as subordinate creatures totally dependent on his own will for all their actions. Hence, the metaphysical and mystical discussions which were led by the apostles, concerning the Divine Being and Will, the Manifestation, the "return" of the saints on earth, and similar esoteric subjects, which so completely scared away the non-initiated masses because of their heretical implications, turned out to be a tour-de-force whereby the

main Babi leaders attempted to socialize theosophical ideas, transforming them into concrete modes of being and action, and thereby justify-
ing in the eyes of naive followers the sovereign claims advanced by
Quddus, Bab al-Bab, and Qurrat al-Ain.

Western observers and hostile Muslim sources reporting on the
Babi movement often make references to the "egalitarian," "socialist,"
or "communist" characteristics of the new creed, doubtless fed by the
venomous rumors spread by its opponents. In conformity with the
Bayan's statement regarding property ownership, the Babi leaders in
Badasht proclaimed that all earthly possessions belonged to the Bab in
his capacity as the Manifestation of the Divine Will, and they counseled
their followers to renounce the properties they had "usurped." However, the added comment that all goods are to be shared equally by all
Babis, as befits true sisters and brothers, is not to be found in the Bab's
writings. Whether it refected a "communism" in the same sense as the
early Christians might be so described, "in a readiness to share their
possessions with one another, and a general liberality in helping each
other,"[78] as Browne put it; or, more appropriately, an attempt to revive
the old egalitarian spirit of the early Muslim conquests, when booties
were distributed amongst the soldiers, the fact remains that the equal
sharing of community wealth was discussed in the Badasht meeting
and implemented during the subsequent revolts. It was an ideal that
conveniently provided the Babis with needed funds and served the
purpose of attracting the economically deprived segment of the population. All Babi sources confirm the practice of communal property by
the leaders.

On the other hand, the reported practice of community of
women and the accusations of immorality seem to have been grossly
exaggerated, though the author of the *Dawnbreakers* admitted to the
"mischief which a few of the irresponsible among the adherents of the
Faith had sought to kindle," and to the "abuse of the liberty which the
repudiation of the laws and sanctions of an outgrown Faith had conferred upon them."[79] Not only is there no reference to the community
of women in the *Bayan*, but the Bab forbade divorce if it was not based
on valid grounds. Moreover, though he allowed men and women
members of an extended family to converse freely, he made it condi-
tional on the topic being "important and serious," reducing the conversation to an exchange of no more than twenty-eight words if it was
not. He pronounced marriage an obligation for all men and women
from age eleven, for the specific purpose of begetting new generations
of Babis.[80] Jani's passage referring to the Bab's authority over his "ser-

vants and maids" was most probably aimed at sanctioning Qurrat al-Ain's discard of her husband.

Immediately after the Badasht meeting, Babi leaders traveled separately to Mazandaran. Qurrat al-Ain and Barfurushi, however, traveled together, taking along their respective followers. According to some sources, they parted once they reached their destination, the young woman in Nur and her companion in his native town. Lisan al-Mulk describes the couple's trip in the Caspian province, where they encountered hostility and harassment which forced them to part, as the mob's anger reached its height at the sight of their lodging together in the same inns and even going to the same public bath.[81] However, we learn from *Zuhur al-haqq*, a Bahai source, that Qurrat al-Ain arrived together with Quddus in Barfurush, where they were able to find help and shelter amongst Babi converts. The author, claiming that Hajj Mulla Muhammad Hamza Shariatmadar Mazandarani (d. 1865), a prominent and highly popular local Shaikhi theologian, was a secret convert, reports that Qurrat al-Ain stayed at his house and even preached in his mosque. Mudarrisi vehemently denies that Hamza ever converted or that Qurrat al-Ain enjoyed his hospitality. Defining Hamza as a humanitarian, tolerant Shaikhi, a "discreet" opponent of Babism, he charged the Bahai author with distortion of facts and misinterpretation of Hamza's work. Yet, the "true version" of the latter, as quoted at length in *Shaikhigiri*, displays too great a tolerance of the Babis for a Shaikhi, and too vehement a criticism of the bloody persecution they suffered. In fact, Mudarrisi himself admits that Hamza was "sympathetic" to their plight and attempted to protect them from the extreme, harsh measures taken by the local authorities.[82]

The fact that Qurrat al-Ain spent some time in Barfurush is confirmed by a passage in *Nuqtat al-Kaf* mentioning Mirza Yahya Nuri's arrival in town, and his first meeting there with the young woman and Quddus. Reportedly it was Yahya who, upon Quddus's command, took Qurrat al-Ain to "an appointed place," most probably meaning Nur, his own family village. There, "that mother of the world," as Jani refers to her, found shelter and protection, as well as "a loving child" in the person of the younger Nuri brother, whom she further instructed in the esoteric doctrine of the Bab. In Nur she was able to continue preaching and corresponding with her fellow Babis. Some of her letters reveal the commanding tone she could assume with other Babi leaders, and a seeming intransigence towards opponents of her faith, along with a perceptible impatience to see the "land of the Babis" finally freed from the nonbelievers. Thus, writing to Mulla Shaikh Ali (Azim), she fiercely protested: "How long wilt thou enjoin on me patience, when the cause hath appeared resplendent, and the Order hath come determined? . . . Patience and endurance are at an end, and there remaineth not aught save reprimand and self-reproach dominant in this moment of just retribution. . . . How long wilt thou make intercession for these drunkards and brutes [i.e., the nonbelievers], all of them? By thy Truth, they will not believe in the signs, neither will admonition profit them as an intimidation . . . Verily, so long as they continue to sojourn in the lands of God they will not humble themselves."[83] Qurrat al-Ain, like some other Letters of the Living, wished to see the Bab's and the Babis' sovereign claims to five Iranian provinces rapidly implemented.

That the Babi leaders in Badasht had planned an armed revolt is absolutely not in doubt. Even Bahai works, in which an obvious effort is made to depict the Babi action as defensive, or aimed only at "demonstrating their belief and their vision," and which maintain that the Babis never "sought holy war, nor contemplated disloyalty to their country and sovereign,"[84]—even these could not entirely overlook the Babis' militancy, nor totally moderate the aggressive tone in their speech and correspondence.

REVOLT AND MARTYRDOM

Mazandaran: October 1848 — May 1849

Mulla Husain Bushrui, after a vigorous campaign in Khurasan to recruit converts to fight the Babi battle, marched to Mazandaran with a force estimated to be over 200 men. Shortly before reaching the province, he reportedly delivered a fiery speech to his followers, inciting them to sacrifice all worldly possessions and ties: "The pursuit of worldly prosperity is incompatible with the perfection of religious life, and the amassing of wealth is antagonistic to the working out of faith . . . close eyes to wealth, wife and child, nay, life itself."[85] He reminded them that only through martyrdom could the faithful find the righteous path to glory and salvation, and asked them to take Imam Husain, "the martyr of the martyrs," as the model to follow, adding: "Ours is the duty to raise the call of the New Day and to proclaim this Divine Message unto all the people. Many a soul will, in this city, shed his blood in this path. That blood will water the Tree of God, will cause it to flourish, and to overshadow all mankind." To appeal further to the masses' sentiment, he included a social message in his talk, encouraging them to pray "that the Almighty may protect Him [the Bab] that, through Him, He may exalt the downtrodden, enrich the poor and redeem the fallen."[86] As the fierce battle raged between the Babis and the opponents' forces, Bushrui kept up their fighting spirit by promising them that Mirza Ali Muhammad would, within a year, conquer the entire globe, reorganize it, establish God's law, and unify all religions.[87]

With the revolt in Mazandaran rapidly spreading, the Babi forces were strong enough to seize the shrine of a local saint, Shaikh Tabarsi, fourteen miles southeast of Barfurush, and construct a fortress around it. From among the recruits there were enough artisans, tailors, sword makers, and masons to help build the fortress and organize a self-sufficient community. Peasants from neighboring villages either joined them, bringing their livestock and grain, or collaborated (out of fear of possible retaliation, or from genuine sympathy for the cause), providing them with provisions and manpower for their raids against enemy camps. It is reported that the Babis thus accumulated a large supply of rice, 200 horses, 40 or 50 cows, and 3–4000 sheep. Bushrui then declared it all communal property, to be equally shared by all members.[88] The egalitarian practice prevailing in the Shaikh Tabarsi fortress confirmed the rumor already spread after the Badasht assembly, that the Babis were "socialist," and even "communists." It was these "principles of fraternity," as Jani put it, that finally prevented Abbas Quli Khan, one of the chief officers of the royalist troops in Mazandaran, who was sympathetic to the movement, from converting.[89]

News was reaching Tehran of the growing strength of the rebels and their alleged intention to establish "communism" with the sword. Wrote the Russian envoy, Prince Dimitri Dolgorukov, to his minister in Moscow, this was a revolution "no matter how you look at it," adding that the Iranian government lacked both the authority and the necessary forces to crush the revolt.[90] His French counterpart in Tehran sent a similar report to the French government, conveying his strong impression that "this religious sect is threatening to become a political party."[91] In fact, state officials in the capital were at first reluctant to carry on a full-scale war against the insurgents, both because they believed the revolt was religiously-oriented, and thus a matter of chief concern to the ulama rather than to the state, and because they feared it might turn into a political rebellion as well, should they react too strongly.

When the newly appointed Governor of Mazandaran wrote to Quddus, asking about the real motives of the revolt, the latter's blunt reply displayed an uncompromising attitude towards the Qajar government. Explaining how he and his fellow Babis were fighting for "the Proof of God," who was at last manifested yet unjustly kept captive, he ended his letter warning the official: "O Prince, misled by worldly glory and the pride of thy youth; know that Nasir ed-Din Shah is no true king, and that such as support him shall be tormented in hell-fire."[92] The message was clear: the Babis were determined to fight the government forces who were preventing them from establishing the rule of their religion throughout the nation.

Led by Bushrui, a brilliant military organizer and fierce fighter, the Babis raided enemy camps, set fire to them, killed and plundered, taking away booty which included guns, swords, horses, even food provisions and herds of sheep. With the exception of the leaders themselves, most of them were on foot, wearing felt hats with white scarves around their necks. They were most successful in attacking at unexpected times of the night or at dawn, thus taking their enemies unaware and unprepared, ferociously screaming their famous war cry, *ya sahib al-zaman* (O Master of the Age), and creating an atmosphere of utter terror and panic among the soldiers, who would then flee their camp. In one such raid, three Qajar princes commanding the royal forces were killed, and the Governor, Mihdi Quli Mirza, ran for his life. The court chronicle of the time, *Nasikh al-tawarikh*, describes how "royal troops were running away from the Babis like a herd of sheep escaping from wolves."[93] The ferocity of the Babi fighters was already well known. Jani relates how a village was sacked whose inhabitants, once friendly to them, had collaborated with the enemy.[94] While victorious, the Babis did no less killing and burning than their opponents: atrocities were committed by both parties.

Judging from Babi sources, the religious zealots who faced death with so much courage, wholeheartedly believed that theirs was a holy war as important as, if not more so, than the battle of Kerbala, where in 680 the third Imam, Husain, suffered martyrdom. There are constant references to earlier Shia martyrs, Mazandaran being compared to Kerbala, and Husain Bushrui to the third Imam. Nevertheless, aspiration for more worldly compensations also helped keep up the morale. To the poorer artisans and peasants, life in the small, tightly knit community of brothers in arms at Shaikh Tabarsi was a pre-taste of what the good life, which the Bab and his representatives repeatedly promised them, might be like. They were offered not equality, but a chance to be evaluated according to their merit as workers and by the degree of their faith. The inflated hopes of people who have nothing to lose, mixed with absolute, unquestioning devotion to the leaders, was skillfully put to utmost use by Babi preachers in a fashion highly reminiscent of the Ismailis. The poor constitute the most valuable class of believers, Ismailis had written centuries earlier, for their faith is the strongest and they are the most willing to sacrifice themselves for a cause.[95]

Elitism characterized the Babi leadership in Shaikh Tabarsi. Sources generally agree that Quddus acquired saintly status, and assumed among the insurgents the position of supreme religious authority. He would rarely appear in public, and would grant audiences concealed behind a curtain. On the rare occasions when he would make a public appearance without cover, the Babis would prostrate themselves at his feet. Even Bushrui would bow to him, acknowledging him as his superior.[96]

Yet it was Bushrui who kept up the fighting spirit with his legendary bravura and charismatic command, leading the Babi forces to victory. When he died on the battlefield in January 1849, the Babis lost courage, despite the efforts of his brother Hasan, who took over his position. By that time, they were put on the defensive, as fresh supplies of troops and a couple of cannons sent from Tehran enabled the royalists to encircle the fortress and besiege it. Even then, the Babis fought valiantly and endured the hardships of ensuing famine stoically, resisting surrender to the very end. The final, decisive defeat occurred as a result of a trap the government officers set for them. The surviving Babis were caught unaware, and a bloody massacre put an end to nine months of insurrection. Quddus was brought to Barfurush, publicly tortured, and burned to death.

Continuing Revolt and Martyrdom

Contrary to government expectations, the defeat in Mazandaran did not put an end to the revolt. As the Russian envoy pointed out, the Babi martyrdom seemed to increase the passion of the zealots, encouraging them to "welcome death with open arms."[97] The year 1850 saw renewed uprisings in Zanjan, Yazd, and Nairiz, along with an aborted one in Tehran. The Babi leaders, Mulla Muhammad Ali Zanjani and Sayyid Yahya Darabi, like their counterparts in Mazandaran, were capable organizers and successful missionaries for their cause. Moreover, the uprisings shared many features in common with the Shaikh Tabarsi revolt. Chief among them was the peculiar blending of genuine religious sentiment, inciting the followers to a selfless readiness for sacrifice, coupled with purely worldly considerations and selfish motives. According to Dolgorukov and Kazem Beg, the *lutis* ("street gangs"), notorious for their role in fomenting public disturbances and fights in the cities and towns throughout the country, constituted an important element in the Babi forces in Zanjan and Yazd.[98]

In Yazd, Darabi at first preached the new doctrine discreetly, converting many local inhabitants and successfully manipulating an existing discontent with the local authorities, before he finally declared open revolt. He directed street riots, and attacked government centers, forcing its officials to flee or resign from their posts. Government forces sent to crush the movement succeeded in doing so after he left Yazd, when he had obviously become aware that there was only a slim chance that the Babis would win. Following his departure, Babis were arrested and cruelly put to death.

However, Yahya's reputation in Fars was rapidly spreading, especially in Nairiz, a small town close to Darab, where his family came from. Many political dissidents welcomed him and rallied to his cause. Nicolas writes that among the converts in Nairiz there were high officials, notables, and mullas, as well as students from the local schools, who adhered to the new faith either secretly or openly. Yahya, chased out of town by the authorities, retired to a neighboring old Sassanian fortress in ruins, from which he conducted regular raids and nightly surprise attacks on Nairiz. He skillfully organized his forces, dividing his followers into small units with specific tasks and responsibilities. The battles were fierce and the losses heavy. The population was terrorized by the gangs and their war cry, "O, Master of the age." However, the Nairiz insurrection ended with the capture and execution of Yahya, by government forces who, as elsewhere, outnumbered and were better equipped than the Babis.

Kazem Beg portrays Yahya Darabi as an ambitious opportunist who, excelling in manipulating people and events for his own selfish political ends, acted chiefly on his own. Though this characterization is to a certain degree true, it obscures the fact that the Bab, from his prison in the North, kept vigilantly in touch with his apostles. Mirza Jani mentions a letter and a talisman Yahya received from the Bab, in Shiraz while on his way to Nairiz from Yazd. There can be no doubt that the Babi leaders acted on the Bab's instruction, though they attempted to achieve their own more personal ends as well. The impact of Darabi's charismatic appeal upon his devoted followers in Nairiz is undeniable.

Despite the fate that befell them and their kin, they kept alive their fond memory of the young, handsome, daring leader, and even attempted to carry on his struggle. Barely two years after his death, the Babis of Nairiz, having taken refuge in a nearby mountain, not only succeeded in resisting enemy assaults, but were also able to raid the town periodically, and kill the governor whom they held responsible for their plight, until finally troops sent from Shiraz stamped out the rebellion. This savage repression did not totally crush the Babi ideal as taught by Yahya. An article published in the *Journal of the Royal Geographical Society* in 1872 mentions that "Niriz is divided into three parishes or mahallas; that to the south termed the 'Mahalla-i Babi' is well known to be peopled almost entirely by Babis, who, though they do not openly profess their faith in the teachings of Siyyid Ali Muhammad the Bab, still practice the principles of communism he inculcated."[99] The inappropriateness of the term "communism" notwithstanding, the Western traveler's observation indicates the survival of the Babi insurgents' communal egalitarianism, as taught not by the Bab, but by Yahya and his comrades in the days of the revolt.

In Zanjan, Mulla Muhammad Ali Hujjat al-Islam, following his swift conversion to Babism, boldly and publicly proclaimed his mission, and laid out plans for a revolt which was to last six months. Like their counterparts in Yazd and Nairiz, he and his followers were well organized and regimented, adopting the same war cry and repeatedly attacking the enemy by surprise. The Zanjan rebels occupied an important segment of the town which, together with a nearby citadel they seized, was fortified and closed off. Watchwords were changed daily for the sake of security. They manufactured their own cannons and gun powder, and struck their own coins bearing the titles of *qaim* (savior) and *sahib al-zaman* (Master of the Age) on each side. The same fighting spirit, the same refusal to surrender despite their inferior numbers and poor equipment, characterized the Zanjani insurgents. The ideal of communal living was also practiced, as Hujjat al-Islam commanded his followers that "they should be as one family and one household, and all things ... should be divided for use."[100] They would periodically assault the royal camps and bring back fresh provisions, water, and arms. Gambling recklessly with their lives, they were promised heaven and spiritual posterity. "God has always willed," their leader would assert, "that in each age the blood of the martyrs shall become the oil of the lamp of religion."[101] Both Babi and Muslim sources mention the active part taken by women in this revolt. Dressed as men, they fought side by side their fellow men with an equally fierce intensity and a fearless willingness to die for the faith. Once again, the Babi revolt lost its momentum with the death of its leader, Hujjat al-Islam, even though his surviving followers continued to fight desperately. Worn out with nearly six months of warfare, they gave in to the treacherous overtures of peace made by the royalist commander, and suffered the same Babi fate: an inevitable, bloody massacre.

Meanwhile, in Tehran, news reached Mirza Taqi Khan Amir Kabir, the new Chief Minister, that the Babis were secretly organizing a major uprising in the capital aimed at murdering government officials, overthrowing the Qajar state, and seizing power. Most Babi sources vehemently deny this allegation and consider such "news" as unfounded rumors spread by their opponents further to discredit them in the eyes of the state authorities, and hence encourage the latter to take more drastic measures to wipe out the new faith. Jani, however, admits that some Babis were actually plotting an uprising, though not of the rumored scope.[102] Kazem Beg identifies Mulla Shaikh Ali (Azim) as the main organizer of the secret Babi group in Tehran, and holds him responsible for masterminding the plot, which he dropped just before the Babis were arrested.[103] Azim may have been involved in the conspiracy, as he definitely was a couple of years later in an unsuccessful attempt on the Shah's life. Be that as it may, the government feared a possible major confrontation in the capital with the religious rebels it had so much difficulty handling in the provinces. Consequently, thirty-seven Babis were arrested and brutally tortured before being given the choice of recanting or facing death. Seven of them, known as the "seven martyrs" in Babi annals, chose death. Among them were the maternal uncle and former guardian of the Bab, Sayyid Ali, a merchant by profession; a mujtahid, Sayyid Muhammad Husain Turshizi; a Sufi master; and a young student.

A recent study of the social basis of the Babi revolts attempts to differentiate the Zanjan and Nairiz uprisings from the Shaikh Tabarsi episode. The author defined the first two as "localized urban upheavals centered on one charismatic personality who had been converted to Babism and succeeded in attracting a large proportion of the populace of the town to a new movement" with no support from the neighboring peasantry or from the Babis of other regions. In contrast, he depicted the Shaikh Tabarsi events as a "definite challenge to the existing order," involving active, large-scale Babi participation from all parts of Iran, its participants representing all different rural and urban groupings in the country.[104] With such a distinction, the author implies that the Shaikh Tabarsi revolt (in comparison with those of Nairiz and

Zanjan, where undeniable non-Babi considerations are discernable) was purely a Babi affair, displaying pure religious motives.

If the available scanty figures are to be taken at face value, then admittedly the Mazandaran uprising included within its ranks a greater number of peasants, as well as artisans and petty shopkeepers, thus constituting a more socially representative movement of revolt. However, such statistics must be used with caution, if only because the distinction between small towns and surrounding villages, with populations constantly fluctuating from one to another, cannot be made in such a clear-cut way. Similarly, the difference between the large-scale Babi participation in Shaikh Tabarsi and the more localized nature of the uprisings in Nairiz and Zanjan was circumstantial, since many of the most important Letters of the Living perished in the North before the outbreak of the revolts in the two towns, and the surviving ones, sources indicate, were busy fomenting trouble elsewhere. Moreover, just as Darabi and Zanjani attracted converts from amongst followers with diverse sociopolitical interests, and just as their respective actions raise doubts as to the purity of their motives, so were Barfurushi and Bushrui open to suspicion, if not actually guilty, of deviation from purely religious considerations.

Social, political, and economic factors were equally at work in all three major uprisings. The spirit of turmoil which facilitated conversion to the new faith was not directly induced by existing socioeconomic dislocations, as Ivanov has it, since the Bab promised neither a new order nor an end to trade with foreign firms. Rather, the new doctrine fulfilled the desires and hopes of individuals, and not groups or classes, who had traditionally shown dissatisfaction with prevailing institutionalized values and systems, whether religio-mystical or sociopolitical. It acted as a catalyst, and by provoking simultaneous action on the part of various discontented elements, it fused into one movement the mystical, political, and social aspirations of the mujtahid as well as the mulla; of the wealthy merchant as well as the petty shopkeeper and artisan; of the landowner and the peasant; of the pious as well as the political agitator. Discontent, traditionally expressed in religious terms, once more galvanized the deep-rooted Shia spirit of messianic enthusiasm and martyrdom, which time and again had led to more or less violent revolts against the established centers of power.

The Bab's Execution

These uprisings and its difficulties in crushing them finally convinced the government that what had first been dismissed as another
inconsequential religious movement in conflict over purely theological
issues, was turning out to be a potentially grave threat to the state.
Mirza Taqi Khan decided to put an end to it by eliminating the root of
the evil, and thus allowed the ulama to pronounce the Bab's death
sentence. The Bab was brought to Tabriz for a public execution.

What, under any other circumstance, could have been just an
annoying, minor incident, reflecting the poor quality of the soldiers'
training, came to add a heightened dramatic touch to the pathetic
"prophet's" last moments of life, and thus increase the awestricken
spectators' unease. On July 9, 1850, as the soldiers shot at him, the
bullets only broke loose the cord tying him, and the Bab ran away. A
loud cry broke the silence and "when the smoke and dust cleared away
after the volley, Bab was not to be seen, and the populace proclaimed
that he had ascended to the skies."[105] At that moment, popular excitement was such, a Muslim source acknowledges, that had the Bab not
run away, and if instead he had capitalized on not having been touched
by the bullets, he would easily have convinced the crowd of a miraculous, divine intervention.[106] "Half the population of Persia would have
become Babis, had the guard house where the Bab ran to contained a
safe hiding place,"[107] wrote a Western observer. The officials watching
the scene, afraid of a possible uprising erupting on the spot, had some
guards encircle the crowd to prevent any disturbance while others
looked for the Bab. Eventually he was found and tied again, and the
soldiers once more aimed, this time more accurately.

The Aftermath

A merciless persecution of the Babis was continued after the
death of Mirza Ali Muhammad by both state and religious authorities,
as well as by individual Muslims. Often personal grudges were
avenged by accusing opponents or rivals of being "tainted by the fatal
doctrines," and, as a contemporary observer has noted, "no time was
lost between apprehension and execution."[108] Nonetheless, the
movement was not crushed, as the surviving leaders were able to keep
up the spirit of revolt and missionary zeal. Babi and anti-Babi accounts
of the history of the sect in the period following the death of the Bab do

not coincide. Both Bahai-Azali mythmaking and Muslim polemical refutations obscure or underrate some significant aspects of the events that marked the second phase of Babism, from July 1850 to the summer of 1866, when Bahaullah proclaimed publicly a new dispensation.*

In most of his writings, including the *Bayan*, the Bab referred to "He whom God shall manifest" in the future as his only legitimate successor, whose revelation, superseding his, would abrogate his own. Though he ordered his followers to expect the new manifestation, he gave no specific information as to its place and time, nor any clues to the identity of the person whom God would choose. He only promised the waiting period would not exceed "1511 or 2001 years." In the meantime, the *Bayan* should retain its authority even after his death, when the "proof and quarantor" would effectively take over the leadership of the community.[109] However, disputes over succession to the Bab, in addition to the individualistic tendencies of some extremists, severely split the community.

There seems to be no doubt that Mirza Ali Muhammad had indeed appointed Subh-i Azal, Mirza Yahya Nuri, to succeed him in leading the Babi community, though Jani's assertion that the appointment was also meant to mark the dawn of a new manifestation is highly debatable. The young Nuri never made such claims nor even attempted to renounce the *Bayan*. However, the new leader, forced as he was to protect himself from public condemnation and arrest, concealed his identity and traveled throughout the country under different guises, while organizing clandestine activities against the state.

The inaccessibility of the leader on the one hand, and the ambitious schemes of Babi opportunists on the other, marked the years 1850–52 as a period of utter chaos and anarchy in Babi annals. Several individual Babis in Tehran, Mazandaran, Azerbaijan, Fars, and even in Baghdad put fourth claims to Babi leadership, either pretending to be the sole representative of Subh-i Azal, or independent "manifestations." Fierce rivalry arose between the various pretenders, with each demanding absolute surrender to his command from the followers. It seems Subh-i Azal was perfectly aware of their contentions and, though publicly disavowing them, he privately approved of some who served him and his cause.[110] For, aside from the blasphemous notions inherent in some of their claims, the "pretenders" were actively fomenting trouble in their respective regions, inciting the populace to

---

*Bahai sources assert Bahaullah first proclaimed the new dispensation in private in 1863.

revolt against the politico-religious establishment, and thus keeping up the original Babi militant spirit. In August 1852, a conspiracy masterminded by Shaikh Ali Azim, which aimed at murdering Nasir al-Din Shah, openly revealed the political nature of continuing Babi activities. The plot, which later was to be denounced by Bahais as the work of a madman deranged by grief over the Bab's death, and as "the cause of shame to mankind,"[111] failed to accomplish its purpose. The would-be assassin, a servant of Azim, only wounded the monarch. Massive arrests and a general massacre of all suspects followed. Qajar officials, alarmed by the potential threat of the "nihilists" and "anarchists," devised "Machiavellian means" for their extermination, best described by Browne: "A partition of the prisoners was made amongst the different classes; if a representative body of each of these classes were made responsible for the execution of one or more Babis; and if it were further signified to the persons thus forced to act the part of executioners that the Shah would be able to estimate their loyalty to himself by the manner in which they disposed of their victims, then all classes, being equally partakers in the blood of the slain, would be equally exposed to the retaliation of the survivors, from whom they would be therefore effectually and permanently alienated, while at the same time the Shah himself would avoid incurring the odium of the massacre."[112] Babi leaders who had survived till then lost their lives in the carnage, amongst them Qurrat al-Ain, Jani, and Azim himself. Bahaullah was imprisoned for four months, then released after proving his innocence. With the permission of the Court, he left Iran for Baghdad. Subh-i Azal, however, escaped arrest by hiding away in remote mountains disguised as a dervish. Later he joined his brother in the Iraqi capital, where a great number of Babis had taken refuge.

Subh-i Azal was still the nominal head of the community, and he was acknowledged as such by most of the adepts, including Bahaullah, who preached and carried on missionary works in his younger brother's name.[113] As the latter continued to lead a secluded life in Baghdad, he rapidly became the most prominent figure of the sect, assuming de facto authority over it. Inevitably, rivalry arose between the two brothers. In 1854, Bahaullah left Baghdad and sought refuge and solitude in mountainous Kurdistan, where he stayed almost two years before his followers brought him back to the Iraqi capital. Sources for this period are scarce and highly polemical, reflecting the biased views of their respective sectarian affiliations. Conspiracy, intrigues, and petty quarrels must have accompanied the loftier activities of the Babis in exile. Such activities continued to alarm the Iranian government, for it finally asked the Ottoman officials to have the Babis extradited or removed from Iraq, because it was considered too dangerously close to Iran. Towards the end of 1863, the Babis were transferred to Turkey. After a four month stay in Istanbul, they were sent to Adrianople, where they spent five years.

It was in Adrianople that the final break between the two Nuri brothers occurred. In the summer of 1866,[114] Bahaullah publicly proclaimed his own dispensation, which was accepted by the majority of the Babis, who then came to be known as Bahais. A relatively small group, referred to as Azalis, chose to remain faithful to the original Babi doctrine upheld by Subh-i Azal. The Babi community in Adrianople, as Browne described it, consisted of "actual exiles and potential martyrs...religious enthusiasts, revolutionary visionaries and speculative mystics."[115] It was of utmost importance to Mirza Husain Ali, a man with charismatic appeal and a talent for leadership, to organize the community and reformulate its doctrines, adjusting Babism to new conditions in order to make it a more viable religion capable of absorbing changes that were needed, given the existing sociopolitical climate.

The new "Prophet of the Age" pronounced the Bab to have been the "Herald," the forerunner whose chief task was to announce the approaching advent of his own manifestation. The new laws he promulgated drastically revised older Babi directives. Essentially, his aim was twofold: to declare the new religion a universal one, transcending national and cultural particularities, and to expand it beyond Iranian frontiers; and to conciliate the Shah and his government, and gain their support against the Muslim clerical opposition. He cancelled or changed earlier doctrines in order to discard elements of mystico-philosophical speculative thought, thus divorcing the new faith more completely from Islamic traditions. He recommended the use of a universal, international language, and exalted humanitarianism over patriotism, insisting on the community of all believers. "Pride is not for him who loves his country, but for him who loves the whole world,"[116] he is quoted as saying. Furthermore, he forbade the use of arms, even for religious purposes, and asked his followers to avoid political involvement, wishing to eliminate totally the militant spirit that characterized original Babism. A spiritual and moral tone came to dominate the new dogma. "Today victory neither hath been or will be opposition to any one nor strife with any person, but rather what is well-pleasing is that...selfishness and lust should be subdued by the sword of the word, of wisdom, and of exhortation." It emphasized "sociability, concord, obedience, submissiveness," counseling the faithful to offer "against the sword the word ... and against the fierceness patience, and in place of oppression submission, and at the time of martyrdom resignation." Yet it encouraged them to profess their beliefs openly, without reverting to the time-honored practice of *taqiyya*, praising sincerity over concealment: "The truth of the matter is not hidden or concealed, but plain and evident."[117]

Bahaullah wrote letters to the Shah explaining the purely spiritual character of the new creed, assuring him of his and his followers' worldly allegiance. "The king is here to rule by divine right. ... He is the refuge of all dwellers upon earth and the asylum of all mankind; it [kingship] is not limited to one party."[118] Thus, contrary to the Babi and Islamic view of the prophet as the absolute sovereign, Bahaullah, the pragmatic leader facing exile and persecution, having lived through the military defeat of the early Babis, expediently declared his religion totally divorced from political concerns. Here, then, Bahaism embraced what no Muslim sect, no Muslim school of thought ever succeeded in or dared to try: the doctrinal acceptance of the de facto secularization of politics which had occurred in the Muslim world centuries earlier. Obviously inspired by Western models, he called for religious tolerance and "equal rights to all peoples and classes," which would help usher in the age of progress; and he warned against continuing religious persecution and its inevitable consequences, political decline and social decay. "Times are changed, and the needs and fashion of the world are changed."[119]

Mirza Yahya, on the other hand, chose to preserve not only the original Babi doctrine, but also the old hostility towards the Qajar state. He gathered around him those who also wished to remain faithful to Babism, as well as those politically minded individuals who, conceiving themselves as Iranians first and foremost and primarily concerned with sociopolitical issues, wished to undertake a revolution. To the latter type, Bahai universalism and pacifism proved to be highly distasteful and irrelevant, whereas Azali Babism provided them with a creed which seemingly justified their political activism and growing nationalist consciousness. In fact, from among the ranks of the Azali faction there emerged individual Iranian nationalists who were to play dominant intellectual and political roles, as individuals and not as Azalis, in the revolutionary movement which culminated in the establishment of a constitutional government in 1906. Fearing both the Muslims and the Bahais, and numerically helpless, Subh-i Azal and his party were more often than not forced to adopt traditional modes of esoteric expression and practice *taqiyya*.

In August 1868, the two religious leaders and their respective followers were once more removed to new destinations. The Turkish government, impatient with fresh attempts at propagandism on the part of the Babis, sent the Bahais to Acre in Palestine and the Azalis to Famagusta in Cyprus. The deadly rivalry between the Nuri brothers was to continue unabated. Azali and Bahai sources accuse each other of envy and vengefulness, intrigues and even murder. The Bahais did kill some Azalis who were allegedly conspiring against Bahaullah, and the Azalis did attempt to undermine the growing influence of the Bahais. Nevertheless, it is interesting to note that, as contact with the West and Western thought increased, both factions were receptive to these influences and attempted to adopt some aspects of Western ideals. Thus, ironically, they both came to demand similar types of Western-inspired social reforms, envisioning a similar ideal of a modern society for Iran (which, incidentally, corresponded to the secularists' view, as we shall presently see). They also expressed an identical anti-clericalism which, again, was to be found amongst the secularists. In practical terms, then, the end was the same, though the means differed.

5

The Secularization of Dissent in Shia Thought

B ETWEEN THE OPPRESSIVE, autocratic Qajar government and a largely illiterate and ill-treated population there came into being in the second half of the nineteenth century a group of educated thinkers, distinct from the ulama, who were committed to the belief that social and political problems were the central issues of life. Declaring that the truly spiritual and religious person was no longer interested in the mystery of life but in pragmatic solutions to particular problems, they rebelled against the great mystical vision of the world and denounced metaphysics and theology as too barren in their abstractions. They were strongly convinced that the principal causes of the social decay, injustice, and oppression they saw in Iran lay in human ignorance and an archaic sense of values, and that only with scientific knowledge could their society liberate itself.

Having witnessed the utter failure of the Shaikhis and the Babis to alter in any fashion the orthodox religious views, yet determined to struggle for change, they looked elsewhere for a source of inspiration and a model to follow. Thus they discovered and were irresistibly attracted to the anti-theological, anti-metaphysical thought of eighteenth-century Europe. However, given the socioreligious climate of the time, and considering the fact that, with the exception of Malkum Khan, all of these thinkers were first brought up in the traditional Shia schools of thought, it is not surprising that they sought, no matter how awkwardly or how unconvincingly, to accommodate Western ideas with Islam, in the same way that previous theosophers had assimilated unorthodox views into their system of thought. This, however, should by no means be taken for Islamic reformism: no serious attempt was made by any one of them either to reinterpret the doctrine as the theosophers had tried, or to show that the Koran anticipates and is fully consonant with the spirit and the findings of basically Western ideas. They all advocated a reform program that would ensure an absolute separation of religious and temporal affairs.

I shall study here five Iranian thinkers whom I consider representative of the new trend: Sayyid Jamal al-Din Asadabadi, known as Afghani (1838–97); Mirza Fathali Akhunzada (1812–78); Mirza Malkum Khan (1833–1908); Abdul-Rahim Talibzada (1834–1911); and Mirza Aqa Khan Kirmani (1853–96). Following a biographical sketch of each individual, I shall analyze their ideas in separate sections. I propose to show how, despite some basically technical differences, they all held in common a faith in the transforming power of enlightened ideas; a belief in change as something not to be feared but to be welcomed; and a self-conception as the new apostles, carrying the message of the age: that of reason, science (in non-religious terms), liberty, and progress. Though they played no major role in the important political events of their time, they laid out the course of future action for their fellow citizens, and therefore are to be held responsible, partly at least, for a number of its consequences.

AFGHANI

Afghani is perhaps the most controversial political figure of the Middle East in the nineteenth century. An Iranian by birth, though during his lifetime he generally claimed to be Afghan, he had a thorough Muslim upbringing, his formal education consisting of the usual religious studies of jurisprudence, the Traditions, and Arabic, as well as philosophy and mysticism, two subjects which tended to attract the attention of the more talented students. In his late teens he visited India, where it seems that he underwent a profound change which helped him develop a newly awakened political consciousness. His stay in the British colony coincided with, or came just before, the time of the Indian Mutiny of 1857, a war that was largely supported by the Muslim population, which had suffered discrimination and a loss of social status with the advent of English rule. It was probably at this time that the young man developed his strong hatred for the British, a hatred which came to characterize his political career throughout his life, and which later led him to proclaim himself champion of the Muslim struggle against British imperialist rule.

Following his stay in India, Afghani traveled to Arabia, then Afghanistan, and in 1870 he arrived in Istanbul. In the Ottoman capital, he delivered a university lecture in which he praised philosophy and discussed prophecy in terms which were considered blasphemous by the Turkish ulama. Upon the latter's demand, he was expelled from the city. From Istanbul, Afghani went to Cairo, where he spent eight most constructive years. He succeeded in gathering around himself a group of young Egyptian and Syrian intellectuals who become his most devoted disciples. Among them was Muhammad Abduh, who was later to play an important role as an educator and legal reformer. Through his informal teaching, his public speeches, and his political intrigues within the Freemasons lodge in Cairo, Afghani established a solid reputation as a leading political and revolutionary figure. His anti-British, anti-government activities caused the Egyptian monarch to order his expulsion in 1879. From Egypt, Afghani went for the second time to India, where he stayed until 1882 when he left for Europe.

In Paris, together with Muhammad Abduh Jamal al-Din, he published an Arabic newspaper, *al'Urwa al Wuthqa* ("The Strong link") which reflected a defensive, pan-Islamic mood and violent anti-British sentiment. He also read Ernest Renan, the French free-thinking writer who had specifically denounced Islam as a backward faith, incompatible with science and responsible for the Muslim world's decay and intellectual stagnation. In a newspaper article addressed to the journalist, Afghani rose in defense of his religion in a manner largely reminiscent of the Muslim philosophers, as we shall presently see.

In London, Afghani became acquainted with Wilfrid Blunt, a pro-Arab amateur politician who had important connections within British government circles, and who introduced him to some leading political figures. After a two-year visit to Russia, where he also managed to talk to leading politicians, he went back to Iran once in 1886–87 and then again at the end of 1889, a most opportune time, for the growing number of concessions given to foreigners and widespread government corruption were causing strong reactions among the merchant and ulama classes. He rapidly became involved in organizing the movement of opposition to the Shah's policies until the latter, alarmed at his activities, forced him into exile. The opposition increased when, in 1891, the court granted a British company a monopoly for the curing and sale of Iran's entire tobacco crop. Afghani helped keep up the spirit of revolt by sending anti-Shah letters from abroad to prominent ulama. However, the success of the revolt (which forced the Shah to revoke the concession in 1892) was primarily due to the unified effort of religious leaders, merchants, and intellectuals, and his own role in it was not so prominent as his followers and admirers claimed it to be. Nevertheless, as Nikki Keddie rightly noted, he was instrumental in the organization of propaganda and mass protest.[1] This protest was the first successful mass movement in modern Iranian history. It also marked the peak of Afghani's career as a revolutionary leader.

The last six years of his life were spent in hopeless struggles to promote his political projects, especially a pan-Islamic scheme calling for the political unification of the Muslims under the rule of one Muslim monarch. Following a short visit to London, where he joined Malkum Khan, who shared his violent hatred for Nasir al-Din Shah and bitterly campaigned against the corruption of the Iranian government, he accepted the Ottoman sultan's invitation to go to Istanbul. Once again he met only disillusionment, for, contrary to his expectations, he was given no major, responsible position. In fact, his relations with Abdul Hamid steadily declined. The crowd of revolutionary Iranians in exile he gathered around himself increased the monarch's suspicion. And even though, after the Shah's assassination by one of Afghani's disciples, Abdul Hamid refused to extradite him as the Iranian government requested, he was closely watched by the Ottoman authorities till he died in 1897, of cancer of the chin.

AKHUNDZADA

Fathali Akhundzada was born in 1812 in Nukha, a small town in West Azerbaijan which was annexed by Russia in 1828. His paternal grandfather was from Rasht (the main town of the Caspian province Gilan), his father from Tabriz, and his mother from Maragha. Despite his Turkic ethnicity and Russian residence, he proudly claimed to be of Persian origin, and considered Iran to be his homeland. When he was barely seven years old, his parents divorced and he went, together with his mother, to live with her uncle in Ardabil, a small town in East Azerbaijan. At the age of thirteen, his great uncle was transferred to a small town in the Caucasus, and he took them along with him. Following the Russo-Persian War of 1828, the small family decided to settle in Nukha, Fathali's birthplace.

Nukha was then a predominantly Shia town, and the young man was given a traditional Shia education. He studied religious sciences, logic, jurisprudence, Arabic, Persian, and Turkish. His family wished to see him follow a religious career. Akhundzada, however, soon decided otherwise. Under the supervision of private tutors and learned friends, he began to study philosophy and Sufi mysticism. At the age of twenty-two, he went to Tiflis where he studied Russian. He then acquired an important position as translator of Oriental languages in the service of the viceroy of the Caucasus in Tiflis, a position which he was to retain for the rest of his life, and which later earned him the title of colonel. From his comfortable and secure post, Akhundzada was able to devote practically his entire time to reading, writing essays and plays, working on a revised script for the Persian and Turkish languages, and keeping up a voluminous correspondence with friends and acquaintances in and outside Russian territory.

Tiflis was then an established cultural center of the Caucasus. Akhundzada had the opportunity to meet many prominent Armenian, Georgian, and Russian intellectuals—mostly revolutionary poets, writers, journalists—who introduced him to Western philosophical and political ideas.

In 1848, Akhundzada visited Iran in the company of General Shilling, the Russian envoy to Nasir al-Din Shah's coronation. In 1863, he went to Istanbul to present his alphabetical reform project to the Ottoman Scientific Society. He stayed at the Iranian embassy, as personal guest of the ambassador, Mirza Husain Khan Mushir al-Daula, whom he had previously met in Tiflis. Apart from these two short trips outside the Caucasus, Akhundzada remained in Tiflis until he died in February 1878.

MALKUM KHAN

Mirza Malkum Khan was born in 1833 in Julfa, the Armenian suburb near Isfahan. At the age of seventeen, his father, Mirza Yaqub, an Armenian convert to Islam who was then working as an interpreter in the Russian embassy, sent him to Paris to study. Within a few years, Malkum acquired a good knowledge of French and English, and, it is reported, of the natural sciences, engineering, and law. In 1851, having completed his education (a commodity that was already much in demand in Iranian government circles), he came back to his native country, ready to set up for himself a brilliant political career. In the early 1850s, Nasir al-Din Shah's court was open to ambitious politicians who, on the one hand, were well versed in European ideas and customs and full of plans and schemes for a rapid modernization of Iran, and, on the other, who were familiar with Iranian court manners and knew how to approach the monarch.

Upon his return to Tehran, Malkum established his first contact with the court by becoming its official interpreter. He also succeeded in getting a teaching position in the very much in vogue Dar al-Funun, a government-sponsored school offering a modern curriculum. In no time at all, he attracted the attention of a then prominent statesman, Mirza Ali Khan Amin al-Daula, whom he accompanied as a consultant on various trips to Europe. In 1856, he went to Paris as an interpreter and political advisor to Farrukh Khan Amin al-Mulk, the Shah's envoy to the Anglo-Persian peace conference.

A few years later, Malkum's first clash with the court occurred, which led to his first enforced exile. In 1858, he had established the *Faramushkhana* ("House of Oblivion"), a society organized into a system of secret cells with a hierarchical administration similar to the Freemason lodges. The semi-secret ways of this organization, which recruited its members from among the aristocracy, royal family, and young students of the Dar al-Funun, aroused the Shah's suspicion, and it was soon banned. Malkum's numerous enemies within the royal circle helped a great deal to undermine his position in the court. There were many ministers and officials who wished to get rid of him, for he had openly attacked them as corrupt and inefficient in the written reform projects he had submitted to the Shah. In 1863, together with other political *personae non gratae,* all labeled "irreligious," he went first to Baghdad, then to Istanbul.

In the Ottoman capital, Malkum remained idle for a while, without work and without influence. It is said about him that during those days he decided to convert to Christianity in order to marry the daughter of an Armenian merchant. He also gave up his Iranian citizenship to become a naturalized Ottoman subject, and thus find employment with the Ottoman government. These actions cast doubt on the depth of Malkum's loyalty to Iran and Islam.

Malkum's star began to shine again when the Iranian ambassador to the Ottoman court, Mirza Husain Khan Mushir al-Daula, a reformer attracted by his ideas, decided to attach him to his service and to seek the Shah's pardon for him. The minister's patronage not only gave Malkum the opportunity to submit his reform projects to the government but also provided him with a sometimes much-needed cover-up for his dubious deeds. Thus, during a brief stay in Cairo as consul-general, when he allegedly accepted a bribe from the Egyptian monach, the Persian embassy prevented the scandal from exploding by immediately recalling him to Istanbul. In 1871, when Mirza Husain Khan became Chief Minister, Malkum was given a position as councilor and an aristocratic title, Nazim al-Mulk. Shortly before the Shah's first visit to Europe, in 1873, which Mirza Husain Khan had advised, Malkum was sent to London as consul to make the necessary arrangements. In 1878, he successfully represented Iran in the Berlin Conference. As a reward for this diplomatic mission, he was promoted to ambassadorial rank and given the title of prince. Four years later, he was once more honored with the Shah's favor, this time receiving the title of Nazim al-Daula.

Malkum's relationship with the court and the Shah began to deteriorate with the notorious issue concerning a lottery concession, which arose in January 1889, and which decisively ruined his career and precipitated his downfall. Nasir al-Din had granted him, in return for the sum of a thousand British pounds, the monopoly for a state lottery. This concession was subsequently bought by a British syndicate for £40,000. Malkum's greatest enemy at that time, the Chief Minister of the time, Amin al-Sultan, had it revoked, thanks to a religious pronouncement from the ulama denouncing the deal as forbidden by Islam because of its gambling nature. Malkum himself was discredited and removed from his position as ambassador.

This break with the court incited the reformer to adopt a less compromising, more revolutionary policy. He founded in London a newspaper called *Qanun* ("Law"), to which he devoted all his energy and attention. The first issue was published on February 20, 1890. The main content of the paper consisted of sharp criticisms against the prevailing social and economic backwardness of Iran and its political corruption, and it called for the establishment of law, a national assembly, and representative government. The paper was banned in Iran, but it succeeded in circulating clandestinely.

It is only after the death of Amin al-Sultan, and during the premiership of Amin al-Daula, that Malkum's position in the court improved. In 1898, Muzaffar al-Din Shah named him ambassador to Rome, and reinstated his titles. Thus, in the last ten years of his life, he enjoyed again the prestige and privileges accorded an Iranian envoy to a European court. He died in 1908 in Lausanne.

ABDUL-RAHIM TALIBZADA

Little is known of Abdul-Rahim Talibzada's life. He was born into a modest family of carpenters in Tabriz in 1834. At the age of sixteen he moved to Tiflis, which had just fallen into Russian hands, where he permanently settled. However, like his fellow Azerbaijani, Akhund-zada, he considered himself an Iranian, kept up his interest in Iranian affairs, and devoted all his works to the discussion of the future of the Iranian nation. His home had become the rendezvous of Iranian statesmen and intellectuals visiting or passing through town. He especially cultivated a friendship with Amin al-Sultan, the controversial politician with whom he kept close ties, even on the eve of the Constitutional Revolution.

Again like Akhundzada, Talibzada discovered Europe and Western European writers through Russian translations and, with the exception of a short trip to Germany, where he sought medical treatment during the last year of his life, he made no attempt to visit those countries he read so much and so avidly about. By profession he was not an intellectual, having spent the greater part of his adult life managing a construction business which he owned. However, once financially established, he turned into a full-time writer. Similarly, he was no professional politician, though he was offered the post of Tabriz deputy in the National Assembly which was set up after the promulgation of the Constitution in 1906. Leading Constitutionalists of Tabriz chose him as one of their most important citizens who had greatly contributed to the dissemination of revolutionary political ideas. He declined the offer, but continued to write about political matters until he died in 1911.

MIRZA AQA KHAN KIRMANI

Abdul Husain Khan, known as Mirza Aqa Khan Kirmani, was born in Mashiz, a small town west of Kirman city, in 1853 or 1854. Both parents were descendants of illustrious families who could trace their genealogies as far back as the Safavid era. On the paternal side, he was the son of Abdul Rahim Mashizi, a wealthy landowner affiliated with the Sufi sect *Ahl-i haq*; the grandson of a close companion of Aqa Khan Mahalati, the Ismaili leader who had been governor of Kirman; and a great grandson of a prominent Zoroastrian community leader who had converted to Islam. On the maternal side, he was the grandson of a distinguished physician of Kirman; the great grandson of a famous jurist and leader of a Sufi order; and a direct descendant of an aristocratic physician from Moghul India who was offered an official position in the Safavid court and had married one of the princesses.

Mirza Aqa Khan's education was traditional, including the study of Arabic and Persian languages and literatures, theology, and philosophy. His teachers were Aqa Sadiq, a disciple of Mulla Hadi Sabzavari, and, more importantly, Haji Sayyid Javad Kerbalai, the noted Babi who introduced him to the writings of Sadra, Ahsai and the Bab, and inspired him to convert to Babism. Kirmani studied elementary French and English with a Zoroastrian instructor, from whom he also acquired a basic knowledge of the ancient Iranian languages, Avesta and Pahlavi. It is reported that from early childhood he had revealed an intense craving for learning and he had set out to pursue his self-education by reading voraciously. A kind of restless intellectual curiosity characterized his endless quest for novel ideas, for he was also a man in pursuit of an ideal, a cause to fight for. He vested his hopes in Babism, which offered him then the most potent contemporary Iranian manifestation of the longing for change. This, however, did not stop him from seeking new ideologies and new faiths elsewhere. His conversion, therefore, remained superficial.

In 1883, following a heated argument with the then governor of Kirman, which brought to an end his brief career as a government official, he left the province, never to return to it again. Kirmani spent two years in Isfahan, where he came to frequent a literary circle which used to discuss controversial theological and philosophical ideas, and afterwards he spent a few months in Tehran. Throughout this period the governor of Kirman attempted without success to have him extradited to his native province. Mirza Aqa Khan finally sought asylum in Istanbul, which he reached in 1886. Except for a short trip that took him to Cyprus (where he met Subh-i Azal and whose daughter he married), Syria, and Iraq, for the last ten years of his life he remained in the Ottoman capital. These were ten industrious and productive years during which Kirmani improved his knowledge of French and English, and thus became more directly acquainted with Western thought, and in which he wrote most of his works and essentially formulated his revolutionary ideas. He mixed socially with a group of Iranian expatriates — merchants, teachers, writers, and poets. He was associated with the Persian language newspaper *Akhtar,* to which he regularly contributed articles on various literary and political subjects, until it was finally closed down by order of the Ottoman authorities in 1895.

Aside from his writings, Kirmani's political involvement in Istanbul was twofold. On the one hand, he helped Malkum Khan to distribute the newspaper *Qanun* amongst Iranian readers; and, on the other hand, he collaborated with Afghani in setting up a pan-Islamic movement and in writing and distributing anti-Shah political propaganda. His relationship with Malkum was based solely on their correspondence, which began in 1890 (that is, at the time Malkum started publishing his *Qanun*), and ended in 1895 when Kirmani was arrested. They never met personally. Kirmani, however, had known Afghani in person since 1892, when the then notorious activist came from London to Istanbul at the sultan's invitation. These pan-Islamic activities, his noted Babi affiliation, his anti-government writings, and open clashes with the Iranian ambassador to the Porte increasingly aroused the Iranian government's hostility. When one of the two hundred letters written by individuals responding enthusiastically to the pan-Islamic organizers' call for revolt was intercepted by the Iranian consul in Baghdad, and Afghani's conspiracy was revealed, an order was issued to arrest all persons involved in the plot. Though the Porte at first refused to do so, and though Afghani himself was left free, Kirmani and two of his companions were arrested in 1895 and sent to Trebizond to await deportation. When Mirza Riza Kirmani shot and killed Nasir al-Din Shah, Kirmani's fate was decisively determined. Since the assassin, an alleged Babi sympathizer, was associated with Afghani and hence with the prisoners, the Iranian government found it convenient to charge them all with murder. In July 1896, Kirmani was executed in Tabriz.

RELIGIOUS THOUGHT

The group of intellectuals under study had, as already stated, rejected as irrelevant the philosophical, mystical, and theological issues which then dominated Iranian thought. They believed free inquiry and religion were incompatible. The Babi and Shaikhi experiences, not to mention the centuries-old dilemma of the theosophers themselves, had clearly revealed to them the futility of any attempt at reconciliation. Consequently they tried, each in his own way, to transcend theological issues in order to concentrate on more immediate social problems.

In a short analysis of Afghani's thought, Muhsin Mahdi discusses the Muslim philosophers' understanding of the "unresolvable" tension between religion and philosophy, and of the religious "walls" they built around the believers to provide a protective shelter from the sense of "terror" which otherwise grips "ordinary" people, who are by nature incapable of understanding. He studies Afghani's view of these "walls" as representative of the Islamic philosophical tradition.[2] However, it is precisely the destruction of these "walls," and their entire mental and social foundation, which the new generation of intellectuals, including Afghani, wished above all to undertake. They fought with all the vehemence and all the strength they could command to wipe out the disastrous consequences of keeping ordinary people in a state of utter dependence on organized religion. They strove to awaken the masses, no matter how brutally, from their "long sleep of ignorance" by tearing apart the "shield" which supposedly protected them from the "fearful," the "vast horizons," the "unknown."

Afghani

No Muslim intellectual of the modern times has been as thoroughly dissected as Jamal al-Din was by both Middle Eastern and Western scholars. He is depicted as a true believer by Gibb,[3] as well as by most Iranian and Arab scholars writing in Persian or Arabic. Kedourie characterizes him as an irreligious opportunist who transformed religion into a political ideology and whose aim was "the subversion of the Islamic religion," adding, "the method adopted to this end was the practice of a false but showy devotion."[4] Keddie surmises that he was probably an Islamic deist,[5] while Pakdaman (among others) saw in him a true nationalist championing the Muslim struggle against Western imperialism.[6] Finally, Muhsin Madhi described Afghani as the "last representative of a great [philosophical] tradition... the first Muslim philosopher to spring up in modern times and give irrefutable testimony to the vitality and formative role of that tradition and to its dedication to the welfare of the Islamic community."[7] One could go on endlessly citing references attesting to his faith or lack of faith, sincerity or duplicity of character. I do not propose to add any new interpretation, nor provide a fresh argument for or against the genuineness of his religious beliefs; my concern is only to clarify a few important points which have been either overlooked or no more than briefly mentioned.

Despite his wide-ranging activities outside Iran, Afghani was through and through an Iranian, and his early formal education was entirely dominated by Shia thought. He had spent four years in the holy cities studying traditional sciences with the ulama whom, in the end, he condemned as shallow, legalistic, and merely interested in the exoteric aspects of religion. He was more attracted to Islamic philosophy, including Sadra's, and to the theology of Ahsai. He even ventured to write a few lyrical poems in the classical Sufi tradition. Analyzing such a poem, where he laments over his condition, Pakdaman speculates that Afghani's departure from Iran might after all have been against his own will, and raises the question of a possible involvement with the Babis.[8] This would be difficult to prove, since he did not write extensively about the sect, apart from a few short sentences in his *Refutation of the Materialists* and in other essays, where he scornfully rejected its adherents as contemporary disciples of the Ismailis of Alamut. But then, so did Mirza Aqa Khan Kirmani, the self-professed Azali Babi, as well as a score of secret converts. Afghani did mix socially with Babis, and had many Babi friends. Moreover, judging from quite a revealing autobiographical note he wrote while in Afghanistan, where he candidly spoke of the multiple charges of heresy made against him by his enemies, he was fully aware of the controversial self-image he projected and of the hostility he aroused so often in individuals and groups alike. The Muslims, he complained, took him for a Christian; the Sunnis for a Shia or a Wahabi (a fundamentalist sect centered in Arabia); the Shia for a Babi. Others accused him of moral corruption, obscurantism, atheism, and materialism. He neither appealed to the nonbelievers nor to the Muslims.

Afghani's views on the origin of the world and on the progressive development of religious belief clearly indicate his unorthodox tendencies.[9] Similarly, his writings display the great impact the Shaikhi school left on his thinking. His notorious lecture in Istanbul, delivered in Persian at the newly-established university in 1870, was almost entirely based on Shaikhism, itself a mere reformulation of medieval Islamic philosophy. Defining prophecy as a craft similar to any other such as medicine, albeit nobler, he contrasted it to philosophy and concluded that, while the former is divinely "inspired," and varies according to times and conditions (hence is primarily "regional," and not always necessary at all ages), the latter is based on reason and is universal, yet it is needed at all times to enlighten humanity. The prophet is infallible, the philosopher is not; but the philosopher is the guide who shows the way out of ignorance, to happiness and well-being.[10]

Similarly, Afghani was merely echoing the Shaikhis when elsewhere he emphatically stated: "There is no doubt that in the present age, distress, misfortune, and weakness besiege all classes of Muslims from every side. Therefore, every Muslim keeps his eyes and ears open in expectation ... to see from what corner of the earth the sage and renewer will appear and will reform the minds and souls of the Muslims." A teacher is indispensable, he added, "some man of high intelligence and pure soul" to help the community of the faithful find the right path.[11] The idea of a "renewer" is not common to the Shaikhis and theosophers alone. The orthodox jurists, both Sunni and Shia, accepted it and even identified individual theologians (such as al-Ghazali in the eleventh and twelfth centuries, Majlisi in the seventeenth, and Bihbahani in the eighteenth centuries) as the "renewers" of their ages. Nevertheless, Afghani's assertion that in each community there must be two groups of teachers—one to guide the intellect and the other the soul, one taking care of the spiritual and the other of the moral aspects of human nature—is more reminiscent of Muhammad Karim Khan Kirmani's two distinct categories of superior beings, the *nuqaba* and the *nujaba*, destined to lead the faithful. Also like the Shaikhis and the theosophers in general, he attacked the organized orthodox religious leadership, both Sunni and Shia, for its anti-intellectualism and the stifling effect it had on scientific and philosophical inquiry. In his famous *Answer to Renan,* he specifically distinguished Islam from "the manner in which it was propagated in the world." Islamic science and philosophy through the centuries made "brilliant and fruitful achievements," he said, despite the "heavy yoke" imposed by the jurists, and should be differentiated from the "Muslim religion" as represented by the orthodox theologians. His eloquent despair ("So long as humanity exists, the struggle will not cease between dogma and free investigation, between religion and philosophy; a desperate struggle in which, I fear, the triumph will not be for free thought, because the masses dislike reason, and its teachings are only understood by some intelligences of the elite"[12]) expressed the centuries-long situation of the Muslim dissenters in opposition to the persecuting jurists, who considered themselves the only true exponents of Islam.

The *Answer to Renan,* which praises the Muslim thinkers who had inherited and eventually transformed Greek and Roman thought, is specifically addressed to a Western audience, and is written in an apologetic fashion for a people, the Arabs, with whom, as a Muslim living in Paris, he chose to identify. In retrospect, it reads like a political statement, not a religious or philosophical one. The message is clear: the Muslims, if they succeeded in throwing off the "heaviest and most humiliating yokes" (that is, blind and unquestioning obedience) imposed upon them by their educators, would "advance rapidly on the road to progress and science." Though aware of tremendous obstacles, he expressed his optimism that Muslim society would "succeed some day in breaking its bonds and marching resolutely in the path of civilization after the manner of the Western society."[13] Reminiscent of the Shaikhis, of Sadra, and of the theosophers and philosophers, both Sunni and Shia, this defiant statement is an open declaration of continued struggle against those who obstruct free inquiry. And there is no mistaking whom he meant: the orthodox theologians, the jurists. Afghani, here and in the rest of his writings, as well as in his political behavior, proved to be a man in revolt against the sociopolitical establishment within the Muslim world. He was not a champion of Islam as a religious system, despite his pan-Islamic ideal. In fact, he rose in defense of religion only when he came to fight the Qajars and needed the support of the Shia mujtahids, and again when he was living in the West and confronting Westerners, who saw in him the "man from the East" and not a freethinker, as he was perceived in Iran, India, Afghanistan, and Turkey. At these times he spoke the traditional language of the Muslim philosopher.

On the other hand, in his Persian essays addressed to Muslims living in Iran and India, Afghani mercilessly condemned his contemporary philosophers and theologians for dealing with issues he considered outdated and irrelevant. He hailed science and deplored the ulama's common practice of dividing it into two artificial spheres, Muslim and European, and of discouraging the faithful from learning from non-Muslims. "They have not understood," he wrote, "that science is that noble thing that has no connection with any nation, and is not distinguished by anything but itself ... men must be related to science, not science to men."[14] He remarked on the ulama's inconsistent attitude: "How very strange it is that the Muslims study those sciences that are ascribed to Aristotle with the greatest delight, as if Aristotle were one of the pillars of the Muslims. However, if the discussion relates to Galileo, Newton, Kepler, they consider them infidels"; and he emphatically stated, "The father and mother of science is proof, and proof is neither Aristotle nor Galileo. The truth is where there is proof, and those who forbid science and knowledge in the belief that they are safeguarding religion are really the enemies of that religion." Thus, he prophetically warned, "The harm of [such] ignorant friend[s] to Islam is greater than the harm of the heretics and enemies of Islam."[15]

Afghani painstakingly attempted to reconcile science and religion, defining the Koran as the Muslim's first teacher of philosophy, and philosophy as the "mother" of all sciences. He severely criticized the works of the Muslim philosophers, which he declared to be faithful copies of the Greeks and the Romans, whom they blindly venerated and imitated. He condemned even more the philosophers of his own time for ignoring relevant issues, such as the cause of the Muslims' poverty and distress or the possibility of reforming the community. He assailed their indifference to the "real sciences" which produced railways, the telegraph, microscopes, and the like. With the world undergoing important changes, he complained, the Muslim philosopher "does not raise his hand from the sleep of neglect. ... He splits hairs over imaginary essences and lags behind in the knowledge of evident matters."[16] And yet, Afghani loudly proclaimed, science is what rules the world. Muslims, who possessed it in the past and hence conquered the world, were now a declining nation. In contrast, the West, who now owned it, was the master of the world. Governments must, he imperatively stated, import science and give it to all their subjects. No reform was possible unless the religious leaders themselves reformed their attitude towards knowledge, and began to learn the "true sciences." Afghani's alarm was loud and clear: Islamic philosophy was no longer able to meet the demands of the modern world, and the Muslims must change their masters. Individuals of learning and science were the only qualified educators. They must be honored and recognized by all. Only they could cure social ills.[17]

Afghani wished to destroy the traditional view of religion, including that of the theosophers. His dedication was not to the "philosophic outlook" in the traditional sense, despite the seemingly traditional rhetoric he adopted so often—a rhetoric he could not easily abandon, given the traditional character of his formal education. In fact, far from being a philosopher, he was a social critic, a polemicist who found in the pre-modern philosophical argument a rationale for his anti-ulama campaign and for his defense of the new sciences against the old. Nor was he aiming at preserving the intellectual tradition of the Muslim world. His few feeble statements regarding the compatibility of Islamic faith and reason were merely an unconvincing repetition of the view of the Shaikhis and other traditional theosophers. Despite his self-appointed mission as the reformer, he did not suggest any possible redefinition or reformulation of the relationship of Islam to the new sciences, besides the old, worn-out theosophers' argument that the Koran is all-encompassing, and what is needed is only a matter of proper understanding.

Thus the theosophers' issues, which the Shaikhis had socialized, were successfully secularized by Afghani. His critique of the orthodox theologians was just as vehement, if not more so, as Hajj Muhammad Karim Khan's. However, unlike the latter, he called for the adoption of Western sciences, and hence universalized the concept of *ilm*. In doing so, he definitely lay the ground for a final, unequivocal secularization of the entire field of knowledge. The Perfect Man, or the Perfect Shia, in Afghani's thought, is well versed in the modern sciences, and is not the theologian, whom he completely dismissed as incompetent and unqualified. Therefore, in the last analysis, there is no ambiguity in Afghani's ideas. Intellectually, he was thoroughly secular. I do not say he was irreligious, nor do I mean to say that he wished totally to eradicate religion from society. On the contrary, Afghani was too sensitive to human spiritual needs, and too aware that science, "however beautiful . . . does not completely satisfy humanity, which thirsts for the ideal and which likes to exist in dark and distant regions that the philosophers and the scholars can neither perceive nor explore."[18] But Afghani was primarily interested in secularizing the most important social institutions, including education, in order to promote knowledge and help raise a new generation of Muslims, who would be aware of the social and political demands of modern times. Hence, his social ideal was a Western type of secularism, where religion and personal faith became an individual matter. Nevertheless, Afghani argued his position in an inconsistent, self-contradicting, often illogical way, anxious as he was to safeguard his Muslim identity and not alarm unnecessarily the ulama, whose opinion he did not respect, yet whose support and cooperation he needed for his political plans. Consequently, out of political expediency and/or fear of *takfir* (being accused of heresy), he failed to part from the traditional mode of esoteric self-expression.

Malkum

Recent studies on Malkum Khan generally portray him as a typical nineteenth-century Iranian politician, ambitious and quick at seizing any opportunity to promote his own financial and political interests; cunning, vain, and egotistic, capable of reaching high positions thanks partly to his intelligence and partly to his ability to maneuver. He is also depicted as an irreligious charlatan whose conversion to Islam was purely expedient and who, determined to "clothe a material reformation in the garb of religion," concealed the "alien and European nature of this progress-worship behind assertions that the ideology of the League (Adamiyat) was derived from the teachings of the Prophet and mystics."[19]

Indeed, Malkum viewed himself as the *prince reformateur* who was going to rescue Iran from its rapid decline, and firmly believed he was the best qualified man to undertake such as task. "I have been to Europe; I have spent ten years of my life thinking about these problems,"[20] he would often state. Similarly, there is no doubt that Malkum, who, of all the group under the present study, had spent more time living in Europe and was thus much more influenced directly by Western thought, did manipulate religion, and religious sentiment, for a secular end. In his search for allies, he befriended, or at least approached, "heretics." An Azali source[21] confirms that while in Baghdad he had contacted the Babis, some of whom had seriously contemplated a joint political action as a good means to promote their cause, given his useful connections in Iran. Further, Malkum was expelled from Baghdad at about the same time as the Babis, upon the request of the Iranian authorities, who watched nervously the large community of expatriates living in the city. Later on, Malkum's correspondence and collaboration with Mirza Aqa Khan Kirmani and Shaikh Ahmad Ruhi, the two self-professed Azali Babis and sons-in-law of Subh-i Azal, certainly proved useful for the spread of his ideas among the sect. On the other hand, in his interviews with the Western press, he never failed to support the Babi cause,[22] and even compared the new religion to Christianity.[23] His close ties with some Babis, in addition to the obviously unorthodox notions implied in his ideas, inevitably led to his condemnation as a Babi by some of his opponents.[24]

In private, Malkum acknowledged, much more openly than any of his contemporary intellectuals, the incompatibility of religious beliefs and scientific knowledge, and admitted that human happiness and success would occur only when reason was "freed from its prison," since human reason is the sole judge and proof. In public, however, his approach was pragmatic. As he explained to Akhund-zada, whom he visited in Tiflis in March 1872, he regarded religion as consisting of three distinct parts: beliefs, rites, and morality, the latter being the basic root and the other two merely its branches. To success-fully implement morality, he argued, one is in need of some Supreme Being, conceived as powerful and merciful, to be worshipped as the Creator and who would act as the ultimate judge. Since religion reigns in Asia (unlike Europe, where science rules), the religious sentiment of the Christians, Jews, and Muslims living in Iran, Turkey and the Caucasus must be respected, for attacking their beliefs would only attract their wrath and mistrust, and one's own ends would not be reached.[25]

In the beginning of his career, Malkum attempted to diffuse his humanist ideal through the House of Oblivion *(Faramushkhana)* he had set up in Tehran, and which had quickly attracted the ulama's fierce hostility. Gobineau took it to be a mere imitation of French Freemasonry;[26] Algar saw it as a base for political action and agitation for reform, a clever, modern means to achieve worldly ends, though he admitted that the organization and its secretive methods of initiation were reminiscent of secret groupings and esotericism in Iran.[27] How-ever, in the last analysis, there was nothing modern or political in the nature of the lodge's activities, with the exception of the promotion of modern sciences. From 1858 when it was founded, till 1861 when it was closed down by order of the Shah, Malkum's ambition was to move up in the sociopolitical echelons of the Qajar court, and his reform projects dating from this period were far from aiming to destroy or even undermine the role and power of the ruling dynasty. To the extent that there were any political elements in his activities, they were directed at the orthodox ulama's social and intellectual influence. And here there is rather a continuity in the tradition of dissent in Shia thought.

In fact, it was the ulama who attacked the society and its founder for disseminating irreligious ideas, sheltering infidels, promoting harmony and peace between Muslims and non-Muslims, and, above all, instituting religious innovation contrary to the Islamic faith. In his defense, Malkum reverted to a rhetoric identical to that of the Shaikhis, the mystics, and the theosophers. He would vehemently deny all charges of heresy, swearing by God and all the Imams that the society only aimed at strengthening the position of Islam, at promoting the interests of the Muslims, and at championing government authority. He emphatically declared its secret method was in conformity with the practice of *taqiyya* honored by the Shia at all times. He defended its innovations as the hidden truths of Islam which could not have been divulged earlier, arguing that the Prophet and the Imams wished to wait till the right time, when humanity was ready to comprehend it, and that their silence over some truth was no proof of its nonexistence.[28] In an eloquent satire, Malkum's denunciation of the ulama closely follows the traditional stand of the Shia dissidents. Scornfully calling them ignoramuses, he held them responsible for widespread cultural and social decline. "Your pride and complacency cause you to stay ignorant of the state of other peoples and the progress they achieve. You have restricted the learning of mankind to a few books of the ancients which you imagine can never be surpassed. The falsity of this belief is apparent to all possessed of true insight. The wisdom of the Creator and sustainer has disposed our powers of intellect in such manner that progress is continuous and perpetual. It is the most signal instance of His creative power that He has inclined the intellect of man to unceasing progress, and this inclination alone secures our superiority over the animal realm. You wish nonetheless to make of the slight and insubstantial knowledge of the ancients, together with the whole mass of their absurdities, the ultimate limit of human progress! The worst of it is that you know nothing even of what they knew!"[29]

Malkum's faith in science led him to call urgently for its widespread teaching in Iran. The time for change had come, he loudly and repeatedly proclaimed. It was no longer the age of national isolation, when a country could "build a wall around itself, or tell outsiders: this is my property, and I do not want to follow the progress of this age," for "world progress concerns all mankind."[30] The present age, he asserted, is the age of fast traveling, of science and technology, and no longer of Arabic expressions and Arabic poetry. However, despite his boundless admiration for science, Malkum, in fact, was more prophetically minded than scientific. His new religion, Adamiyat, which he developed during the revolutionary phase of his life and thought, though obviously influenced by Auguste Comte's *religion de l'Humanité,* reflected more the messianic tendencies inherent in Shia traditional thought than it did Comte's scientism. It was directed toward the establishment of the reign of the just who would overthrow the oppressor. It called for open revolt. "Where am I? In the prison of oppression. What must be done? The walls of this prison must be destroyed. With what power? With the power of Humanity."[31] However, his humanism was by far more anthropocentric than any traditional theosopher's. For the new "faith," which attempted to combine

Judeo-Christian and Muslim teachings, would proclaim the right of people to worship freely whatever suited them best, as long as it followed the "law of the world order," and as long as they were guided by reason. It hailed humans as the most perfect of all beings, capable of progress and self-improvement, and it set forth his ultimate goals in life: to avoid evil and accomplish good; to abolish oppression and maintain a harmonious relationship with his fellow humans; and to seek knowledge and promote the cause of humanity. "Humanity means serving the world," he wrote. "Man means he who seeks true life. Man means savior of the world."[32]

Malkum dedicated his newspaper *Qanun* to the "cause," and used it as a means to propagate his "call."

Akhundzada

Akhundzada's self-appointed mission was, along with his contemporary intellectuals, to "awaken" the Muslim nations from what they generally viewed as a centuries-long social and intellectual torpor, and to guide them to what they believed to be the path of civilization and progress. However, Fathali Akhundzada chose to abandon the cautious ways and means that characterized the action and style of the others, and adopt instead a brutally frank language to express his criticism. Hence, he categorically refused to abide by the centuries-old rules of esoteric writing, and upheld his right to a free, assertive, unambiguous self-expression. "If I write in a mild and veiled way," he wrote in answer to a publisher in Bombay who counseled him to adopt a more cautious style, "then my writings will be similar to . . . all our past *urafa's* [mystics] works. Have those works borne any fruit?" he asked. Nay, in their philosophical exposés the mystics behaved like cowards, keeping ordinary people in utter darkness as to the true nature of their thought, which they concealed through a bewildering style. Philosophically, Akhundzada insisted, they were as "materialist" as Voltaire and other European philosophers were centuries later.[33] In an interesting though highly speculative study of Jamal al-Din Rumi, he went so far as to claim that the thirteenth-century poet, despite an outward belief in the Sufi concept of unity of Being, had faith in neither Heaven nor Hell; neither Prophecy nor Imamate, for he viewed the "unity of Being" as an eternal matter. Truly materialist statements, Akhundzada explained, were inserted here and there in the narration, confusing the ordinary reader yet enlighten-ing the adept.[34] Vehemently denouncing the esoteric mode of self-expression, he vowed to bring to light the "true" thought of Iranian thinkers, "to liberate the mind of our philosophers and sages which was kept captive for 1287 years," to "rescue" human beings from blindness, and thus become the cause of happiness and good fortune in Asia. Thus he announced he would expose his ideas to the common people with utmost honesty, without fear and "without hiding behind veils," in the manner of the European thinkers.[35]

Far from fearing *takfir*, or even his readers' shocked reactions, Akhundzada was deliberately provocative in all his political essays. Fear and shock, he wrote to a young Iranian correspondent, are the best means to awaken, reform, and preach. Paternalistic counsels, sermons, and even the threat of hell or promise of heaven are not effective ways to implement ideas. "The time of Sadi," he said, refer-ring to a thirteenth-century poet, "has passed. This age is a different age...human beings have outgrown the childhood phase and now are reaching manhood."[36] He loudly proclaimed, "I perceived that the Islamic faith and fanaticism represented an obstacle to the diffusion of civilization among the Muslim peoples. I therefore set myself the task of sundering the foundations of the faith, of extirpating fanaticism and dissipating the dark ignorance of the peoples of the East."[37]

In "Sa Maktub," an interesting though highly controversial es-say, he questioned the very existence of God, and argued there can be only two possible explanations for the existence of the world:

1. The world exists on its own, regulated by its own rules and in no need of a Creator. If this is so, the author surmises, one can assume, together with Petrarch and Voltaire, that all beings constitute one complete Force, that is, one complete Existence, which manifests itself in various shapes and forms, deterministically governed by fundamen-tal laws. These laws control all life, be it animal, vegetable, or human. In the latter case, the man fertilizes the woman; for nine months the child leads a vegetatitng life; then it is born, leads an animal life, grows old, dies, and is transferred to the world of matter. This one and complete Existence has no beginning and no end. Nothing has pre-ceded it and nothing will follow it. It is both its own creator and its own creature. it is composed of numerous atoms, the interrelation of which is regulated by universal laws.

2. The world might owe its existence to a total, complete Being, with all existing things part of that whole. Hence this Being is the source of everything, the place where everything starts and where

everything ends. In fact, the whole and the parts are but One Being, which manifests itself in various shapes and forms following its own rules and regulations. In that case, then, the existence of the parts is still determined by the same set of rules and regulations as in the first assumption. In both cases, neither the whole nor the parts have any choice. There can be no difference between the part and the whole. It is like a human body with its different members: one cannot exist without the other. How, then, can a part worship a whole?

Having thus attacked the orthodox religious conception of God, the author similarly condemned the religious notion of divine justice as conceived in the common belief in heaven and hell. Let us suppose, he argued, that the Creator has created me, allowing me one hundred years to live. No matter how much power, and no matter how much wealth I possess, I would still not be free from experiencing all sorts of pains and sufferings. If, however, I spend those hundred years in sin, committing all kinds of crime, the Just Creator will, of course, punish me. I accept the fact that, for those hundred years, He may have me burned for one hundred, two hundred, six hundred, nine hundred or even a thousand years. Does the Creator have the right, in the name of justice, to have me burn for longer than that? Can the worldly pleasure of a hundred years be equivalent to the sufferings of one day in hell? Akhundzada strongly challenged this notion of divine justice. "We have to believe that the Creator is merciful and forgiving. Yet, a Creator who owns such a hell, a Creator who is such a revenger, is the cruelest of all beings. If He had to treat me this way, why did He create me at all? When did I ask life from Him?"[38] And he concluded that if such a hell exists, then God must be an unloving, hateful, cruel being. If, on the other hand, there is no hell, then why, he wondered, do the ulama deprive the people of the pleasures of this world; why do they frighten them, and thus prevent them from improving their way of life, and from following the path of progress together with other nations? For, after all, humans have to indulge, within reasonable limits, in the pleasures of this world, such as dance, music, theater—all forbidden by Muslim laws. And people should set their own limits, since each human being is born with a natural ability to differentiate good and evil. Moreover, fear of hell and hope for heaven cannot prevent crime. Akhundzada also denied the existence of the soul, and therefore rejected the concept of an after-life.

The author's denunciation of religious beliefs did not end here. He pursued the subject further by expressing his disbelief in the divine nature of the prophetic revelation, which he preferred to interpret in socio-anthropological terms. He stated that religions and prophets have appeared in the world in times of ignorance, when Nature was feared. Now, the modern world offers science and knowledge to answer questions and to calm people's fear. Since science can explain everything, there is no need for a prophet. What have the Arabs gained from Islam? he asked. "Nowadays, there is no people that is more ill-famed or more wretched than the Arabs. Why hasn't Islam been a cause of happiness to them? Barefoot and hungry, they are now isolated, deprived of science and art. Most probably it is the tales of their Muslim creed that have kept the wretched ones apart from the civilized nations." This does not mean, Akhundzada hastened to admit, that other religions are better than Islam. On the contrary, Islam is the most acceptable of them all. But he openly declared, "I consider all religions to be meaningless and mythical."[39]

That Akhundzada was a professed atheist, there is no shade of doubt. All his works and his private correspondence attest to it. However, despite his frank confession of unbelief, despite his "radical antagonism to Islam,"[40] as Algar put it, it was not the faith itself he wished to uproot from Iran as much as the way it was taught, interpreted, and practiced. He wished to reform and not to abolish. And here his attack on the orthodox religious leadership echoes the theosophers. Like them, he condemned *taqlid* (following the rulings of a mujtahid) and *ijtihad* (the legal function of a mujtahid) as the two main sources of ignorance prevailing in the country. A *muqallid* (one who practices *taqlid*), he wrote elsewhere, "is a person who, upon the order of his mulla, gulps a morsel of food without chewing it, whether it tastes delicious or like poison."[41] Similarly, when a new Minister of Education was appointed in Iran, he warned him: "*Taqlid* has ruined us. It is high time we shake off its yoke and escape from darkness and ignorance, so we enter the land of light and knowledge."[42] He stressed the necessity to free the believer "from the imposed servitudes of the so-called religious obligations," such as pilgrimage to Mecca, which he felt was of no national interest, and the performance of *taziyya* (religious play reenacting the martyrdom of the Imam Husain at the battle of Kerbala), which he dismissed as a fruitless legacy of the past and a symbol of cultural backwardness.[43] He admired England and France for their effective secularization of society, and their success in curbing the social and political influence of the clergy. He referred to the Protestant movement in Europe as a perfect example of a rational interpretation of religion and the elimination of superfluous and superstitious beliefs. He emphatically asserted that Islam could survive only if it was rationally understood in a similar fashion, and when its laws concerning peoples' rights were reformed and adapted to the needs of the nation.[44]

Talibzada

Talibzada, the Muslim believer whose discreet piety, in contrast to Afghani's showy devotion, marked his private life so profoundly, was no less concerned with the prevailing state of religion. But while he was fully aware of the clash between the ideal and the harsh reality, he firmly refused to dwell on such theological and metaphysical issues. The law of creation and the mysteries of life cannot be rationally understood he argued, since human reason is deficient and hence human knowledge must perforce remain limited. All that humans need to understand is the meaning of good and evil, knowledge and ignorance, the useful and the harmful.[45] Nonetheless, his approach to religion was as pragmatic and rationalistic as that of other intellectuals of his time. "True religion is one that is rationally accepted and scientifically proven right,"[46] he would often write. Revealed books, he would point out, aim at helping our existence in this world, and guide people to the right path. The right path, according to Talibzada, the devout Muslim, must run parallel to human development; since everything created undergoes change with time, laws must change accordingly, the old ones being cancelled and new ones enacted. "It is obvious," he wrote, echoing the Shaikhis, "that the laws of each age, promulgated in order to facilitate man's life, must fit the times. What was needed in the Abbasid period no longer fits this present age of progress. We must leave them aside ... and establish new ones that are needed for today."[47] Like his fellow reformers and the theosophers before them, Talibzada refused to recognize the basic contradiction inherent in his demand for the abrogation of the old laws and his adherence to Islamic law. Vehemently denying any possible charge of heresy, he emphatically explained, "We do not touch our Muslim law nor do we add anything to it." God and the Koran are eternal, but all the rest is changeable. "It is time for us ... to learn to distinguish reform from innovation, and to believe that all religious laws are there to guide ... and not to spread ignorance or to obstruct" the path to progress.[48]

Again like the traditional dissidents and his own contemporaries, Talibzada accused the high-ranking clerics, whom he derogatorily referred to as "God's attorneys," of worldliness and hypocrisy, and of using their alleged "closeness to God" to justify their own self-importance. Deploring the "self-evident truth" that science and technology, and human progress in general, were to be found in Europe but not in the Muslim countries, he held the ulama responsible for the Iranian nation's ruin and corruption. He categorically dismissed them as unqualified to rescue the nation from its moral, scientific, economic, and political backwardness, since their teachings, he claimed, ran counter to true worship of God, self-knowledge, and the acquisition of science.

Kirmani

Mirza Aqa Khan wrote abundantly but without system. The voluminous, disorderly corpus of his works, which included newspaper articles, poems, historical and philosophical treatises, political pamphlets, and theological essays, are a trial to anyone who attempts to discover in them a logical sequence of ideas. He claimed to be a Muslim, a Babi, and an agnostic philosopher all at the same time. As a result, his works constitute a hopeless amalgam of the most disparate philosophical and social ideas.

As a Babi, Mirza Aqa Khan attested his belief in a Supreme Being, creator of all things, who manifests his will to humanity through successive revelations, the Bab's being the most recent and hence most perfect. He upheld the doctrine of the eternity of the world, which makes existence absolutely dependent on God, the Necessary Being. As a materialist philosopher, he believed matter to be the essence of existence, the material world being governed by natural laws, and he claimed that all earthly events are products of the world of matter, and thus there is no need to suppose another cause for the changes and transformations occurring on this planet. However, anxious as he was to reassure his readers of the "respectability" of his thought, or to avoid at all costs the threat of *takfir*, he would often lapse into an "orthodox" tone, and profess his belief in Islam, in Muhammad as the Seal of the Prophets, and in the Koran as the Book of God. "I myself am Muslim," he would write, "and am in no need of proofs to have faith in Islam."[49] While citing Voltaire at great length, he would remark: "It is true that Voltaire was irreligious and was an enemy of all prophets. Even now I still tremble in fear of admitting his ideas, for my sense of religiosity is appalled."[50]

Despite the inconsistencies and paradoxes inherent in his thought, Kirmani's main goal, like that of his fellow intellectuals, was to uphold reason and modern science, both of which he conceived as incompatible with religious truth. In fact, throughout his numerous writings he remained consistent only in a kind of worshipful confidence in these two. At times he was willing to accept the traditional Muslim philosophical view of "truth" as ultimately but one, expressed in rational abstract terms to the "elite," and in imaginative, religious form to the masses. At other times, he boldly refuted all divine revelations. Obviously influenced by contemporary Western sociological studies, he interpreted the origins of primitive religions (hence all religions) in terms of human ignorance and fear of the natural environment. Humans came to attribute supernatural power to objects and individuals, and thus gradually the notion of a supernatural being evolved from animism and idolatry to prophecy and monotheism. Prophets appeared in all nations, bringing messages suitable to the time and conditions of their followers. Although these religions, he asserted, were apparently different one from the other, basically they were all one and the same: their aim was to create a deity and a faith. Reason was not involved in the process.[51]

Similarly, his own conception of religious law as something which undergoes endless evolutionary changes in order to meet the demands of a constantly changing world reflects the Ismaili, Shaikhi, and Babi views. And although his argument that religion functions as a medical treatment for social maladies ("whether the doctor is called Docteur Muhammad, or Monsieur Issa or Mirza Musa, the purpose of the prescription is to cure"[52]) recalls Muhammad Karim Khan's own words, Kirmani departed further from orthodoxy than his predecessors ever did. For he dramatically stripped religion of its universal spiritual claims, and reduced its function to a mere social service, to be discarded as soon as the nation reached a "civilized stage," since, he emphatically remarked, Europe has once and for all shown that "the existence of philosophers and learned men has rendered the existence of prophets unnecessary. They say that science is more honorable than faith, and that it is better to understand than to believe."[53]

Moreover, whereas prior theosophers spoke of changing conditions in time, Kirmani emphasized changing conditions in space, in terms of national differences. "A religion is declared solid and best," he wrote, "when it is based on, and is compatible with, the nation's nature and particular living conditions; and when it is the cause of that nation's progress, culturally as well as morally."[54] However, he warned, if religion is the cause of the nation's ruin and misfortune, then it is to be considered false and useless. Again and again he would stress the need to test the efficiency of a given religion in curing national ills, and would state that each nation must have its own prophet whose message would best fit the peoples' needs of the time.[55]

Kirmani shared the distaste felt by Akhundzada, Afghani, and Malkum for traditional learning as it was taught in the local schools. He expressed his utter disillusionment with the "daily meal" served to the young by their instructors. "Any wretched fellow who had drunk this soup," he exclaimed, "remained hungry, poor and distressed."[56] He assailed the traditional curriculum, asserting that the study of Arabic grammar and vocabulary corrupted the Persian language; that the study of the Traditions reinforced the prevailing intellectual stagnation; and the study of theosophy and Koranic commentary raised fruitless questions concerning trivial matters. "What do I gain, I an Iranian, from knowing about early Arab Muslim rulers such as Khalid ibn Walid or Yazid ibn Muawiya? What do I gain from reading all about Ali and his sons or the love and hate of Abbas?"[57] Echoing Akhundzada's vehement attack on Islamic, and especially Shia, practices, he dismissed the pilgrimage to Mecca as a superstitious habit to worship "a few rotten bones in dusty graves," and he deplored its high cost. "And what for? . . . to go several times around a black stone like crazy people, in the heat of the sun, to kill a thousand poor beasts, and then to come back to their country having lost all of their possessions, hungry and barefoot, having gained the title of *hajji* ("pilgrim"). . . . I swear by the God of Mecca that, apart from a house, a mosque, a black stone, a burning soil, bitter water, and a handful of lizard-eating, merciless and rude Arabs, they have seen and understood nothing."[58] In the same vein, Kirmani condemned the annual commemoration during Muharram of the death of Husain at Kerbala, arguing that the believers' energy was misplaced and misused, their moans misdirected, and their attention distracted from the gruesome reality of their world. Hence, he commented, "If those thousands of screams and moans they utter for the Imams were uttered instead for their own miserable conditions, all the injustice and backwardness of their country would be removed."[59]

Not content with a mere denunciation of Shia practices, Kirmani undertook to blame the Arabs and Islam for the general decline of the Iranians. Before Islam, he wrote, the Arabs were a handful of ignorant, savage, lizard-eating, bloodthirsty, barefoot, camel riding, desert-dwelling nomads who lived through theft, raid, and plunder.

Muhammad revealed the Koran to them in order to enlighten their minds, refine their mores, organize their political community, and provide them with a sound code of laws—in short, to civilize them. Hence, he argued, the Islamic rules befit only a "barbarian nation." However, contending that the Koranic laws, written down by an Arab primarily for Arabs, did not and could not meet the needs of the Iranians, who already had a highly sophisticated civilization and an elaborate political system of their own,[60] Kirmani wholeheartedly rejected Islam as an alien religion, which he held responsible for all the cultural ills of Iran. Not only did the Iranians suffer from the Arab conquest of their land, he lamented, not only were they forced to adopt the "creed of Arabism," not only did they witness the burning of the ancient books and find themselves compelled to study, in a foreign language, a "mixed-up Koran that has no beginning and no end," but also they remained culturally backward, for all Iranian studies proper had been entirely neglected ever since.

Besides the Arabs and Islam, Mirza Aqa Khan denounced the ulama for the "destructive" role they played in society. "This faith, which the Iranians were forced to accept at the point of the Arab sword, today is still apparently accepted out of fear of the ulama's *takfir*. Formerly fearing the sword, today [they] fear the pen."[61] Again echoing prior theosophers and his contemporaries (though adopting a more excessively violent tone), he dismissed the religious leaders as selfish, ignorant men who corrupted, misunderstood and misinterpreted the religious precepts, mainly in order to promote their own interests. "While European learned men are busy studying mathematics, sciences, politics and economics, the rights of man, in this age of socialism and of struggle for the improvement of the conditions of the poor, the Iranian ulama are discussing problems of cleanliness and the ascension of the Prophet to heaven."[62] And he loudly sounded the alarm: "What is left of Islam is only a name, hollow and dried up. With utter sorrow I warn the ulama that in a few years even the name of Muslims will be taken away from us, and we will then perish as a community."[63]

Kirmani found in Babism the religious rationale for his rejection of the autocratic fanaticism of which he accused the ulama, while he hoped it would furnish the means to help bring about an Iranian cultural renaissance. Thus, in some essays he hailed the Bab as the redeemer who would liberate Iran from the Islamic faith he despised so passionately. Yet, a careful study of *Hasht Bihisht*,[64] the commentary of the *Bayan* which he wrote together with his close companion, Ahmad

Ruhi, clearly reveals the authors' social and national interests in the controversial creed. Their frankly nonreligious interpretation (which, when compared with the original *Bayan,* might appear on the verge of heresy) displaced the central emphasis from religion to the moral and political aspects of life in society. Moreover, in his non-Babi essays, while he persistently condemned the massacre and general persecution of the Babis and fiercely defended their cause to his Muslim readers, he simultaneously assailed the Babis with the same intensely felt scorn with which he rejected religion in general. Similarly, in his *Qahvakhana-yi surat,* where he sketched an idealized portrait of his former Babi master, Sayyid Javad, to whome he attributed the similarly idealized features of a European Renaissance humanist, and whom he offered to his readers as a perfect model to follow, Kirmani's hymn to reason and science comes through loud and clear.

"Truth means service to mankind; means order; means enlightening the minds; means establishing equal rights among all members of the human race; means protecting the children of our race; means tall buildings, industrial inventions, factories, expansion of the means of communication, promotion of knowledge, general welfare, implementing of just laws.... Religion is concerned with concrete issues, not with abstractions. It is not enough to utter a few words attesting the oneness of God. One has to establish unity of human beings, either through scientific knowledge or through love. What is the use of crying over Imam Husain, if one is cooperating with the oppressors and wishes the worst for the oppressed? One has to destroy the oppressor and become the champion of the oppressed. What is the use of cursing Yazid the dead? One has to help the living not the dead.... Reason and scientific proofs are the sources of my words and the basis of my deeds. Man's reason is the first prophet sent to him by God ... I believe in Islam, in the holy Koran. But which Islam? That true Islam that brings peace and security to all.... That Islam that is the attestation and the proof of all religions, that is the sum total of all holy laws, the origin of all sects. ... That Islam that sanctifies science, and does not see in ignorance a necessary religious duty."[65]

Thus to Kirmani rationalism, religious tolerance, and intellectual broadmindedness are the ultimate rules that lead to the straight path. The religions that have been revealed by different prophets, when correctly interpreted according to the needs of the time, place and people, stand as mere variations on the same theme in order to meet the demands of a constantly changing world.

REFORMS

The divergences of religious opinion which differentiate Afghani, Akhundzada, Malkum Khan, Kirmani, and Talibzada from one another are not found in their respective conceptions of reform. Their critique of traditional learning was not concerned with any allegedly false assumptions so much as it was with the lack of commitment to solving the social and political problems of the modern Muslim. They rejected the traditional religious conception of knowledge not because they denied its essential truth, but because they rejected its exclusiveness over all other fields of inquiry. More importantly, they hailed humans as rational, responsible beings capable of shaping their own destinies and qualified to enact laws that would either supersede or complement divine directives. In their search for models to follow, all five intellectuals under study turned to Europe and the European sciences.

Thus, Malkum dramatically sounded the alarm by predicting that, if reforms were not immediately undertaken to modernize the country, Iran would perish. He warned against the Western powers' invasion of the "barbaric nations": "This overpowering flood [the West] is pushing its way across the entire globe, beginning with the most rotten soil. Algeria, Egypt, Morocco, China, Japan, Kabul . . . India . . . were all flooded. See how ignorant we are to want to stop this world-conquering flood with our bare hands. . . . With such a low budget, with such Ministers, with such a government, and with such a poor science, we wish to confront the might of Europe. . . . By God, it is impossible! By God, it cannot be! We either have to lift ourselves from this base level up to that of Europe within the next two or three years, or from now on we should consider ourselves as already drowned and buried under the European flood."[66] Aware of the difficult and, in fact, dangerous position his call for modernization would put him in, he cautiously assured the ulama and Iranian officials that imitating the West would by no means run counter to Islamic law. Politics and religion, he argued, are two separate realms, and borrowing a political system would in no way affect the religious life of Iran. He firmly believed that the Western system of government could be imported as easily as the telegraph was, and political progress would be achieved "without committing any injustice, without opposing the Muslim law, without problems and without losses."[67]

Both Kirmani and Akhundzada shared Malkum's blind faith in Europe's political superiority over the Muslims in general and Iranians in particular. "Muslim Sultans have brought to Iran nothing but ruin, nothing but promotion of their own self-interests,"[68] wrote Akhund-zada, and he was echoed by Kirmani, who never failed to refer to Europe as the guide to prosperity, progress, and happiness, as the authority to consult, and as the ultimate proof for all his arguments. "O ignorant fathers of today!" he passionately pleaded. "You who are not willing to let your children learn the language of the Europeans and study their sciences because it is heretical, soon this ignorance of yours will reduce them to servitude, and you shall see this abjectness with your own eyes."[69] Talibzada, the most pious practicing Muslim of the whole group, equally vested his hope for a more efficient, better organized, and more just government in the Western parliamentarian system and Western concepts, including liberty, equality, freedom of opinion and of worship, free elections and a free press — all to be guaranteed by a Western-type constitution to be enacted by elected representatives. "The days of fanaticism and ignorance are over,"[70] he loudly proclaimed.

It is interesting to note here that, despite their constitutional ideal, when it came to discussing concrete programs of reform and the means to establish them, the intellectuals suggested Peter the Great of Russia and Frederick the Great of Prussia as the best models of en-lightened monarchs dedicated to national reconstruction. In one of his essays, Akhundzada appealed to the Shah to cooperate with the re-formers in their struggle against the ulama's power, to liberalize his rule, and to promote secular education. "History has proven" he stated, "that as long as ignorance and superstition reign supreme, no despotic rule can last long. For the credulity of the people makes it very easy for any religious imposter to appeal to the masses, assume power and depose the despot. . . . Hence the survival of a dynasty depends on education and on national liberation from erroneous beliefs."[71] It is of great national interest, he wrote elsewhere, that a harmonious rela-tionship be established between the people and their monarch, a relationship based on mutual trust and cooperation. To this end, the government must free itself "both outwardly and inwardly" from the ulama, and severely reduce the latter's role in its administration. In fact, he bluntly added, the monarch must become the sole *marja-i taqlid* himself (the model to be followed by the faithful). However, he cautioned, the monarch must carefully use the correct means and employ the right officials to carry on important tasks, and thereby gain the people's trust.[72]

As Nasir al-Din Shah appointed new ministers who were in favor of reforms, such as Mirza Husain Khan Mushir al-Daula, who in turn chose Mirza Yusif Khan Mustashar al-Daula as his deputy, Akhundza-da's counsels seemed to bear fruit. Yusif Khan, a native of Tabriz, had begun his official career as a clerk in the British consulate there before joining the Iranian Ministry of Foreign Affairs. For eight years, he held a position in a small town in Azerbaijan until, in 1860, he was called to Tehran and then sent to St. Petersburg as temporary chargé d'affaires, before finally being nominated consul general at the Iranian legation in Tiflis. He met Akhundzada there, with whom he established close ties and with whom he extensively corresponded from the various posts he subsequently held in Europe and Iran. Similarly, while in Tiflis, Yusif Khan established contacts with Malkum Khan and Mirza Husain Khan, who was then the ambassador in Istanbul, sharing in common with both officials an admiration for the Ottoman Tanzimat (reforms) and a strong wish to accomplish parallel projects in Iran. The exchange of ideas among the three and their mutual support for each other's projects intensified through the late 1860s. Mirza Yusif Khan's most famous work, *Yak Kalama*, written in Paris in 1870, undeniably bears the mark of Malkum's thought, just as his own work influenced Mal-kum. Both used the expedient of identifying *mashrutiyyat* ("con-stitutionalism") with *mashruiyyat* ("holy law") in order to sell their ideas to the authorities and assure the ulama of their respectability.

However, while Malkum and Afghani carefully adopted a reli-gious rhetoric to promote secular ends, Akhundzada, Kirmani, and Talibzada more decidedly abandoned all caution and called for the outright secularization of the educational and judicial systems. In his *Kitab-i Ahmad*, Talibzada, severely criticizing the traditional system of education and denouncing the dominant social and intellectual influ-ence of the ulama, hailed freedom of thought as "the first cause of progress and knowledge."[73] In all his works, he expressed his firm belief in a Western-type, secular code of laws which could effectively complement and/or supplement the Islamic law, seeing it as the only way out of "backwardness," since it would put an end to religious intolerance, guarantee freedom of opinion and of worship, and thus lay the foundation of a free society. Gone would be the age of sectarian rivalry and religious imposters. In fact, Talibzada, as well as Kirmani in his non-Babi essays and Akhundzada, blamed the rise and rapid spread of religious movements such as Babism on the predominance of religion in Iran, where people easily fell prey to "lunatics" masquerad-ing as prophets. "Who is responsible?" Talibzada asked, "the corrupt ulama."[74] His fellow intellectuals shared his belief that a secularized society could effectively block the spread of the imposters' influence.

Akhundzada explicitly took Europe as the best example of a society that had successfully curbed clerical power and therefore had eliminated the source of superstition. "Nowadays in Europe," he wrote, "if someone came up with supernatural claims, he would be immediately detected as crazy or as a charlatan, and would be duly taken care of so he would not harm the nation."[75]

Akhundzada was in favor of setting up a ministry of justice which would assume all judicial functions traditionally held by the ulama, leaving to the latter jurisdiction over purely religious concerns such as prayer, fasting, sermons, marriage and divorce, and burial rites. He did not rule out the possibility of hiring "responsible and qualified" ulama as judges and legal counsels, provided they were no longer involved with religious affairs proper. To ensure the successful implementation of the reforms, Akhundzada asserted, illiteracy must be eliminated and education spread.[76]

Akhundzada was aware of the futility of the court reforms. In a sarcastic letter addressed to Yusif Khan who was then involved, together with Mushir al-Daula and Malkum, in granting a concession to a British firm headed by Baron de Reuter for the right, among others, to construct railways in Iran, he fully expressed his skepticism: "Tanzimat and reforms are all fine, but they are without foundation. They are ephemeral. Sciences must first be taught to all Iranians of all classes, all walks of life, without exception, so that all people can participate in all affairs of government. For the moment, have fun with some toys, there is no harm in it. Sure, railways will help develop the country. ... But the complete happiness of people has other conditions."[77] It was this fundamental concern with educational reforms that made Akhundzada give priority to education and devote less attention to political matters. He repeatedly warned that one must first train people to accept European ideas and technology, that European books must be translated.

The fall of Mirza Husain Khan's cabinet (which included Yusif Khan) in 1872, as a result of the conservative ulama's opposition to the Reuter concession, convinced Akhundzada of the futility of accommodation. In a brutally frank letter addressed to his fallen friend, Akhundzada endeavored to dismiss the idea of identifying *mashruiyyat* (Islamic law) with *mashrutiyyat* (constitutionalism), and totally dismissed Islamic law as incompatible with the spirit of justice. How can a law be just, he asked, if it allows the veiling and seclusion of women, and treats non-Muslims as inferior beings? Contending that it was not yet possible to plant the roots of French constitutionalism in the present Muslim world, he reiterated his conviction that "one has to educate the nation until it is ready on its own to establish true justice and a constitution."[78]

Twenty years after Akhundzada's death, observing the failure of the few feeble attempts at reform made during the long reign of Nasir al-Din Shah (d. 1896), Talibzada realized that no reforms could effectively be undertaken prior to a change in the political system itself. Thus, he wrote repeatedly and extensively about the Western type of government by law, which consisted of a parliament with two houses and a cabinet of ministers directly responsible to parliament, and which he wished to see established in Iran. In his *Masail* and especially in *Masalik*, published respectively shortly before and after the outbreak of the Constitutional Revolution of 1905–06, he discussed the merits of constitutionalism, of the right of the majority of the people to legislate through their representatives, and of the duty of the elected officials to ensure the implementation of reforms. He suggested Japan as a model for all Asian nations to follow, since, he argued, its victory over Russia in the 1905 war had demonstrated how a "backward nation" could defeat a major power once it reformed its institutions. He was almost extravagant in hailing Japan, "the country of science and freedom," and its recently established constitutional government, which he contrasted to Russia, the land of "ignorance, oppression and absolute monarchy."[79]

Whereas the theosophers, the Shaikhis, and the Babis had struggled to adapt their individual and metaphysical perceptions to a standardized and basically inflexible system of rituals and beliefs, the secularists attempted to voice their concern to see religion adapt itself to new social and cultural conditions. They called for change, which they accurately perceived as a moral necessity arising from the dire needs of their own society, and not from a mere desire to emulate the West. They perpetuated the argument of the traditional philosophers that religion is a social necessity, since popular morality was still tied to religious beliefs. Far from wishing to destroy Islam, they wished to use it as a vehicle for change as Muslim thinkers had attempted previously, though less successfully.

However, in the case of the theosophers, the whole process of selective adoption and adaptation of elements of the Islamic faith was privately undertaken by individuals, who jealously safeguarded their esoteric knowledge within a small circle of adepts, and who ensured the smooth and discreet transmission of ideas through successive generations of followers. Change was barely perceived by the society at large or, more importantly, by the ruling establishment. In contrast, the case of the secularists, especially Malkum, who was the most westernized, was potentially more explosive. The ideas they introduced not only originated in societies regarded as infidel for being non-Muslim, but they also constituted a vital threat to the social system which the orthodox ulama had dominated for so long. For the mood for change had already crossed the intellectual boundaries and had begun to assume a political dimension. The secularists' controversial ideas were no mere intellectual disputes, but made up a forceful and vehement social movement clamorously demanding change and demanding a curtailment of the ulama's influence and control over those institutions they wished to reform.

NATIONALIST THOUGHT

With the exception of Afghani, who chose a more traditional path in seeking solutions to the problems resulting from Western encroachment in the Muslim world, and who attempted to restate the old concept of the Islamic community as a sociopolitical entity, this group of Iranian intellectuals spoke more of Iran, the nation, than of Islam. Their message was secular and nationalist, in spite of their concern to see religious reform. Religion was actually identified with a nationalist movement of change and revolution. Whereas Malkum used Islam as a vehicle for introducing European-inspired reforms, and Talibzada frankly called for a separation of religion from secular affairs, Kirmani focused on what in the Babi teachings could be presumed to have some general validity beyond the spiritual values of the religious movement. Through his own interpretation, he believed that Babism could be absorbed into the mainstream of newly founded Iranian nationalist thought. By promoting the adoption of Persian as a holy language to replace Arabic, of Shiraz (the birthplace of the Bab) as the new Mecca, and Nauruz (the ancient festive day celebrating the spring equinox) as the first day of a revised calendar, he expressed his wish to see Iran reassume its past cultural supremacy. Moreover, it was because of his vision of a revolutionary Iran developing along purely nationalist lines that he championed the Azali sect, which, following the death of the Bab, kept up the spirit of revolt against the established socioreligious and political order, in contrast to the Bahais, who adopted a pacifist and universalist religious tone. It was his quest for national heroic action that, to a large extent, drew him to Babism in the first place, and led him to proclaim proudly that the Babis' noble feelings constituted a force "surpassing the power of ten thousand English naval cannons," and that "the tales of Farhad and Shirin [ancient Iranian legendary lovers] are but a small part of the tale of our exciting love."[80] Finally it was his worldliness and secularism that motivated him in his non-Babi works, where he openly attacked all religions and prophets, to condemn the Bab as well and to attribute to Babism the same defects he found objectionable in Islam.

Though Afghani, Talibzada, and even Malkum upheld the Islamic cultural identity of Iran, Akhundzada and Kirmani sought to restore the pre-Islamic cultural legacy and attribute to it due credit for past grandeur, while condemning Islam as the cause for national decadence. They wished to discover ancient Iranian history which, as they honestly admitted, they hardly knew. Influenced by Jalal al-Din Mirza, a freethinking Qajar prince with whom he regularly corresponded, and who introduced him to a Zoroastrian native of Bombay by the name of Manikji who was living in Tehran, Akhundzada confessed to both his desire to write about the subject in order to reveal the "calamities and ruin our fatherland has suffered in the hands" of the Muslim Arabs. "My hope," he wrote to Manikji, "is to have Iranians realize that we are the children of Parsees and our fatherland is Iran. We should side with those who share our race, our language, our fatherland, and not with bloodthirsty aliens."[81]

Akhundzada, and Kirmani, in whom he found an enthusiastic follower, painted a glittering picture of ancient Iran, honored by great Achaemenid and Sassanian monarchs, adorned by great artists and poets, finally "raped" by "savage Bedouins." Kirmani nurtured a passionate hatred for the Arabs: "I spit on the Arabs! Shame on those cowards who have attacked such a great state ... Iran," he would write.[82] Such violent anti-Arab sentiments incited him to dismiss not only Islam but also Iran's Islamic culture as unworthy of its ancient Zoroastrian glory. Both men showered scorn upon all the famous Iranian literary figures excepting Firdausi, since the *Shahnama* celebrates the glorious deeds of legendary ancient Iranian kings and heroes. "The result of their metaphysics and mysticism," Kirmani contemptuously proclaimed, "has been nothing but a crop of brutish idleness and sloth, and the production of religious mendicants and beggars; the result of their odes to roses and nightingales has been nothing but a corruption of our young men's morals and the impelling of them toward smooth cheeks and red wine."[83] Akhundzada and Kirmani's grand portrayal of the past, however, bears the marks of modern Western concepts. In the Western racist theories of the time, they found a rationale for the contempt they felt for the Arabs, and a positive argument for the glorification of Iran, "the noble Aryan nation," of the "good Aryan people of good extraction." What Kirmani praised Mazdak* for—"Mazdak the pure... the learned... Mazdak the powerful philosopher, the founder of just law and right creed, who, two thousand [sic] years ago lay the foundation of republicanism and *égalité*"[84] (in transliterated French in the text) — were, in fact, the eighteenth and nineteenth-century European ideas of human rights, freedom of speech, and republican socialism. Similarly, despite their cult of the pre-Islamic past, neither Akhundzada nor Kirmani really wished to see it resurrected. In fact, in a letter to Manikji, whom he hailed as the "reminder of our ancestors... from whom we have been separated," Akhundzada promised the Zoroastrian community, "who have suffered eclipse for 1280 years," better social conditions and eventual full recognition as equal members of the Iranian society, yet specifically maintained that neither the old religion nor the old laws would be restored. "Islam will prevail, though not in the same way," he asserted.[85] Kirmani, more violently anti-Islamic in tone than Akhundzada, and who simultaneously sought answers to the problems he raised in contradictory schools of thought, viewed the "new Iran" in very much the same fashion.

Stripped of the irrational judgments they often passed and of the irrational emotions they displayed, (despite their claims to be rational), Akhundzada and Kirmani's vision of the future of Iran appears to be virtually the same as Malkum and Talibzada's, who did not indulge in the glorification of a mythical past. The vision was of a modern, thoroughly secular, Western type of nation-state, ideally to be governed by human laws which acknowledge the effective separation of religion from temporal affairs (without necessarily eradicating religion from society), and grant freedom of opinion and of worship to all citizens, who would be equally treated regardless of their religious

---

*Mazdak was the founder of a reformist religious sect in Iran which had great political influence during the years A.D. 488–531. The best-known feature of his teaching was the endeavor to remove every cause of discord among men by making women and possessions common property.

affiliation. More importantly, both Akhundzada and Talibzada, the Turkish-speaking Azerbaijanis, as well as Malkum and Kirmani, agreed on the need to stress the importance of one common national language, Persian, as a vital bond superseding religion.

THE LEGACY OF THE SECULARISTS

Because of the radical reforms they called for, because of their blunt anti-clericalism, and, more importantly, because of the aggressive campaign they relentlessly carried on to spread their ideas and influence in government and court circles, the secularists suffered persecution from the religious authorities. Akhundzada and Talibzada were declared infidels; Kirmani had been declared one upon his conversion to Babism; Malkum, while enjoying royal favor and patronage, was beleagured; and Afghani, while still in Iran in his youth, experienced similar harassment, which pushed him to leave his native land. Only his later ambitions, which led him to embrace the political cause of the Muslims, kept him safe from persecution and even earned him the title of champion of Islam in Muslim annals. In fact, throughout the second half of the century, any attempt at reform that directly challenged the traditional position of the established ulama was immediately branded as heretical and suffered the consequences. It would be no exaggeration to say that nineteenth-century social thought was interpreted according to the religious affiliation of its author or follower. Was the person a Babi? An Azali or a Bahai? A freethinker? Undeniably, the secularists, rising against time-honored standards they deemed inadequate and uninspiring for progress into the future, attacked religious orthodoxy and called for change in a style and language sometimes reminiscent of the Babis and the Shaikhis. Talibzada was a pious, practicing Muslim and Akhundzada was a self-professed atheist. Kirmani, a Babi convert who did not hesitate to collaborate with Afghani on his pan-Islamic project, was in reality a freethinking agnostic. Malkum was an Armenian who did not hesitate to switch back to his ancestors' religion when circumstances demanded it, while Afghani was a Muslim believer, despite his association with the Babis. They admitted to their circle of *civilizés* (a French term they often used) Babis, Zoroastrians, nationalists infatuated with the pre-Islamic past, and bitter enemies of Islam and the Muslims in general.

The religiously heterogeneous composition of the group points to its non-religious, rather than antirreligious, concerns, and to the priority it gave to secular issues. They wished to transcend their respective affiliations, or lack of affiliation, to any particular religion or sect, in order to form a joint, common cause. They met whenever they could, in Iran, Turkey, the Caucasus, or Europe, and corresponded when they couldn't. They introduced their friends and acquaintances to each other as men they could trust and with whom they shared a common outlook. Akhundzada was introduced to Manikji the Zoroastrian by the Qajar prince Jalal al-Din Mirza; Malkum was introduced to the latter by Akhundzada. They freely associated with Azali Babis such as Malik al-Mutakallimin, a preacher from Isfahan who had secretly converted to Babism and who was to play a leading role in the Constitutional Revolution. Talibzada first met the Isfahani preacher, who helped him establish in Baku a new school for Iranian children which offered a modern curriculum. Mutual respect and a sense of camaraderie as avant-garde thinkers characterized the intellectuals' relationships. They read and promoted each other's works, and provided each other with new lists of Russian and European, as well as Turkish, books. They made intensive use of the newspapers as a medium to propagate their ideas. They were keenly interested in seeing their works read and possibly published in translation by Western Orientalists. The French scholar A. L. M. Nicolas and the Englishman E. G. Browne, both of whom knew the secularists either in person or through correspondence, were interested in progressive Iranian thought, and helped the authors to smuggle their illicit works to Europe.

They greatly influenced one another, to the point of presenting identical arguments concerning identical issues, with only slight variations in the religious tone they each adopted. A good example of this mutual influence is to be found in the introduction to *Kitab-i jadid,* the Babi historical account which was based on Jani's earlier chronicle, the *Nuqtat-al kaf.* As Browne explained, the book was compiled by, among other individuals, Manikji the Zoroastrian, who showed great interest in the controversial creed. Manikji himself, as Browne assured us, most probably was the author of the introduction and the last section of the main text. A careful reading of these two parts clearly reveals the non-Babi author's Western-inspired reformist ideas, which not only are not to be found in the original Jani text, but, more importantly, were adopted by Bahais as Bahai views. In fact, the Bahais, who had commissioned its composition, accepted the *Kitab-i jadid* in its entirety as their own account of early Babi history.

To condemn them all as heretics plotting to destroy religion would miss the central issue of the secularists' thought. True, Afghani and Malkum often revealed themselves to be dubious manipulators instead of the altruistic reformers they claimed to be, oscillating as they did between a craving to serve and a craving for fame and influence. True, Kirmani and Malkum remained religiously ambivalent throughout their adult lives, and practiced *taqiyya* to the point of abuse. Nonetheless, the question to ask is not whether they were religious or irreligious, genuine or showy, orthodox or heterodox, but rather, given the socioreligious climate of Qajar Iran, why and how they reverted to traditional Islamic rhetoric.

Similarly, to denounce them as traitors ready to sell out their national cultural patrimony would amount to studying history backwards. A historian's criterion of judgment should not be whether or not someone's actions are justified in the light of subsequent developments. Twentieth-century issues, resulting from a growing social complexity and a heightened self-awareness among the Muslims, are entirely different from those of the nineteenth century or the pre-modern era. Similarly, present-day ideological analyses and solutions are inapplicable to pre-Pahlavi society. At the dawn of the nationalist era, the founders of nationalist thought were absolutely free of the existential and national anxiety that characterizes twentieth century thinkers: free of the need to reject "the other" (the West) in order to assert the "self," and free of the morbid love-hate passion that consumes the minds of contemporary traditionalists. They accepted the fact that, politically as well as scientifically and technologically, Europe was superior, and they were backward. They naively and wholeheartedly took Europe as their model, even suggesting that to fail to do so would be tantamount to national death. Yet the openness and honesty of their attitudes in no way reflected self-debasement or servility. It was a harmonious self that diagnosed the ills and, full of confidence and optimism, prescribed the cure.

Doubtless, their diagnosis and the cure itself projected a simplistic perception of Europe. Undeniably, they saw their future society in the mirror of that Europe. However, for nineteenth-century intellectuals who had not experienced "the dislocation of the self" which modernized, contemporary thinkers have been living through, the root of the sociocultural problem was not Europe, but the prevailing religious and intellectual conditions that they deplored. Here they joined ranks with theosophers, Shaikhis, and Babis in their opposition to the orthodox ulama, whom they held responsible for holding back free inquiry. The difference was, with them, that the tenets of rationalism were translated into the language of secularism and nationalism. It was a new language aimed at dispelling some forms of superstition and deference to religious authority, and it found certain kinds of intellectual oppression no longer tolerable. Above all, it encouraged the growth of individual self-respect and political consciousness.

Prominent contemporary writers like Jalal Al-Ahmad contend that the ideas which the nineteenth-century modernists so passionately promoted were not their own, but were ones borrowed from the West and imperfectly understood at that, and that in their harsh criticism of their inherited value system and their attempts to build a new society, they promoted the destruction of Iran's traditional culture. Admittedly, Adkundzada and Kirmani's nationalist thought already carried the germ of twentieth-century Iranian cultural ideology. Their recognition of the Muslim world's "backwardness," as compared to Western Europe, motivated them to seek a more "authentic" self-definition in the ancient past, and to find in Islam a convenient scapegoat for the "tarnished" world image of their country. Thus, national consciousness was, to a great extent, born out of the combined perception of a highly idealized West and a mythical past. Since neither Akhundzada nor Kirmani knew much about ancient Iran, and since their knowledge of Europe, acquired through unsystematic and disparate reading of European books, was no less deficient, the definition of their culture and nation rested on a distorted conception of reality. It led to their deliberate effort to wipe out, or at least undermine, traditional sociocultural values, and substitute for them an ideology that inevitably created a severe cultural and, eventually, political gap that was to alienate the nationalists from Iranian Muslim society at large. One can, therefore, certainly justify the twentieth century intellectuals who contemptuously and angrily dismissed the nineteenth-century modernists as the *gharbzadas* (intoxicated by the West) who first bore the germs of a contagious disease that was to reach epidemic proportions by the 1950s.

However, the so-called modernist thought of the turn of the century, despite its loud call for westernization, was in spirit and form, if not in content, deeply rooted in tradition, bearing as much the mark of the Irano-Islamic heritage outwardly rejected by some of its spokesmen, as of the European systems it strongly wished to emulate.

The *ilm* (knowledge) that the nineteenth-century modernists spoke about so eloquently differed from the theosophers' conception of it. It was given a broader, more modern, scientific meaning. The modernists turned against the ulama's division of knowledge into a Muslim knowledge and a secular European one; they wished to see a more universal approach given to it by erasing the notion that Western science was incompatible with the Islamic faith. Yet, here again they reflected their deep-rooted traditional outlook. They argued that each person's history is characterized by an unfolding of higher mental attributes and an attainment of wisdom by degree; that humans, the center and summit of creation, are capable of perfectability; and that there is order and equilibrium in the universe. These arguments, reflecting not only the seventeenth and eighteenth-century European philosophers, but essentially a classical Islamic view, clashed with the more contemporary, more "modern" concepts of the Positivists and the Social Darwinists, who dismissed the Age of Reason ideal as an antiquated illusion.

In fact, Kirmani, who wholeheartedly accepted Darwin's theory, still did not adopt the ideas of the war of nature, natural selection, and survival of the fittest among random variations, which make humans along with other forms of life, "the children of chance." Rather, he identified Darwinism with Sadra's notion of the substantive movement that lies behind the progressive evolution of all beings toward perfection. But where Sadra's moving force was the human mystical yearning for divine love, Kirmani's was humanity's thirst for knowledge and social progress.[86] Darwinism could be reconciled with a faith in the power of reason among fully evolved and socialized people, and Kirmani may have intended such a reconciliation, but he did not argue it consistently.

In their attempt to define the new society, despite their conscious or unconscious desire to emulate some of the sociopolitical practices of Western Europe, nineteenth-century reformers projected the neo-Platonic view of the heavenly city on earth, the classical "Virtuous City" of the medieval philosophers, where the Perfect Man, the philosopher-king, rules over the masses, rather than the concept of a pluralistic society where the sovereignty of the people is recognized and where a representative government implements the will of the majority. Though Talibzada was aware of and wrote, albeit briefly, about the ideological differences existing between liberalism, radicalism, and conservatism, he failed to understand the significance of a multi-party system, misinterpreting the role of the opposition by limiting it to censoring the ruling party, and preparing itself to take over should it find the latter corrupt or defective. Otherwise, he remarked, in all issues related to national interests there is and never was any conflict. Such a fundamental misconception of the nature of the British political system, which he chose as a perfect example to emulate, reflected Talibzada's own personal view of national unity and the priority he deliberately gave to it. Thus, he never missed any occasion to state emphatically, "Iran is one country, one nation, one religion. Its needs and its interests are one and only one."[87]

Similarly, although Afghani quoted a Koranic verse, "Verily, God does not change the state of a people until they change themselves inwardly," which he interpreted in a truly modern sense to mean that people must rely on their own individual efforts to change positively,[88] paradoxically he often expressed the traditional philosophers and Shaikhis' view that the masses, ignorant and corruptible, must be guided in order to attain a civilized stage and to control their base animal condition. Like them he recognized the essential role of the ulama in instructing the masses (whom he believed "incapable of discerning good from evil" or of tracing "causes or to discern effects"[89]), and in commanding surrender and obedience.

Malkum Khan himself, the most modern of them all, who is considered the father of constitutionalism in Iran and who introduced the Western concept of law to the Iranians, adopted a traditionally elitist, paternalistic attitude towards the people. He, Kirmani, Akhundzada, and Afghani thought of themselves as united by something more than mere interest in ideas; they conceived themselves as being a dedicated, special class of Perfect Men, devoted to spreading a new revelation. They highly praised Martin Luther and his Reformation, and wished to see a similar Islamic reform movement established in the Muslim world, which would usher in the age of "Islamic renaissance"; and each one envisioned himself as the Reformer. Hence, their view of society was still a traditionally monist view, expressing a passionate longing to discover one unitary truth encompassing all existence and impregnable to attack from within and without. Their thought, in spirit if not in content, represented a secularized form of the quest for the True Prophet.

6

Conclusion: The Triumph of Secularization

IN 1889, SYDNEY CHURCHILL, a member of the British legation in Tehran, described what he saw as the ability of individual Iranians to affiliate themselves with any new creed, provided they found in it, "as one of its fundamental principles the liberty of thought and the expression thereof," as well as the potential to combat oppression and "existing evils." He then raised the question: "What are the real ideas of most of those professing Babism? Do they look upon themselves as followers of a new religion, or as members of a new society for political and social reform?"[1]

In the preceding chapters, I have dealt with controversial theological and theosophical issues and movements of revolt, contending that—aside from their individual attraction to religious leaders who seemingly symbolized "the perfection of humanity" and appeared to manifest the ultimate expression of truth they so earnestly sought—basically what the followers more often than not aimed at were more concrete, more tangible sociopolitical goals. Imami Shia Islam, which has dominated Iranian thought for so many centuries, has proved to be an important vehicle for intellectual continuity and change. Despite the great hostility displayed by the organized, orthodox leadership towards heterodoxy, especially in the Safavid and Qajar periods, it has accommodated to a remarkable degree the novel and radical ideas raised by progressive-minded individuals in revolt against the "stifling narrow-mindedness" of the official religion. It constantly kept a door open to divergent outlooks that reflected the changing conditions and mood of the time, and thus periodically offered a more or less direct challenge to the conservative views of the sociocultural establishment.

Dissent in Iranian intellectual history almost always expressed itself in terms and a fashion relevant to the sociopolitical situation of the age. In the Safavid and early Qajar periods, when individual consciousness and identity were so indistinguishable from the Shia consciousness, both at the mass and elite levels, mystics and philosophers channeled their opposition exclusively into metaphysics and theology, aiming at the orthodox ulama's intellectual dominance. The Shaikhi reform movement, progressive as far as dogma was concerned, was politically and socially conservative, reinforcing the traditional elitist conception of knowledge and leadership. In the middle of the nineteenth century, the Babi episode both represented the tradition of messianic revolts in Iranian history, as well as marking the politicization of religious dissent.

By the end of the nineteenth century, when fresh ideas were gradually being imported from the West, and when, simultaneously, national consciousness was aroused by contact with the same European countries which also endangered the political and economic independence of the country, the secularization of Shia dissent effectively took place. Appalled by their nation's scientific and political backwardness, late nineteenth-century thinkers turned both against the traditional sciences of theology and metaphysics and their exponents, and also the corrupt, traditionally despotic Qajar government. The secularists introduced a new genre, social criticism, to Iran's literary world, which was used both as a weapon to discredit the establishment, and as a torch to "enlighten" and "awaken" their compatriots from their "long sleep of ignorance." These pursuits, together with Shia dissent, were diverted to national social action and political demonstrations. The last decade of the nineteenth century and the first years of the twentieth saw the effective polarization of the different expressions of dissent—socioeconomic, religious and political—into one movement of revolt, which culminated with the Constitutional Revolution of 1905–11. Both the secularists and the religious dissidents, as well as some mujtahids, appalled by the growing corruption of the court, the government's chronic financial crisis, and its increased reliance on the unwise practice of granting concessions and receiving loans, which established foreign economic domination in the country, demanded a constitution for their nation.

Much has been written about the Constitutional Revolution. Iranian historians, basing their studies on standard sources, eyewitness accounts, memoirs, and biographies of famous participants, generally tend to perceive the role played by religion in a highly conventional fashion, in terms of orthodox Shia Islam as expressed by well-coordinated, "liberal" clerical leaders whose sole purpose was to champion the cause of Islam and of the Muslims. Nikki Keddie, in an early article,[2] sought to rectify this monolithic picture of the religious dimension of the revolution, and pointed at the "irreligious" elements which were covertly so active in the political scene. She did not, however, analyze those elements in the context of the long tradition of dissent in Shia Islam.

The religious and political situation in Iranian society at the time was far more complex, more multiform in its diversity, than is generally conveyed. I do not intend to offer here a comprehensive study of the revolution, for it would be beyond the scope of the present volume. I merely wish to discuss a few points which are not only relevant to the subjects treated so far, but also might possibly clarify the position of the Constitutionalists, both the religious ones and the secularists.

One essential matter should be discussed here, namely, the failure of the controversial schools and sects which we have studied not only to gain broad-based public recognition, and thus be allowed to implement the basic doctrinal reforms they advocated, but, more importantly, to succeed in implementing those very changes within their own communities.

Though individual Bahais and Azalis were beginning to reform some aspects of their own intellectual and social views and mores, they were chiefly motivated by their desire to modernize in the manner of the West with which they increasingly came in contact, rather than by a wish to follow the models set by their leaders. In his extensive writings on the two rival sects, E. G. Browne notes the quasi-traditional outlook of both Bahaullah and Subh-i Azal, whom he visited in their respective places of exile in Palestine and Cyprus. For instance, he described the seclusion and the aura of semidivinity surrounding Bahaullah. He was revered by his followers, who, if ever honored with an audience, would enter his room on their knees and prostrate themselves at his feet.[3] Subh-i Azal's image was no less "holy," no less awesome. Similarly, while visiting Iran in the year 1887–88, Browne noticed that the reforms advocated by the Bab regarding personal matters such as divorce, polygamy, and fuller freedoms for women, "at present ... have only met with partial success."[4] In fact, as Browne noted elsewhere, Subh-i Azal strongly recommended the use of veils by women.[5] Of greater importance to an understanding and correct appraisal of the spread and survival of Babism in Iran is Browne's perceptive analysis of some Sufi converts, whom he characterized as being "attracted by the prestige and influence of the Bab or Bahaullah, but really retaining their original beliefs almost or quite unmodified and, as it were, reading these into the doctrine to which they have attached themselves, rather than deriving them from it."[6] He had met many of this kind, especially in Kirman, where they were vehemently condemned by other Babis.

It was only after the death of Bahaullah in 1892 and Subh-i Azal in 1912 that the leadership of the sects fell into the hands of individuals who decisively undertook important changes. The Western-inspired innovations promulgated by the new Bahai leader, Abdul Baha (also known as Abbas Effendi), further accentuated the universal, apolitical characteristics of Bahaism, and thus isolated the majority of the Bahais even more from Iranian political life. On the other hand, the new Azali leader, Mirza Yahya Daulatabadi (the son of Haji Mirza Hadi Daulatabadi, who was Subh-i Azal's original choice until the former's untimely death[7]), followed a nationalist, secularist path and, together with other individual Azalis, played a predominant role in the revolution. Here, however, it must be emphasized that the Azalis' actions cannot be interpreted as representing a collective policy, but rather personal choice that more and more drew them away from the original Babi creed which had, at first, seemed so attractive. It is also worthy of note that no individual Azali, not even the leader himself, strove for an ascension to temporal power, nor aimed at creating a Babi-Azali state.

There exists no single study of presumed Azalis who were active in the revolution, chief among them: Mirza Nasrullah Malik al-Mutakallimin, the preacher from Isfahan, and his fellow revolutionary comrade, Mirza Jahangir Khan, the journalist-editor of the highly popular newspaper of the day, *Sur-i Israfil*, Mirza Yahya Daulatabadi himself, and scores of other "secret converts." Doubtless, the rigorous self-doubt and self-questioning which they, like many other Iranian thinkers of the time, were subjected to, initially propelled their conversion to the controversial theosophical doctrine. Once exposed to the outside world, their new perspectives and broader intellectual horizons renewed their challenge to the established order, although it was no longer expressed in the language of religious dissent. An increasingly pluralistic outlook upon the multiform world which they were becoming conscious of disengaged them from the philosophical and theological controversies they had found so absorbing before. They began to view the new Western-inspired learning as superior in its accomplishments, and, most importantly, as novel, different, and radically opposed to the traditional form of education. To their minds, it was also the secret of European progress. They hoped, therefore, to achieve through a political revolution the change which the religious controversies had failed to bring about. And here they joined the ranks of the secularists studied in the previous chapter. They were neither free-thinkers nor Azalis any longer, but secular nationalists fiercely fighting a war on two fronts: at once against the despotic government, and against the orthodox clerical establishment. Like Malkum, Afghani and Kirmani, at times they felt the need to use religious rhetoric in order to reach a wider audience and, above all, not to scare away those members of the ulama class willing to lend them an ear.

The Kirmani Shaikhis, for their part, failed even more completely to implement any kind of doctrinal reforms. Unlike the Babis, they did not produce a new generation of progressive-minded adepts who could elaborate and develop the original doctrine further. Quite to the contrary, they seemed to stagnate intellectually by stubbornly upholding their original views, which they taught in private, while publicly professing orthodoxy. Hajj Muhammad Karim Khan's denunciation of modern European science as corrupt and corrupting was perpetuated by his successor, who kept up the spirit of resistance to foreign, "unIslamic" ideas. Thus, paradoxically, the Kirmani Shaikhis at the turn of the century drew further and further away from the original Shaikhi view, which held that religion and religious laws must undergo constant change in order to meet the demands of a constantly changing world. Instead, they drew closer to the orthodox religious position, while politically the Shaikhis proved to be even more conservative.

Following the death of Muhammad Karim Khan, a dispute over the succession to leadership split the Kirmani community.[8] Two of his sons were rival contenders: his eldest, Muhammad Rahim Khan (d. 1889), and Muhammad Khan, son of Karim Khan's favorite, Qajar-born wife. The latter son finally succeeded in attracting the allegiance of the majority of the sect's followers. Nevertheless, his leadership was marred with strife between himself and his followers, and also with the sons of his father's old rivals in the city of Kirman. Among his opponents, Hajj Shaikh Abu Jafar, son of Aqa Ahmad, ranked highest in terms of the intensity and the persistence of his feud, which often led to violent clashes in the streets. When Abu Jafar died, his son, Hajj Mirza Muhammad Riza, took over the leadership of the Balasari camp. The Shaikhi-Balasari war intensified during the entire year of 1905.

Aside from the basic theological issues which continually pushed the orthodox ulama to declare the Shaikhis to be heretics, serious political considerations lay behind the struggle. As a result of the considerable wealth he inherited, along with the right to administer the Ibrahimiyya bequest, Muhammad Khan attained a social status equal to his father's at the height of the elder's influence. He enjoyed the total support and allegiance of his relatives and dependents, as well as the loyalty of less wealthy followers who sought the benefits which Shaikhi membership and patronage might entail. Like his father, he led the life of a Qajar grandee, rather than that of a religious leader. And, again like his father, he was politically highly ambitious.[9] As a Qajar, he was close to the center of power in Tehran, and had easy access to the court. In fact, most of the princes, Muzzafar al-Din Shah included, adhered to the Shaikhi school of theology.

As the struggle between the state and the ulama intensified throughout the first decade of the twentieth century, the Shaikhis were increasingly fought not only as heretics but, by then, essentially as members of the hated ruling dynasty. The fact that, on the eve of the revolution, Muhammad Khan declared himself in opposition to constitutionalism added fuel to the hatred of those Balasari ulama who were its partisans, or at least fighting on the side of the "freedom-seekers." Repeatedly the Shaikhis were pronounced heretics by the Balasari ulama; they were banned from public places, especially baths, and they were not allowed to bury their dead in Muslim cemeteries. Outbreaks of violence in the streets led the central government to send royal forces into Kirman to put an end to the strife. Aqa Muhammad Riza, leader of the Balasaris, was publicly beaten by the soldiers and expelled from the city. General protest followed. The Balasaris mobilized the populace, including women and children, to stage massive demonstrations and call for the return of the expelled religious leader. Tension was so high, harassment so hazardous to personal safety, that Muhammad Khan felt compelled to leave town and retire to the family's country estate in Langar.

It is interesting to note here that, in addition to the Balasaris, the Shaikhis encountered the hostility of the Azali residents of Kirman. While Hajj Muhammad Karim Khan was still alive, Subh-i Azal had written to him to warn him and his followers of "hell and damnation," and of eternal enmity.[10] After the execution of Ahmad Ruhi and Mirza Aqa Khan Kirmani, Ruhi's brothers, who were also Azalis and close associates of Mirza Riza Kirmani, Nasir al-Din Shah's assassin,[11] joined the raging war against the Shaikhis as chief organizers. The late Muhammad Hashimi reports in his lengthy accounts of Kirman politics at the turn of the century that one of the brothers, Mihdi Bahr al-Ulum (who was to be elected a deputy to the first Majlis or National Assembly in 1906), had forged a telegram bearing the signature of the leading orthodox mujtahid of Najaf and addressed to Balasari mujtahids in Kirman. Claiming it was carrying out the Imam's order, it cursed Muhammad Karim Khan, his children, and his followers, pronouncing them all heretics. Bahr al-Ulum allegedly instructed a simple-minded man who worked in the local cemetery to reveal the telegram to the populace and announce it was given to him by the Imam himself. Copies of the telegram were found posted on the walls all over town. It further inflamed the mobilized masses' hostility to the Shaikhis.[12] Whether or not one can totally rely on Hashimi's account of the forged telegram, the fact remains that anti-Shaikhi rioting reached its climax. Government forces had to intervene once more to restore public order. Those held responsible for spreading the rumors and causing public agitation, including the Azalis, were beaten and forced to pay a heavy fine. A semblance of quiet ensued without, however, putting a success-ful end to the strife. Hajj Muhammad Khan was unable to return to Kirman city. He died towards the end of 1905, just when the revolution was about to break out, thus terminating the Balasari-Shaikhi war. With the downfall of the Qajars, Kirmani Shaikhism turned into a school of theology in the manner of a Sufi order.

Doubtless the action of the Azalis in Kirman was motivated by personal and sectarian grudges against the Shaikhis. Doubtless they wished to avenge the Bab's death, and, in a sense, belatedly assert the righteousness of the Babi cause. Nevertheless, sectarian differences were minimal in comparison to their increasing commitment to nationalist and revolutionary issues. By participating in the Kirman war, and by outwardly espousing the Balasari, they were able to bring their underground political activities out into the open, and seize the occasion to foment even more trouble in the volatile situation created by the long sectarian dispute. To incite the masses to revolt against the local Qajar establishment, declared heretical because of their religious views, was a well-calculated move benefiting not just the Azalis, but most contemporary politicians, lay as well as clerical, because it served to attract the support of the religious community, giving them the religious legitimacy which they needed for the revolu-tion they wished to undertake. The Shaikhi-Balasari war of Kirman went down in some Iranian annals as the spark that first set the fire of the Constitutional Revolution.

The theosophers, the Shaikhis, and the Babis attempted to offer their own views of religion as alternatives to official Shia Islam. All three types of dissidents directly challenged the office of mujtahid, and the power it had acquired as a result of the centralizing policies ruthlessly implemented by the Bihbahanis, father and son, in the eighteenth and early nineteenth centuries. By the second half of the nineteenth century, new socioeconomic forces and external pressures in the form of British and Russian involvement in domestic affairs, added a new political dimension to the religious controversies. Leaders of various religious factions, orthodox or otherwise, began to voice their concern with political issues which came to overshadow theological disputes. There came into being a peculiar system of alliances that were not intended to outlive their immediate goal, the establishment of a national assembly. Men and women belonging to diverse interest groups and religious affiliations were loosely associated in this single, common cause, but for different reasons.

While the Kirmani Shaikhis defended the Qajars, the Azerbaijan branch of Shaikhism sided with the Constitutionalists. Influential orthodox mujtahids such as Fazlullah Nuri gave their support to the Shah's effort to safeguard his dynastic interests. Lower-ranking, freethinking ulama, including Malik al-Mutakallimin and Sayyid Jamal al-Din Isfahani (who had co-authored an essay critical of the orthodox ulama[13]), as well as Majd al-Islam Kirmani, joined ranks with orthodox mujtahids in calling for a constitutional government. There exists no detailed study on the background of the proconstitution mujtahids. Though they were by no means "freethinking," some of them were in touch with and, and to varying degrees, influenced by religious dissidents and the secularists.

Sayyid Sadiq Tabatabai was the sole mujtahid member of Malkum Khan's "House of Oblivion" *(Faramushkhana)*, [14] and Shaikh Hadi Najmabadi allegedly had advised Afghani to teach "the concept of freedom... by means of instruction in Koranic exegesis."[15] In fact, both mujtahids were Afghani's most important clerical contacts in Tehran. Moreover, the celebrated mujtahid Muhammad Tabatabai, one of the two leading clerical proponents of the revolution, had, through his father, Sadiq, connections among the freethinkers, including Malkum and Afghani, as well as among members of the *anjuman*s or secret societies that were to prepare the way to the open revolt. It is also significant that Nazim al-Islam, the clerical author of the famous *Tarikh-i bidari-yi iraniyan*, which chronicles the revolution, and founder of one such society, himself professed unorthodox views. He never failed to express his admiration for Mirza Aqa Khan Kirmani and

Ahmad Ruhi (though without mentioning their well-known Azali affiliation), and he admitted that he considered himself the disciple of the former.[16]

He had studied with Muhammad Tabatabai in Tehran and, together with the latter's son, administered a newly established school which viewed the "new learning" with greater tolerance than other schools run by orthodox ulama. In fact, apparently the school was founded to counter the ulama's opposition to the "new studies" and new type of schools.[17] Most probably it was also planned as a religious counterpart to the state-sponsored new school, Rushdiyya, which had recently opened by order of Amin al-Daula, the reform-minded statesman, and had been denounced by the orthodox clerics.

Nizam al-Islam further displayed his "liberalism" when, upon his return to his native city a few years after the outbreak of the revolution, he found himself appalled by the "fanaticism" and "narrow-mindedness" of the local religious establishment and set up for himself the difficult and hazardous task of denouncing the mujtahids' views in public, hence antagonizing both the Shaikhis and the Balasaris. Muhammed Hashimi, editor of the posthumously published *Tarikh-i bidari*, explicitly states his unwillingness to reveal the nature of Nizam al-Islam's views or the content of his opponents' refutations, for fear of offending Kirmani personalities still alive at the time he prepared the manuscript for publication.[18]

Was Nizam al-Islam, one of the respected clerical leaders of the revolution, an Azali? Or was he merely a man in favor of a new social and political order? His activities in the pre- and post-revolutionary years; his high praise, not only of Mirza Aqa Khan Kirmani and Ahmad Ruhi, but also of Afghani, Malkum, and Iranian reformers in general; his close collaboration with Sayyid Muhammad Tabatabai, the mujtahid leader whom he described as a man who "wished to increase his knowledge of the Europeans,"[19] (as contrasted to the conventionally orthodox ulama, who reacted so strongly to anything European) prove he was essentially a reformer sharing other reformers' conceptions of the "new Iran." It was this unity of purpose that gathered together men of different intellectual backgrounds to establish the famous *anjumans*, or secret societies.

No doubt exists about the actual purposes of the secret societies set up by various groups and individuals: to "awaken," to disseminate revolutionary ideas, and, above all, to call for reforms. Of the two *anjumans* which are important for the present study, one, known as the

Islamic Society *(shirkat-i islami)*, was founded by the freethinkers Malik al-Mutakallimin and Sayyid Jamal al-Din Isfahani, who were in favor of modernization and of curbing clerical influence. Although it recruited members from among the ulama themselves, and although it counseled all its members to refrain from associating themselves with any religious assembly that was not Muslim to avoid accusation of heresy, it deliberately and knowingly opened the door for Western concepts and ideas. The public speeches and newspaper articles which were sponsored by the society and lists of reading materials recommended to its members clearly reflect the views of Afghani, Malkum, Talibzada, and other secular reformers.

The second society, named the Secret Society *(anjuman-i makhfi)*, which was founded by Nazim al-Islam, among others, followed a similar pattern of recruitment and programming. While it, too, attempted a strenuous blend of Western concepts with Islamic rhetoric, equating *mashrutiyyat* (Constitutionalism) with *mashruiyyat* (Islamic law), it proposed the same reforms the secularists had been clamoring for: the spread of education, limiting the despotic power of the Qajar government, establishing a code of law *(qanun)*. Direct references to the secularists were often made in the meetings, and their "patriotism" and "enlightened commitment" was hailed as a model to imitate.

Of greater significance was the members' attempt to emphasize the national rather than religious character of the homeland. A clause included in the charter of the society declared all religious minorities, Zoroastrians, Jews, and Christians, eligible for membership, provided they were Iranian "by birth and race." Another clause specifically stated that the task of protecting and preserving the homeland was not restricted to the Muslim jurists alone, but to "all ulama," whether learned in jurisprudence or any other science; they could be Muslim or non-Muslim ulama, as long as they considered Iran their homeland. "In this sense and for that [national] purpose, they shall agree and cooperate with the Muslim ulama."[20] Though they made a point of referring to Islam constantly, it was Iran the nation they were mainly concerned with. Their practice of *taqiyya*, if one is justified in calling it that, aimed at softening the bluntness of their secularist goal rather than concealing "heretical" or "freethinking" tendencies. National secular interests clearly emerged as superseding religious differences. No Islamic rhetoric, not even the sanction and support the societies gained from some mujtahids of the time, could conceal this fundamental feature of the revolution.

The Constitutional Revolution marked the culmination of dissent in Shia Iran, for it was the very foundation of the traditional system of thought that was so decisively shaken as a consequence. The whole program of reforms, in spirit and in content, aimed from the beginning at severely curbing clerical influence, and once the Constitutional government was established, measures were immediately taken to secularize those very institutions the ulama had controlled for so many centuries. At the time, rare were the orthodox ulama who could have foreseen such drastic consequences. Fazlullah Nuri, the "notorious" mujtahid who, despite an initial support of the Constitutionalists, turned against them and championed the cause of Qajar government instead, and who paid with his life for his "betrayal" once the Shah was finally defeated, stands out almost alone in revolutionary chronicles.

There were some orthodox ulama who genuinely attempted to revise Shia views on political matters and to incorporate the notion of constitutional law into Muslim law, just as, throughout the centuries, others had discreetly assimilated Sufi ideas. However—and there lies the tragedy of modern Iranian Shia thought—they failed to realize the fundamental difference between speculative metaphysics (whereby strictly unorthodox concepts could be safely absorbed through the devices of *taqiyya* and esoteric modes of expression) and the novel sociopolitical ideas that were so important in shaping national policies affecting the lives of millions of citizens. This inability to draw a sharp line between what could be adopted without causing any sociopolitical or cultural tremors, and what could eventually have dramatic repercussions, led to the ulama's loss of influence in the postrevolution period. Hence, the clerical members of the first Majlis bitterly clashed with their lay colleagues over most of the legislative issues brought before the assembly, loudly denouncing their colleagues' positions on those issues as sheer emulation of the Europeans. Talibzada's exasperated, blunt response expressed the reality of the situation: "No one," he wrote, "wants to admit that [the idea of] this Majlis is after all imported from Europe, and the Constitution is a translation of a European one."[21]

The orthodox mujtahids who supported the Constitutionalists believed they were combating the Qajar state. The revolution which they led ironically provoked a social explosion with fatal consequences for their traditional role and interests. By directly participating in revolutionary politics they only succeeded in turning the political energies of the dissidents against themselves. Strong enough to destroy the Qajar power, the mujtahids could not master the social forces which that destruction released and which generated new impulses to undermine the traditional order even further. Modernist politicians and intellectuals challenged the religious leaders' trusteeship of society and sought to exclude them from political power.

Epilogue

IT WOULD BE ERRONEOUS and highly misleading to leap over nearly three-quarters of a century of a nation's cultural, social, economic, and political development, in order to examine the current Islamic Revolution in the light of the events that led to the promulgation of the Constitution of 1906. Observers might indeed find striking similarities between the two movements, such as the effective coalition of the clerical, mercantile, and intellectual oppositional groups; the role of religion as a powerful force successful in undermining the authority of the state, which it declared corrupt and un-Islamic; and the predominant anti-Western stand of the revolutionary leaders. Hasty analysts might conclude that the ulama, after fifty years of the Pahlavis' anti-clerical repression, were finally able to rise once more and resume their national task, which had been so abruptly, and so brutally, halted by the imperialist powers and the Pahlavis in the second decade of the century. Some historians, anxious to discover clear-cut dialectical sequences in historical events, might be tempted to study twentieth-century Iranian social and political history in terms of the rise, temporary eclipse, and triumphant return of clerical leadership. Scholars of "resurgent Islam," opponents of modernizing theories, and Third Worldists who view the contemporary Islamic political movement purely from the perspective of its struggle against Western imperialism might find this thesis especially attractive. However, a more careful study of the current Islamic Revolution would prove this analysis wrong.

This epilogue is a summary of my article, "Islam in Pahlavi and post-Pahlavi Iran," in John Esposito, ed., *Islam and Development: Religion and Sociopolitical Change* (Syracuse: Syracuse University Press, 1980).

189

In the preceding chapters, I have described and analyzed the tradition of religious dissent in Iran. I have argued that the messianic impulse and revolutionary tendencies so characteristic of early Shia Islam were combated by law-minded mujtahids who, more often than not, constituted an integral part of the ruling establishment, rather than an opposition force. I have shown how progressive and even radical Shia ideas were kept alive in the works and, as in the case of the Babis, in the actions of the dissidents. I have concluded that the Constitutional Revolution of 1906, despite the vital role played by some leading mujtahids, marked the ascendency of the dissident element, both lay and clerical, as well as the advent of secular nationalism in Iranian politics. The Constitutionalists' most lasting contribution, in that it deeply affected the future course of Iranian social history, lay in the secularization of social thought. Prominent decision makers not only demanded the secularization of the educational and parts of judicial systems, which previously were under the full control of the religious establishment, but, more importantly, divorced their sociopolitical views from Islam. Most of them sought a model to emulate in Western Europe. The opposition to the jurists, which had expressed the religious dissidents' resentment of the orthodox theologians' intransigence and anti-intellectualism, turned into frank anti-clericalism. The Constitutionalists generally wished to confine religion and religious views within the walls of the mosques and of the *madrasas*-turned-seminaries.

Furthermore, the dismissal of the theological restraints and taboos which the jurists had for centuries imposed upon Iranian thought, broke down the fences that artificially contained together different groups of intellecuals and professionals within the loosely defined class of the "turbaned," or educated elite. A new lay class of intellectuals and professionals, writers, journalists, lawyers, teachers, politicians, orators, and philosophers came into being, with separate interests and group allegiances. Their anticlericalism did not mean they were antireligious, or that they wished to eradicate religion from society. Rather, their secular, nationalist ideals transcended their Muslim identities. For a great number of them, Islam had become a matter of private conscience.

As a result of secularizing policies, the ulama emerged as one separate professional class of religious leaders who were specialists in Islamic jurisprudence. Limited by their traditional expertise, they proved to be vulnerable in comparison with the secular professionals, whose education better prepared them to assume political and social leadership.

Nevertheless, doctrinal conflicts with aspects of the new learning and the new sociopolitical systems that were adopted nationally in the postrevolution period, were left unresolved. Similarly, the Constitution of 1906, which marked the culmination of socioeconomic and cultural forces at work separate from the official religion, paradoxically granted the mujtahids even greater potential power. It gave a council of five mujtahids the right to supervise all legislation in the parliament. Thus, ironically, modern forces and modern political concepts achieved for official Shia Islam what the traditional Imami leadership had continually frowned upon—that is, direct participation in temporal affairs. Such was the price that the lay modernists and their natural clerical allies (the religious dissidents who secularized their dissent and closely identified with the secularists) had to pay for the leadership, support, and legitimacy the religious institution provided in their struggle against the Qajar state.

The secularist revolutionaries did not develop a modern army and government bureaucracy in order to preserve their gains from destruction by hostile forces (both domestic and foreign). Thus, they proved powerless to construct a new society with well-founded, modern sociopolitical institutions. It was not until the Pahlavis came to power in the 1920s, and actually implemented the Constitutionalists' secularizing reforms, that the clerics suffered major setbacks and were finally pushed back to their mosques. With the exception of a brief interlude (1951–53) when they and other, secular parties were allowed political freedom, the religious opposition was politically ineffectual. Education was made compulsory in the secular state schools, and the judicial system was brought under the jurisdiction of the Ministry of Justice, headed and staffed by secular-educated lawyers and jurists. The modernization of the educational and judicial systems, using mostly Western models, was the Pahlavi regime's effective weapon for secularizing society and implementing radical, nationalist reforms. Inspired by the ideas of nineteenth-century nationalist intellectuals such as Mirza Aqa Khan Kirmani and Akhundzada, and their followers in the twentieth century, the Pahlavis sought to emphasize the pre-Islamic cultural heritage of Iran. Nauruz, the ancient Zoroastrian festive holiday celebrating the spring equinox, was adopted as the day marking the beginning of the Iranian new year in a revised calendar. School textbooks stressed ancient Iranian history, glorified the "genius of the Aryan culture," and traced a national historical continuity from pre-Islamic times to the present through the institution of the monarchy.

Thus dispossessed of their traditional function in society, the ulama rose in defense of Islamic law, so severely displaced by modern reforms. Whereas, in the past, the ulama had accepted the necessary existence of monarchal power, by the 1960s leading clerical opponents of the Shah adamantly refused to sanction his authority. Similarly, the changes made in the name of modernization finally provoked the mujtahids to reverse their long practice of suppressing extremist messianic activism, and to raise the banner of the Imam in self-defense against a state determined to annihilate their social influence. Hence, messianic features so characteristic of the original Shia sect, and which the orthodox theologians had kept checked for centuries, were reactivated. All the old elements were fully invoked: the call for *jihad*, holy war, against the infidel and the heretic; the readiness to die a martyr for the holy cause; the strong conviction that a true and pure Islamic order would and should replace the corrupt and evil government; the charismatic appeal of the leader who lays claim to the Hidden Imam's deputyship. The mujtahids who previously were instrumental in the depoliticization of Shia Islam and the secularization of politics, now turned into messianic figures aiming at establishing a theocracy. Thus, in the 1960s and '70s, the revolution of the ulama who, as a result of the Constitutional Revolution and the Pahlavis' policies, had emerged as a distinct, socially defined and cohesive class of their own, was more than just a revolution for the sake of religion. It was a social and cultural revolution as well. The message of Ayatollah Khomeini's often-quoted book, *Hukumat-i islami,* ("Islamic Government") written in the early '70s, leaves no doubt as to the author's aim: to restore the lost power of the *fuqaha* (jurists); while upgrading and reformulating their function in society.

The role Khomeini attributes to the *faqih* is truly revolutionary, not only in the context of Pahlavi Iran, but also in the context of the Imami Shia political views written down and upheld by generations of jurists. In Khomeini's view, the *faqih* is both the interpreter of Islamic law and the only legitimate ruler of the community in times of the Occultation of the Imam. Thus, he declared the Constitution of 1906 un-Islamic, just as Fazlullah Nuri, the Constitutionalists' fiercest opponent, had done at the turn of the century. However, whereas Nuri defended the Qajar monarchy, Khomeini turned decisively antimonarchist. In Islam, he argued, God alone is the legislator. The Prophet and, after him, the Imams were the executors who implemented the divine law. In the period of Occultation, the Muslim jurists assume their task. Hence, the old theocratic doctrine which, since the death of the Prophet had survived only as an ideal coexisting with a pragmatic justification of secularized politics, is now threatening the balance that has traditionally existed—even though strained at times—between the religious and political centers of power. Ironically, lay revolutionary ideologists helped the ulama to advance their claims successfully.

The harsh, coercive means the Pahlavis used to implement their policies eventually succeeded in alienating not only the ulama, but also the lay professionals, who began to view the lack of political freedom as too high a price to pay for the national programs they and their predecessors at the turn of the century had so hopefully called for. Because of their modern educations and professional occupations, they were different from and, more often than not, opposed to the traditionally oriented ulama. However, with many, opposition to the Pahlavi regime came to acquire a religious undertone. Expressing a deeply-felt disillusion and disenchantment with the West and Western values, with which they are by far better acquainted than their predecessors in the nineteenth century, they chose to champion Islam and Islamic moral and cultural values. Having witnessed some of the excesses of Westernization at home, looking for the ideology needed for a national struggle against dictatorship at home and its supporters abroad, they turned to Islam. Neither group, however, ever contemplated a return to the old socioreligious order, not even those who, like Mihdi Bazargan, the first prime minister of the Islamic Republic, cultivated close ties with clerical opponents of the Shah. In the 1940s and '50s, they chose to side with Muhammad Musadiq (Mossadegh), the prominent nationalist leader, until the 1953 CIA-staged coup brought about his downfall.

Both Mihdi Bazargan and Ali Shariati (d. 1977), the two most widely read Muslim ideologists in the 1960s and '70s, differentiated their concept of Islam, renewed and reformed, from traditional Islam. Shariati often talked about the need for an "Islamic Protestantism" to help make Islam once more a viable sociopolitical force, and to usher in the "Islamic Renaissance." Using a tone and a rhetoric highly reminiscent of the religious dissidents in past centuries, he depicted "the deceit of long-bearded official clergy" as one of the three forces of evil—political, economic and spiritual—that had oppressed the masses for centuries. He denied doctrinal legitimacy to the ulama's authority in society, beyond what they acquired as scholars and teachers of their special discipline. He thus challenged their right to be called the Imam's deputies, arguing that the Imam had not appointed anyone to that position. He accused the ulama of reducing Islamic knowledge to the narrow discipline of jurisprudence and the Traditions, which he contemptuously defined as "repeating the repeated." Whereas Khomeini and his fellow clerics proclaimed an almost divine right to rule, Shariati spoke of the duty of the *raushanfikr* (the "enlightened thinker," i.e., those having secular educations) to lead the nation to the path of progress. Khomeini spoke of the superiority of Islam over all other religions; Shariati candidly admitted he viewed Islam not as a tradition or a particular dogma, but as an ideology, a faith generating social consciousness, which would rally believers as well as nonbelievers in the national struggle against the oppressor.

While the revolution was in the making, these fundamental differences between the ulama and the lay ideologists were minimized by practically all involved, in order to achieve a common goal—namely, the overthrow of the Shah. The deep divisions that subsequently split the ranks of the revolutionaries into rival factions represent more than the inevitable convulsions and upheavals that normally accompany any revolution, once its first target is reached. Rather, they are symbolic of the dichotomy that has traditionally existed in Imami Shia circles between proponents of the jurists' orthodoxy, and those in favor of religious renewal. Just as, in the past, the two opposing camps fiercely fought for the right to promote their respective views of religion, at present the clerics and their supporters on the one hand, and Muslim secularists on the other, are engaged in a battle the outcome of which might decide the fate of Islam in Iran, and of the political future of the nation.

To consolidate their power and establish a hegemony firmly based on religious populism, the clerical leaders have reverted to their traditional, law-minded role as the protectors of orthodoxy. They mercilessly wage war against "deviators," the modern, educated professionals who do not abide by their rulings, as well as their political opponents. They have turned into fundamentalists, since currently their very *raison d'être* in Iranian politics in religion interpreted in a most traditional fashion. Islamic law must, therefore, be fully restored and enforced according to fundamentalist tenets. Polygamy, male-biased divorce procedures, the veil for women, an archaic penal code, and other aspects of the law pertaining to the private lives of Muslim men and women are in the process of being reinstated. Education must return to the Islamic fold, which means that the entire system must be "purged" and "Islamized." Although Khomeini declares he does not intend to divide knowledge into Islamic and non-Islamic categories, he insists it must be founded on Islamic morality and values. The so-called cultural revolution of the Islamic Republic is, in fact, establishing severe clerical censorship of the kind that the Constitutionalists at the turn of the century had eliminated. In the last analysis, the clerics, acting as the champions of Islam, symbolize the erosion of national secular values which were first espoused by the nationalist intellectuals in the second half of the nineteenth century.

In pre-Pahlavi Iran, both Shia speculative thought and orthodoxy coexisted within a large, loosely defined association of ulama, with the secular state acting as a neutral outsider capable of regulating and even manipulating the interaction of the two trends. Hence, differences of opinion and a pluralistic religious outlook survived the jurists' persecution. The current politicization of Shia Islam, and the fusing of political and religious authorities into one, leave no room for dissent, not even a mild Islamic reformist trend.

Notes

1—SHIA AND THE TRADITION OF DISSENT IN ISLAMIC THOUGHT

1. Cited in Husain M. Jafri, *The Origins and Early Development of Shi'i Islam* (London: Longman, 1978), p. 299.

2. Abdulaziz Sachedina, *Islamic Messianism: The Idea of the Mahdi in Twelver Shi'ism* (Albany, N.Y.: SUNY Press, 1981), pp. 32–34.

3. Ibid., p. 108.

4. W. M. Montgomery Watt, "The Reappraisal of Abbasid Shi'ism," in *Arabic and Islamic Studies in Honor of Hamilton A. R. Gibb*, edited by F. Makdisi (Leiden: Brill, 1965), p. 369.

5. Henry Corbin, *En Islam Iranien: aspects spirituels et philosophiques*, 4 vols. (Paris: Gallimard, 1971–72) 1:7, 15.

6. Marshall Hodgson, *The Venture of Islam*, 3 vols. (Chicago: University of Chicago Press) 1:472.

7. Muhsin Mahdi, *Alfarabi's Philosophy of Plato and Aristotle* (New York: Free Press of Glencoe, 1962), p. 00.

8. Muhsin Mahdi, *Ibn Khaldun's Philosophy of History* (Chicago: University of Chicago Press, 1964), pp. 56, 90.

9. Ibid., pp. 126, 132.

10. Reynold A. Nicholson, *Studies in Islamic Mysticism* (Cambridge: Cambridge University Press, 1922), p. 18.

11. Rom Landau, *The Philosophy of Ibn Arabi* (London, 1959), p. 58.

12. Nicholson, pp. 78, 79.

13. Joseph Eliash, "Ithna Ashari Shi'i Juristic Theory," *Studia Islamica* 29 (1969):24–25.

14. Marshall Hodgson, "Batiniyya," *Encyclopedia of Islam*, New Edition.

15. Marshall Hodgson, "The Ismaili State," in *Cambridge History of Iran*, edited by J. A. Boyle (Cambridge: Cambridge University Press, 1968), p. 459.

16. Sachedina, *Islamic Messianism*, pp. 102–3, 106.

17. Ibid., p. 37.

18. On the controversy over Tusi's sectarian affiliation see W. Ivanow, ed., *Tasaw-wurat ya rauzat al-taslim* (Leiden: Brill, 1950) and M. Mudarrisi, *Sarguzasht va aqaid-i khaja tusi* (Tehran, 1956).

19. Alessandro Bausani, "Religion under the Mongols," in *Cambridge History of Iran*, edited by J. A. Boyle (Cambridge: Cambridge University Press), p. 539.

20. See Tusi, "Risala-yi dar rasm-i ayyin-i padishahan-i qadim," in *Majmua-yi rasail* (Tehran, n.d.), pp. 28–35; and Tusi, "Nasihat nama," in Mudarrisi, *Sarguzasht*, pp. 48–50.

21. Sachedina, *Islamic Messianism*, p. 63.

22. Ibid., pp. 107–8.

23. See Ann K. S. Lambton, "Quis Custodiet Custodes: Some Reflections on the Persian Theory of Government," *Studia Islamica* 6 (1956).

24. Vladimir Minorski, trans. and ed., *Tadhkirat al-Muluk: A Manual of Safavid Administration* (London: Luzac, 1943), p. 110.

25. Sachedina, *Islamic Messianism*, p. 101. The account by J. Chardin, the often-quoted eighteenth-century French traveler to Iran, of some mujtahids' claim to political rule must be regarded as an exception rather than the rule at the time. If there was political confrontation between the two centers of power, state and religion, it did not necessarily mean that the mujtahids were acting in unison, following a formulated policy with a definite plan of action to implement it. In fact, history shows the contrary. With the disintegration of the Safavid state and its final collapse in the Afghan invasion in 1722, leading mujtahids left Iran for the holy cities in Iraq. They made no attempt to rise in defense of their religion against the invading Sunni Afghans or, later, against the controversial religious policies of Nadir Shah.

26. Ibid., pp. 139, 140, 145.

27. See Eliash, "Ithna Ashari Shi'i Juristic Theory"; and Robert Brunschvig," Les Usuls al-Fiqh Imamites ã leur stade ancien (X^e et XIe siècles)," in *Le Shi'isme Imamite*, Proceedings of the Colloque de Strasbourg, 1970.

28. M. B. al-Khansari, *Rauzat al-janat fi ahwal al-ulama wa al-sadat* (Isfanhan, 1962), pp. 308–52.

29. Hamid Algar, *Religion and State in Iran, 1785–1906: The Role of the Ulama in the Qajar Period* (Berkeley: University of California Press, 1969), pp. 7, 36; G. Scarcia, "Interno alle Controversie tra Ahbari e Usuli presso gli Imamiti di Persia," *Rivista degli Studi Orientali* 3 (1958):223, 237.

30. M. Mudarrisi Chahardihi, *Shaikhigiri va babigiri* (Tehran, 1972), pp. 35–37.

31. Algar, *Religion and State*, p. 8.

32. Ibid., p. 20.

33. G. Scarcia, "Kerman 1905: la 'guerra' tra Seihi e Balasari," *Annali del Instituto Universitario Orientale di Napoli* 13 (1963), p. 200.

34. Henry Corbin, "Imamologie et Philosophie," *Le Shi'isme Imamite*, p. 146.

35. *Al-Hikma al-muta'aliya fi'asfar al-aqliya al-arba'a* (Tehran, 1958), p. 1, p. 8. Hereafter referred to as *Asfar*.

36. Corbin, *En Islam Iranien*, 4:36–46; and by the same author, *Le Livre des Pénétrations Métaphysiques* (Tehran, 1964), p. 12.

37. Fazlur Rahman, *The Philosophy of Mulla Sadra* (Albany: SUNY Press, 1975), p. 4.

38. *Kasr asnam al-jahiliya* (Tehran, 1961).

39. *Sa fasl* (Tehran, 1961), pp. 82–84.

40. Rahman, *The Philosophy,* pp. 9, 13–16.

41. Corbin, *En Islam Iranien,* 4:86.

42. *Kasr asnam,* pp. 132, 133.

43. Rahman, *The Philosophy,* pp. 10, 36.

44. Ibid., pp. 12, 36–37, 97, 115, 117, 206.

45. *Sa fasl,* p. 64; *Asfar,* p. 1, p. 7.

46. Corbin, *En Islam Iranien,* I:89–91.

2—THE RADICALIZATION OF DISSENT IN SHIA THOUGHT: EARLY SHAIKHISM

1. Ahmad Ahsai, *Fihrist-i kutub-i marhum ahmad ahsai va sayir-i mashayikh-i izam* ed. Abul Qasim b. Zain al-Abidin, (Kirman, 1957), pp. 166–79.

2. Henry Corbin, *L'École Shaykhie en Théologie Shi'ite* (Tehran, 1957), p. 14. For a description of his dreams see Shaikh Abdullah, *Risala-yi sharh-i ahval-i shaikh ahmad* (Kirman, 1967), pp. 9–17.

3. Abidin, *Fihrist,* p. 178.

4. Ibid., p. 179.

5. A. L. M. Nicolas, *Essai sur le Sheikhisme* 4 vols. (Paris: Geuthner, 1910), 1:xi, xii.

6. M. Mudarrisi, *Shaikhigiri va babigiri* (Tehran, 1972) p. 30, 48–49.

7. Corbin, *L'École Shaykhie,* pp. 19–20.

8. "Dalil al-mutahhayarin" (Manuscript no. 5161, Tehran University Library).

9. "Dalil"; also cited in Nicolas, *Essai,* 2:12.

10. Nicolas, *Essai,* 2:19.

11. Ibid.

12. Ibid., p. 28.

13. Corbin, *Terre Céleste et Corps de Résurrection* (Paris: Buchet-Chastel, 1961), pp. 14, 129.

14. Ibid., pp. 135, 137, 141. See also Corbin's report in *Annuaire de l'École Pratique des Hautes Études: section des Sciences Religieuses* (Paris, 1967–68), pp. 138–39.

15. M. Baqir Majlisi, *Haqq al-yaqin* (Tehran, 1968), Book VI, pp. 368–534.

16. Corbin, *En Islam Iranien*: aspects spirituels et philosophiques, 4 vols. (Paris: Gallimard, 1971–72), 4:85–116.

17. Rahman, *The Philosophy of Mulla Sadra* (Albany: SUNY Press, 1975) pp. 225, 252, 254.

18. Corbin, *Terre Celeste,* pp. 146–64, 310–31; Nicolas, *Essai,* 3:23–45.

19. Majlisi, *Haqq al-yaqin,* Book VI, pp. 301, 331, 368–83.

20. Corbin, *L'École Shaykhie,* p. 43.

21. Cited in Lambton, "Quis Custodiet Custodes: Some Reflections on the Persian Theory of Government," *Studia Islamica* 5–6 (1956):128.

22. Abdulaziz Sachedina, *Islamic Messianism* (Albany: SUNY Press, 1981), pp. 49–50.

23. See his *Al-Babul-hadi ashar,* trans. W. M. Miller (London: 1928).

24. Rahman, *The Philosophy of Mulla Sadra,* p. 185.

25. Ibid., p. 260.

26. Corbin, *En Islam Iranien,* 4:82.

27. Ibid., pp. 270, 273.

28. Cited in Nicolas, *Essai,* 3:3.

29. "Risala-yi sir va suluk," *Majmua-yi rasail* (Tehran, n.d.), pp. 51, 52; see also Tusi's *Tasawwurat ya rauzat al-taslim,* trans. W. Ivanow (Leiden: Brill, 1950), pp. lxxix–lxxx, 98, 129.

30. Kazim Rashti, "Usul al-din," (manuscript no. 2692, Tehran University Library); Corbin, *En Islam Iranien,* 4:273; Nicolas, *Essai,* 3:3, 5.

31. Nicolas, *Essai,* 3:4, 6.

32. Ibid., pp. 51–57.

33. Rahman, *The Philosophy,* pp. 111–13.

34. Ibid., pp. 128–33, 141–45.

35. Henry Corbin, *Le Livre des Pénétrations Métaphysiques* (Tehran, 1964) p. 48; Nicolas, *Essai,* 3:10; Mudarrisi, *Shaikhigiri,* p. 97.

36. Rahman, *The Philosophy,* p. 141.

37. Corbin, *En Islam Iranien,* 4:209–10, 258.

38. Corbin, *L'École Shaykhie,* p. 5.

39. Abidin, *Fihrist,* p. 127.

40. "Risala-yi fiqhiyya" (Manuscript no. 3993, Tehran University Library).

41. Corbin, *En Islam Iranien,* 4:279.

42. Cited in Nicolas, *Essai,* 3:67.

43. Mudarrisi, *Shaikhigiri,* pp. 45–47, 85–86; Corbin, *En Islam Iranien,* 4:263.

44. Corbin, *L'École Shaykhie,* pp. 14–15.

45. W. Ivanow, *Studies in Early Persian Ismailism* (Leiden: Brill, 1948), pp. 5–8.

46. W. Ivanow, *Kalami Pir: a Treatise on Ismaili Doctrine* (Bombay, 1935), pp. xliii, 21. See also A. M. al-Abd, *al-Insan al-kamil fi fikr ikhwan al-safa* (Cairo, 1976), p. 282.

47. Ivanow, *Kalami Pir,* p. 106.

48. Nicolas, *Essai,* 1:lv, v.

49. Mudarrisi, *Shaikhigiri,* p. 90.

50. Nicolas, *Essai,* 2:39–40.

51. Cited in Nicolas, *Essai,* 2:38–44, 52–55.

52. Ibid., pp. 60–61.

53. Rahman, *The Philosophy,* pp. 169–79, 180–85.

54. Ibid., p. 169.

55. Ibid., pp. 181, 183, 185.

56. Ivanow, *Kalami Pir,* pp. xxxiii, 70.

57. *Fusul* (Tehran, 1956), p. 36.

58. Nicolas, *Essai,* 2:44, 52, 55.

59. Corbin, *Le Livre des Pénétrations Métaphysiques,* p. 47; *L'École Shaykhie,* pp. 3, 6.

60. Abidin, *Fihrist,* pp. 242–52.

61. Mudarrisi, *Shaikhigiri,* pp. 51–52.

3—THE SOCIALIZATION OF DISSENT IN SHIA THOUGHT: KIRMANI SHAIKHISM

1. Murtiza Mudarrisi, *Shaikhigiri va babigiri* (Tehran, 1972) pp. 49–50, 176.

2. Sayyid Muhammad Hashimi, "Mazahib dar kirman," *Mardum Shinasi* 2 (1958).

3. Ahmad Ali Khan Vaziri, *Tarikh-i kirman ya salariyya* (Tehran, n.d.), pp. 346–50. The editor of this volume, Bastani-Parizi, asserts that Mushtaqali Shah's death was solely due to doctrinal disputes.

4. Hamid Algar, "The Revolt of Aqa Khan Mahallati and the Transference of the Ismaili Imamate to India," *Studia Islamica* 29 (1969):74; Firidun Adamiyat, *Amir kabir va iran* (Tehran, 1969), pp. 251–58; Vaziri, *Tarikh-i kirman,* pp. 383–93.

5. Comte Arthur de Gobineau, *Trois Ans en Asie* (Paris: Leroux, 1905), p. 309.

6. E. G. Browne, *A Year amongst the Persians* (Cambridge: Cambridge University Press, 1927), pp. 476, 573.

7. Printed in Abul Qasim b. Zain al-Abidin, *Fihrist-i kutub-i marhum ahmad ahsai va sayir-i mashayikh-i izam* (Kirman, 1957), pp. 76–92.

8. Ibid., p. 78.

9. Shaikh Abdullah, *Tazkirat al-auliya* (Kirman, 1967), pp. 70–72, 74.

10. Hajj Muhammad Karim Khan, *Hidayat al-talibin* (Kirman, 1960), p. 156.

11. Al-Abidin, *Fihrist,* pp. 80–83.

12. Ibid., pp. 84–85.

13. M. Karim Khan, *Hidayat al-talibin,* p. 156; M. H. Hashimi, "Nazari bi intikhabat-i kirman," *Ittihad-i Milli* 322 (1954–55).

14. M. Karim Khan, *Hidayat al-subyan* (Kirman, 1967).

15. Ibid., p. 29.

16. Ibid.

17. Ibid., p. 32.

18. M. Karim Khan, *Hidayat al-talibin,* p. 176.

19. Ibid., p. 175.

20. Ibid., p. 82.

21. Ibid., pp. 174–75.

22. Ibid., pp. 25–26.

23. Ibid., pp. 61–62.

24. Ibid., pp. 105–106.

25. Ibid., pp. 14, 28–29, 74, 86.

26. M. Karim Khan, *Irshad al-awwam*, 4 vols. (Kirman, 1934–36), 3:259–60; vol. 4:53–60, 204–5, 384–86.

27. M. Karim Khan, *Irshad*, 2:4, 43–47, 131–32, 86–87. See also his *Rujum al-shayattin* (Kirman, n.d.), pp. 73–81; and "Dar javab-i sualat-i shaikh muhammad kurdistani," *Majma al-rasail farsi* (Kirman, n.d.).

28. M. Karim Khan, *Irshad*, 1:280–317.

29. M. Karim Khan, *Rujum*, p. 165.

30. M. Karim Khan, *Irshad*, 3:155.

31. Ibid., 1:18–24, 50–51; see also M. Karim Khan, *Si fasl* (Kirman, 1948), p. 23.

32. See, for instance, *Irshad*, 3:239–44, 274–75.

33. Ibid., 1:261.

34. Henry Corbin interprets Karim Khan's view of the ascent of men in metaphysical terms as a purely spiritual venture, a "progressive reversion" back to the point of origin. See *Terre Celeste et Corps de Résurrection* (Paris: Buchet-Chastel, 1961), pp. 356–57; *En Islam Iranien: aspects spirituels et philosophiques*, 4 vols. (Paris: Gallimard, 1971–72), 4:288–89. However, Karim Khan's idea was borrowed from the theosophers, and especially from Mulla Sadra. Mulla Sadra's notion of "substantive change" is definitely conceived as irreversible and evolutionary, oriented toward greater perfection (see chapter one). Moreover, Karim Khan does not discuss the acts of the fall and the ascent as occurring simultaneously, but successively, implying a chronological process in time.

35. *Irshad*, 1:81–82, 164–67, 170–71; 4:44–49.

36. Ibid., 3:3–5, 13, 186–87.

37. Ibid., 3:172–74; 4:52–53, 286–90; idem, *Tir shahab dar radd-i bab khasran maab* (Kirman, n.d.).

38. *Irshad*, 3:14–15.

39. Ibid., 4:288.

40. *Tir shahab*, p. 174.

41. *Irshad*, 3:243.

42. Ibid., 1:136–42; 4:52, 62, 64–66, 290.

43. Ibid., 3:21–28.

44. Ibid., 4:40–51.

45. Ibid., 1:90; 2:201-4; 3:7–10, 14; 4:11–14, 253–57, 269–70.

46. Ibid., 4:17–18.

47. Ibid., pp. 109, 116–38, 166, 174, 258–76, 279–87.

48. Ibid., 1:143–44.

49. Ibid., 4:240, 291–92, 312.

50. *Tir shahab*, p. 176.

51. *Irshad*, 1:53, 194–95.

52. Ibid., pp. 136, 164; 2:179–80; 3:61, 275; 4:19, 43–44, 211.

53. Ibid., 1:9–10.

54. Ibid., 4:20–22.

55. Ibid., pp. 23–25.

56. H. M. Balyuzi, *The Bab* (Oxford: George Ronald, 1973), p. 33.

57. M. Karim Khan, "Nazari."

58. Bastani-Parizi, *Ajdha-yi haft sar* (Tehran, 1973), pp. 191–95.

59. Ibid., p. 191.

60. *Irshad*, 1:156.

61. Ibid., pp. 154–62; 4:141.

62. Ibid., pp. 228–29.

63. See his "Nasiriyya," *Majma al-rasail;* and *Sultaniyya* (Kirman, 1963).

64. M. Karim Khan, *Chahar fasl* (Kirman, n.d.).

65. Ibid., pp. 16–19.

66. Ibid., p. 29.

67. M. Karim Khan, *Rukn-i rabi* (Kirman, 1948); "Dar javab-i sualat-i mulla jamal," *Majma al-rasail.*

68. *Sultaniyya*, pp. 82–83, 148–49, 165, 175–82, 221–31.

69. *Tazkirat al-auliya*, pp. 113–21.

70. *Irshad*, 1:131–32.

71. Ibid., pp. 29–30, 382–83.

72. Ibid., pp. 151–52; 3:180–85, 188–89.

73. Ibid., 2:21–41; 3:213; 4:76; *Rujum*, pp. 32–33; "Nasiriyya," pp. 315–32; *Sultaniyya*, pp. 49–54.

74. *Irshad*, 3:48–59; 4:290; and "Dar javab-i marhum abdulla ali khan," *Majma al-rasail.*

75. *Nasiriyya*, pp. 383, 385–92, 395–96.

4—THE POLITICIZATION OF DISSENT IN SHIA THOUGHT: BABISM

1. He apparently experienced an earlier vision shortly before Rashti's death in January 1844. See Denis MacEoin, "From Shaykhism to Babism: A Study in Charismatic Renewal in Shi'i Islam" (Ph.D. thesis, Cambridge University, 1979), where the author states the important call occurred on May 4, 1844. Yet another source, Moojan Momen, *The Babi and Baha'i Religions, 1844–1944: Some Contemporary Western Accounts* (Oxford: George Ronald, 1981), p. xxviii, explains the Bab first proclaimed himself Bab on May 23, 1844, when he met Bushrui.

2. Cited in Hasan M. Balyuzi, *The Bab* (Oxford: George Ronald, 1973), p. 65. See also Mirza Yahya Nuri Subh-i Azal, "Tarikh-i badi," manuscript in the Babi Collection, Princeton University Library, Princeton, N.J.

3. Lord Curzon, *Persia and the Persian Question*, 2 vols. (London: Longmans, 1892), 1:497, n. 2.

4. A. L. M. Nicolas, *Seyyed Ali Mohammad dit le Bab* (Paris: Geuthner, 1905), pp. 273–76.

5. Mirza Jani, *Kitab Nuqtat al-kaf*, ed. E. G. Browne (Leiden: Brill, 1910), p. 140.

6. "Tarikh-i babiyya," manuscript in the Babi Collection, Princeton University Library, Princeton, N.J.

7. Balyuzi, *The Bab*, pp. 25–26.

8. *A Traveller's Narrative: written to illustrate the episode of the Bab,* trans. E. G. Browne (Cambridge: Cambridge University Press, 1891), p. 309.

9. Nicolas, *Seyyed Ali Mohammad,* pp. 212–13; Balyuzi, *The Bab,* p. 71. See also the Bab's own "Kitab bain al-haramain," manuscript in the Babi Collection, Princeton University Library, Princeton, N.J.

10. Nicolas, *Seyyed Ali Mohammad,* p. 225.

11. Wednesday, November 19, 1845. For the text of the Bab's confession see E. G. Browne, *Materials for the Study of the Babi Religion* (Cambridge: Cambridge University Press, 1918), pp. 256–58.

12. Cited in A. L. M. Nicolas, trans., *Le Beyan Persan,* 2 vols. (Paris: Lerout, 1911), 1:xvii–xxv.

13. Mirza Kazem Beg, "Le Bab et les Babis ou le soulèvement politique et religieux en Perse de 1845 a 1853," *Journal Asiatique* 7 and 8 (1866):382–84, 464–69.

14. Denis MacEoin, "The Concept of Jihad in the Babi and Baha'i Movements" (Paper read at the Third Annual Seminar on Bahai Studies at the University of Lancaster, April 1979), p. 12.

15. "Bayan-i farsi," manuscript in the Babi Collection, Princeton University Library, Gate V, unit 5.

16. Nicolas claims it was Mirza Aqasi who had sent for him (*Seyyed Ali Mohammad,* p. 242).

17. MacEoin, "The Concept of Jihad," p. 12.

18. Balyuzi, *The Bab,* p. 125.

19. MacEoin, "The Concept of Jihad," p. 17.

20. See the Bab's letter addressed to him in E. G. Browne, trans., *Tarikh-i jadid; or New History of Mirza Ali Muhammad the Bab* (Cambridge: Cambridge University Press, 1893), p. 351; also cited in *Nuqtat al-Kaf,* pp. 125–27.

21. *Bayan,* II, 1.

22. *Selections from the Writings of the Bab* (Haifa: Bahai World Center, 1976), pp. 11–17.

23. Ibid., pp. 18–23.

24. Ibid., pp. 24–28.

25. Cited in Kazem Beg, "Le Bab et les Babis," p. 371.

26. Cited in Murtiza Mudarrisi, *Shaikhigiri va babigiri* (Tehran, 1972), pp. 307–17.

27. Balyuzi, *The Bab,* p. 145.

28. *Bayan,* II 1; III 13.

29. A. L. M. Nicolas, trans., *Le Livre des Sept Preuves* (Paris: Leroux, 1902), Proof 4.

30. Ibid., Proof 7; see also *Selections,* p. 139.

31. Nicolas, *Seyyed Ali Mohammad,* p. 219; see also MacEoin, *From Shaykhism,* p. 160.

32. "Sahifa-yi adliyya," manuscript in the Babi Collection, Princeton University Library, Princeton, N.J.

33. Introduction to *Le Livre des Sept Preuves.*

34. *Bayan,* I, 2.

35. Roger Arnaldez, "Insan al-Kamil," *Encyclopedia of Islam,* new edition.

36. *Bayan,* I, 2.

37. Ibid., III, 13.

38. *Le Livre des Sept Preuves,* introduction.

39. *Bayan,* II, 15.

40. Ibid., II, 7.

41. Ibid., I, 1, 15.

42. Ibid., II, 11.

43. Ibid., I, 3, 14.

44. *Bayan,* II, 7.

45. Ibid., II, 8.

46. Ibid., II, 1, 6, 7.

47. Ibid., II, 4, 6, 7.

48. Ibid., III, 8, 15; see also *Selections,* pp. 144–45.

49. *Bayan,* IV, 12, 16.

50. Mikhail S. Ivanov, *The Babi Uprisings of 1848–52* (Moscow: Trudy Instituta Vostokvedeniya 30, 1939).

51. *Bayan,* V, 7.

52. Ibid., III, 1, 12; VII, 13.

53. Ibid., II, 9; III, 16; V, 6.

54. Ibid., IV, 8, 18; V, 7.

55. Ibid., V, 16.

56. Ibid., VI, 9; VII, 13.

57. Ibid., V, 18.

58. Ibid., VIII, 5, 16, 17; IX, 1.

59. Ibid., V, 6.

60. Ibid., V, 19.

61. Ibid., VII, 16.

62. *Selections,* p. 57.

63. *Bayan,* IV, 5; V, 5; *Selections,* pp. 41–43.

64. Kazem Beg, "Le Bab et les Babis," p. 393.

65. E. G. Browne, "The Babis of Persia," *Journal of the Royal Asia Society* 21 (1889):504–5.

66. MacEoin, *From Shaykhism,* p. 202.

67. *Bayan,* V, 7, 14.

68. Balyuzi, *The Bab,* p. 164. The author, however, omits mentioning the real cause of the Babis' alarm; see also MacEoin, *From Shaykhism,* pp. 203–207.

69. MacEoin, *From Shaykhism,* pp. 210, 215.

70. *Tarikh-i jadid,* p. 274; *Nuqtat al-kaf,* p. 142.

71. *Bayan,* IV, 5; VIII, 15.

72. *Tarikh-i jadid,* p. 275; *Nuqtat al-kaf,* p. 142.

73. MacEoin, "The Concept of Jihad," p. 27.

74. *Nuqtat al-kaf,* pp. 144–155. For a Bahai evaluation of this account see Balyuzi, *Edward Granville Browne and the Baha'i Faith* (London: George Ronald, 1970).

75. *Nuqtat al-kaf,* p. 144.

76. Subh-i Azal, quoted by Browne, denied she ever removed her veil. "Sometimes, when carried away by her eloquence, she would allow it to slip down her face, but she would always replace it after a few moments." *Traveller's Narrative*, p. 314.

77. Other Babi eyewitness accounts confirm Jani's report; see MacEoin, "The Concept of Jihad," pp. 27–28.

78. Browne, "The Babis of Persia," p. 502.

79. Nabil Azam, *The Dawnbreakers: Nabil's Narrative of the Early Days of the Bahai Revelation*, trans. and ed. Shoghi Effendi (Wilmette: Bahai Publishing Trust, 1932), p. 298.

80. *Bayan*, VI, 12, VIII, 10, 15.

81. Lisan al-Mulk, *Nasikh al-tawarikh* (Tehran, 1965), vol. 3, p. 239.

82. Mudarrisi, *Shaikhigiri va babigiri*, pp. 142–44, 158–66; *Nuqtat al-kaf*, p. 201. Jani also mentions Hamza's sympathy for the Babis and his categorical refusal to denounce them as heretics, until he was forced to "keep quiet."

83. *Tarikh-i jadid*, pp. 434–41.

84. Balyuzi, *The Bab*, pp. 172, 174, 177, 187.

85. *Tarikh-i jadid*, pp. 45–46.

86. Balyuzi, *The Bab*, p. 56.

87. Nicolas, *Seyyed Ali Mohammad*, p. 301.

88. *Tarikh-i jadid*, pp. 55, 78; *Nuqtat al-kaf*, p. 159.

89. *Nuqtat al-kaf*, pp. 162–63.

90. Cited in Mudarrisi, *Shaikhigiri va babigiri*, pp. 271–72.

91. Nicolas, *Seyyed Ali Mohammad*, p. 320.

92. *Nuqtat al-kaf*, p. 166; see also MacEoin, "The Concept of Jihad," pp. 29–30; *Tarikh-i jadid*, p. 362, appendix 2. The text of *Tarikh-i jadid* includes parts of Quddus's letter to the governor, where he emphasizes the religious rather than political aim of the revolt, and omits the more overt political statements.

93. *Nasikh al-tawarikh*, 3:251.

94. *Nuqtat al-kaf*, pp. 161–62.

95. Abdul Latif Muhammad al-Abd, *al-Insan al-kamil fi fikr al-ikhwan al-safa* (Cairo, 1976), p. 137.

96. Nicolas, *Seyyed Ali Mohammad*, pp. 301–2; Kazem Beg, "Le Bab et les Babis," pp. 490–92.

97. Cited in Mudarrisi, *Shaikhigiri va babigiri*, p. 275.

98. Ibid.; see also Kazem Beg, "Le Bab et les Babis," p. 351.

99. Cited in *Traveller's Narrative*, p. 261.

100. E. G. Browne, "The Babi Insurrection at Zanjan," *Journal of the Royal Asia Society* 29 (1897): 793.

101. Nicolas, *Seyyed Ali Mohammad*, p. 342.

102. *Nuqtat al-kaf*, p. 215.

103. Kazem Beg, "Le Bab et les Babis," pp. 243–47.

104. Moojan Momen, "The Social Basis of the Babi Upheavals (1848–1853): A Preliminary Analysis" (Paper read at the Third Annual Bahai' Studies Seminar, University of Lancaster, April 1979).

105. Cited in Balyuzi, *The Bab*, p. 202.

106. Cited in Nicolas, *Seyyed Ali Mohammad,* p. 375.

107. Arthur Arnold, *Through Persia by Caravan,* 2 vols. (New York: Harper, 1877), 2:279.

108. Cited in *Traveller's Narrative,* p. 120, note 1.

109. *Bayan,* II, 16, 17; III, 16; VII, 10.

110. See one of his works cited in Browne, *Materials for the Study of the Babi Religion,* p. 218; *Nuqtat al-kaf,* pp. 260–261.

111. *Traveller's Narrative,* pp. 49–51.

112. Ibid., p. 328.

113. Some Bahai sources assert that Bahaullah had asked the Bab to designate Subh-i Azal as the "outward" leader, so that he, the "true hidden" successor, would be protected from harm while being seen and known by the faithful: *Traveller's Narrative,* pp. 62–63; see also Mirza Muhammad Javad of Qazvin, "An Epitome of Babi and Bahai History to A.D. 1898," *Materials for the Study of the Babi Religion,* pp. 19–20.

114. M. Momen, *The Babi and Baha'i Religions,* p. xxii.

115. *Tarikh-i jadid,* p. xxi.

116. *Traveller's Narrative,* p. 152.

117. Ibid., p. 114.

118. Ibid., pp. 69, 74, 78.

119. Ibid., pp. 158–164.

5—THE SECULARIZATION OF DISSENT IN SHIA THOUGHT

1. Nikki R. Keddie, An *Islamic Response to Imperialsim: Political and Religious Writings of Sayyid Jamal ad-Din "al-Afghani"* (Berkeley: University of California Press, 1968), p. 29.

2. "Islamic Philosophy in Contemporary Islamic Thought," in Charles Malik, ed., *God and Man in Contemporary Islamic Thought* (Beirut, 1972), p. 104.

3. Sir Hamilton A. R. Gibb, *Modern Trends in Islam* (Chicago: University of Chicago Press, 1947), p. 28.

4. E. Kedourie, *Afghani and Abduh: An Essay on Religious Unbelief and Political Activism in Modern Islam* (London: Frank Cass, 1966), p. 45.

5. "Religion and Irreligion in Early Iranian Nationalism," *Comparative Studies in Society and History* 4 (1962), pp. 265–95.

6. Homa Pakdaman, *Djamal-ed-Din Assad Abadi dit Afghani* (Paris: Maisonneuve et Larose, 1969).

7. "Islamic Philosophy," pp. 104–5.

8. Pakdaman, *Djamal-ed-Din,* pp. 37–38.

9. See Keddie, *Islamic Response,* pp. 13–14.

10. Pakdaman paraphrases a Muslim's refutation of the lecture in *Djamal-ed-Din,* p. 47.

11. "Tafsir-i muffasir," *Maqalat-i jamaliyya* (Tehran, 1933), p. 99; English translation in Keddie, *Islamic Response,* pp. 215, 172.

12. Keddie, *Islamic Response*, pp. 172, 182, 183–4, 187.

13. Ibid., pp. 182–83.

14. "Dar talim va taalum," *Maqalat*, pp. 88–96; *Islamic Response*, p. 107.

15. Ibid.

16. "Favaid-i falsafa," *Maqalat*, pp. 134–48; *Islamic Response*, pp. 113–14.

17. "Dar talim va taallum." See also "Dar talim va tarbiyyat," *Maqalat*, pp. 113–19.

18. "Answer to Renan," *Islamic Response*, p. 187.

19. Hamid Algar, *Mirza Malkum Khan: a Biographical Study of Iranian Modernism* (Berkeley: University of California Press, 1973), p. 229.

20. M. Tabatabai, *Majmua-yi athar-i mirza malkum khan* (Tehran, 1948), p. 103.

21. "Tarikh-i babiyya," manuscript in the Babi Collection, Princeton University Library, Princeton, N.J.

22. "A Talk with a Persian Statesman," *Contemporary Review* (London, July 1896): 73–77.

23. Wilfred S. Blunt, *A Secret History of the English Occupation of Egypt* (London: Unwin, 1907), pp. 82–87.

24. As he himself complained in *Qanun*, no. 11, 1890.

25. Akhundzada's report of his conversation with Malkum Khan, H. Muhammadzada, ed., *Mirza Fathali Akhundov: alifba-yi jadid va maktubat* (Baku, 1963), p. 292 (hereafter *Maktubat*).

26. Arthur de Gobineau, *Religious et philosophie dans l'Asie Centrale* (Paris, 1865), p. 306.

27. See Algar, *Mirza Malkum Khan*, chapter 2.

28. "Risala-yi faramushkhana," cited in Homa Natiq, *Az mast ka bar mast* (Tehran, 1975), pp. 175–76.

29. "Sayyahi guyad," H. Rabizada ed., *Kulliyat-i Malkum Khan* (Tehran, 1936), pp. 187–212; English translation in Algar, *Mirza Malkum Khan*, pp. 278–99.

30. Tabatabai, "Kitabcha-yi ghaibi," *Majmua-yi athar*, p. 8.

31. Firidun Adamiyat, *Fikr-i azadi dar iran* (Tehran, 1951), p. 216.

32. Ibid, pp. 104, 201.

33. Letter to Mirza Yusif Khan, Dec. 17, 1870, *Maktubat*, pp. 183–87.

34. Firidun Adamiyat, *Andishaha-yi Mirza Fathali Akhundzada* (Tehran, 1970), pp. 259–64; see also introduction to H. Muhammadzada, ed., *Maqalat-i farsi* (Tehran, 1976).

35. *Maktubat*, pp. 174–85.

36. Letter to Mirza Jafar Khan, March 25, 1871, *Maktubat*, pp. 206–10.

37. Cited in Hamid Algar, "Malkum Khan, Akhundzada and the Proposed Reform of the Arabic Alphabet," *Middle Eastern Studies* 5 (1969):122.

38. "Sa Maktub," manuscript in the Milli Librari, Tehran, p. 83.

39. *Maktubat*, p. 31.

40. Algar, *Mirza Malkum Khan*, p. 81.

41. Cited in H. Sadiq, ed., *Maqalat-i falsafi* (Tabriz, 1978), p. 70.

42. Letter to Minister of Sciences, September 1868, *Maktabut*, pp. 131–32.

43. "Sa Maktub," pp. 142, 154, 167.

44. Ibid., pp. 142–43.

45. *Masalik al-muhsinin* (Tehran, 1968), p. 150; *Masail al-hayat* (Tiflis, 1906), pp. 35, 41.

46. *Masalik,* pp. 183–84.

47. Ibid., pp. 94–95.

48. Ibid., p. 99.

49. "Sad khitaba," Browne Collection, Cambridge University Library, letter 7; see also letters 25, 37.

50. "Sa Maktub" (not to be confused with Akhundzada's essay of the same title), manuscript owned by Professor Nikki R. Keddie, University of California at Los Angeles, p. 74.

51. "Sad khitaba," letters 6, 7, 8.

52. Kirmani "Sa Maktub," p. 24.

53. "Hikmat-i nazari," manuscript owned by Mr. Ali Muhammad Qasimi, Tehran, folio 87.

54. "Sad khitaba," letter 17.

55. Ibid., letter 18.

56. Kirmani, "Sa Maktub," p. 45.

57. "Sad khitaba," letter 27.

58. Kirmani, "Sa Maktub," p. 80.

59. "Sad khitaba," letter 31.

60. Ibid., letter 15; Kirmani, "Sa Maktub," pp. 24–26.

61. Kirmani, "Sa Maktub," pp. 88, 74.

62. "Sad khitaba," letter 37; see also letter 24; and Kirmani, "Sa Maktub," pp. 29, 30, 53.

63. "Risala-yi insha allah masha allah," manuscript in the Browne Collection, Cambridge University Library.

64. *Hasht Bihisht* (Tehran, n. d.).

65. *Qahvakhana-yi surat, ya haftad va dau millat* (Tehran, 1969), pp. 33–34.

66. Tabatabai, *Majmua-yi athar,* p. 99.

67. Cited in Adamiyat, *Fikr-i azadi,* p. 126.

68. In a letter to the minister of sciences, Sept. 1868, *Maktubat,* pp. 25–26.

69. "Sad khitaba", letter 39.

70. *Masalik,* p. 181.

71. Kirmani, "Sa Maktub," p. 71.

72. Letter to Yusif Khan, March 25, 1871, *Maktubat,* p. 201.

73. *Kitab-i Ahmad* (Istanbul, 1893), pp. 3, 10, 11.

74. *Masalik,* p. 186.

75. Letter to Hajj Shaikh Muhsin Khan, Feb. 1869, *Maktubat,* p. 139.

76. Letter to Yusif Khan, March 1871, ibid., pp. 199–200.

77. N.d., ibid., p. 310.

78. *Maqalat-i falsafi,* pp. 33–40.

79. *Masail,* pp. 72, 117, 118.

80. *Hasht Bihisht,* pp. 267–68.

81. Letter to Manikji, July 29, 1871, *Maktubat,* pp. 249–51.

82. See Mangol Bayat, "Mirza Aga Khan Kirmani: A Nineteenth Century Persian Nationalist," *Middle Eastern Studies* 10 (1974).

83. Cited in E. G. Browne, *Modern Press and Poetry in Persia* (Cambridge: Cambridge University Press, 1924), pp. xxxiv.

84. "Sa Maktub," p. 88; see also *Ayin-iskandari* (Tehran, 1947), p. 165.

85. Letter to Jalal al-Din Mirza, May 20, 1871, *Maktubat,* pp. 220–23.

86. Kirmani, "Sa Maktub," pp. 90, 98–99; *Hasht Bihisht,* p. 154.

87. F. Adamiyat, "Andishaha-yi Talibov," *Sukhan* 16 (1966):692, 817.

88. *Islamic Response,* p. 173, n. 24; see also his "Chira islam zaif shuda," *Maqalat,* pp. 164–72.

89. "Answer to Renan," *Islamic Response,* p. 182.

6—CONCLUSION: THE TRIUMPH OF SECULARISM

1. Cited in E. G. Browne, *Materials for the Study of the Babi Religion* (Cambridge: Cambridge University Press, 1918), p. 293.

2. "Religion and Irreligion in Early Iranian Nationalism," *Comparative Studies in Society and History* 4 (1962):265–95.

3. E. G. Browne, "The Babis of Persia," *Journal of the Royal Asia Society* 21 (1889):519.

4. Ibid., p. 499.

5. Browne, *Materials,* p. 212.

6. Browne, "The Babis of Persia," p. 883.

7. "Tarikh-i babiyya," manuscript in the Babi Collection, Princeton University Library, Princeton, N.J.; see also Browne, *Materials,* p. 312.

8. For a detailed account of this dispute, and further events related to the Shaikhis, see Muhammad Hashimi Kirmani, "Nazari bi ikhtilaf va intikhabat-i kirman," *Ittihad-i Milli* 11 (1954–55):320–66.

9. Ibid., no. 327.

10. Murtiza Mudarrisi, *Shaikhigiri va babigiri* (Tehran, 1972), pp. 202–7.

11. See Nazim al-Islam, *Tarikh-i bidari-yi Iraniyan,* 2 vols. (Tehran, 1967), 1:100–16.

12. "Nazari," no. 352–56.

13. See Muhammad Ali Jamalzada, "Tarjuma-yi hal-i Sayyid Jamal-al-Din Vaiz," *Yaghma* 3 (1950–51).

14. Firidun Adamiyat, *Andishaha-yi taraqi va huKumat-i qanun: asr-i Sipahsalar* (Tehran, 1972), pp. 68, 70, 71.

15. Cited in Hamid Algar, *Religion and State in Iran, 1785–1906: The Role of the Ulama in the Qajar Period* (Berkeley: University of California Press, 1969), pp. 199–200.

16. *Tarikh-i bidari,* I:19.

17. Ibid.

18. Ibid., p. 23.

19. Ibid, p. 62.

20. Ibid., pp. 46–47.

21. Cited in Firidun Adamiyat, "Andishaha-yi talibov," *Sukhan* 16 (1966):816.

Bibliography

Abd, Abdul Latif Muhammad al-. *Al-insan al-kamil fi fikr ikhwan al-safa* [The Perfect Man in the Thought of the Brethren of Purity]. Cairo, 1976.

Adamiyat, Firidun. *Afkar-i ijtimai va siyasi va iqtisadi dar athar muntashir nashuda-yi dauran-i qajar* [Social, Political, and Economic Ideas in Unpublished Documents of the Qajar Period]. Tehran, 1977.

———. *Amir kabir va iran* [Amir Kabir and Iran]. Tehran, 1969.

———. *Andishaha-yi mirza aqa khan kirmani* [The Thought of Mirza Aqa Khan Kirmani]. Tehran, 1967.

———. *Andishaha-yi mirza fathali akhundzada* [The Thought of Mirza Fathali Akhundzada]. Tehran, 1970.

———. "Andishaha-yi talibov" [The Thought of Talibov (Talibzada)]. *Sukhan* 16 (1966):454–64, 549–63, 691–701, 815–35.

———. *Andishaha-yi taraqi va hukumat-qanum: asr-i sipahsalar* [Progressive Thought and the Rule of Law: The Sipahsalar Period]. Tehran, 1972.

———. *Fikr-i azadi dar iran* [The Idea of Freedom in Iran]. Tehran, 1961.

———. *Idiulugi-yi nihzat-i mashrutiyyat-i iran* [The Ideology of the Constitutional Movement in Iran]. Tehran, 1976.

Abdullah, Shaikh. *Risala-yi sharh-i ahval-i shaikh ahmad* [Biographical Essay of Shaikh Ahmad]. Kirman, 1967.

———. *Tazkirat al-auliya* [A Biography of Leaders]. Kirman, 1967.

Afghani, al-, Sayyid Jamal al-Din Asadabadi known as. *Maqalat-i jamaliyya* [Jamal's Essays]. Tehran, 1933.

Afshar, Iraj, ed. *Majmua-yi asnad va madarik chap nashuda dar bara-yi sayyid jamal al-din mashhur bi afghani* [Collected Unpublished Documents on al-Afghani]. Tehran, 1963.

213

———. "Talibov" [Talibov (Talibzada)]. Yaghma 4 (1951) 214–21.

Akhundzada, Fathali. Alifba-yi jadid va maktubat [A New Alphabet and Letters]. Edited by H. Muhammadzada. Baku, 1963.

———. Maqalat-i falsafi [Philosphical Essays]. Edited by H. Sadiq. Tabriz, 1978.

———. Maqalat-i farsi [Persian Essays]. Edited by H. Muhammadzada. Tehran, 1976.

Algar, Hamid. "Malkum Khan, Akhundzada and the Proposed Reform of the Arabic Alphabet." Middle Eastern Studies 5 (1969):116–30.

———. Mirza Malkum Khan: A Biographical Study in Iranian Modernism. Berkeley: University of California Press, 1973.

———. Religion and State in Iran, 1785–1906: The Role of the Ulama in the Qajar Period. Berkeley: University of California Press, 1969.

———. "The Revolt of Aqa Khan Mahallati and the Transference of the Ismaili Imamate to India." Studia Islamica 29 (1969):55–81.

Arjomand, Said Amir. "Religion and Political Action and Legitimate Domination in Shi'ite Iran: Fourteenth to Eighteenth Centuries A.D." European Journal of Sociology (France) 20 (1979):59–109.

Arnaldez, Roger. "Insan al-kamil." Encyclopedia of Islam, 2nd. ed.

Arnold, Arthur. Through Persia by Caravan. New York: Harper, 1877.

Aubin, Jean. "La Politique Religieuse des Safavides." In Le Shi'isme Imamite. Paris, 1970.

Bab, Mirza Ali Muhammad known as the. "Bayan-i farsi" [Persian Bayan]. Manuscript in the Babi Collection, Princeton University Library, Princeton, N.J.

———. "Kitab bain al-haramain" [The Book of Bain al-Haramain]. Manuscript in the Babi Collection, Princeton University Library, Princeton, N.J.

———. "Sahifa-yi adliyya" [Essay on Justice]. Manuscript in the Babi Collection, Princeton University Library, Princeton, N.J.

———. Selections from the Writings of the Bab. Haifa: Baha'i World Center, 1976.

Balyuzi, H. M. The Bab. Oxford: George Ronald, 1973.

———. Edward Granville Browne and the Baha'i Faith. London: George Ronald, 1970.

Bastani-Parizi, M. Ajdaha-yi haft sar [The Dragons of Haft Sar.]. Tehran, 1973.

Bausani, Alessandro. "Religion in the Seljuq Period." The Cambridge History of Iran, edited by J. A. Boyle. Cambridge: Cambridge University Press, 1968. Vol. 5.

———. "Religion Under the Mongols." The Cambridge History of Iran, edited by J. A. Boyle. Cambridge: Cambridge University Press, 1968. Vol. 5.

Bayat, Mangol. "Continuity and Change in Modern Iranian Thought." In *Modern Iran: The Dialectics of Continuity and Change,* edited by Michael Bonine and Nikki R. Keddie. Albany: SUNY Press, 1981.

——. "Islam in Pahlavi and Post-Pahlavi Iran: A Cultural Revolution?" In *Islam and Development: Religion and Sociopolitical Change,* edited by John L. Esposito. Syracuse: Syracuse University Press, 1980.

——. "Mirza Aqa Khan Kirmani: A Nineteenth Century Persian Nationalist." *Middle Eastern Studies* 10 (1974):36–59.

——. "A Phoenix Too Frequent: The Concept of Historical Continuity in Modern Iranian Thought." *Asian and African Studies* 12 (1978):203–20.

——. "Religion and Government in the Thought of Mirza Aqa Khan Kirmani." *International Journal of Middle Eastern Studies* 5 (1974):381–400.

——. "Shi'ism in Contemporary Iranian Politics." In *Towards a Modern Iran,* edited by Sylvia Haim and Elie Kedourie. London: Frank Cass, 1981.

Blunt, Wilfrid S. *A Secret History of the English Occupation of Egypt.* London: Unwin, 1907.

Browne, Edward G. "The Babi Insurrection at Zanjan." *Journal of the Royal Asiatic Society* 29 (1897):761–827.

——. "The Babis of Persia." *Journal of the Royal Asiatic Society* 21 (1889):485–526 and 881–1009.

——. *Materials for the Study of the Babi Religion.* Cambridge: Cambridge University Press, 1918.

——. *Modern Press and Poetry in Persia.* Cambridge: Cambridge University Press, 1924.

——. *The Persian Revolution of 1905–06.* Cambridge: Cambridge University Press, 1910.

——. *A Year Amongst the Persians.* Cambridge: Cambridge University Press, 1927.

——, trans. *Tarikh-i jadid or New History of Mirza Ali Muhammad the Bab.* Cambridge: Cambridge University Press, 1893.

——, trans. *A Traveller's Narrative Written to Illustrate the Episode of the Bab.* Cambridge: Cambridge University Press, 1891.

Brunschvig, R. "Les Usuls al-Fiqh Imamites à leur Stade Ancien." In *Le Shi'isme Imamite.* Paris, 1970.

Corbin, Henry. "Le Combat Spirituel du Shi'isme." *Eranos-Jahrbuch* (Zurich) 30 (1961):69–125.

——. *L'École Shaykhie en Théologie Shi'ite.* Tehran, 1957.

——. *En Islam Iranien: aspects spirituels et philosophiques.* 4 vols. Paris: Gallimard, 1971.

——. "Imamologie et Philosophie." In *Le Shi'isme Imamite.* Paris, 1970.

——. "Pour une Morphologie de la Spiritualité Shi'ite." *Eranos-Jahrbuch* (Zurich) 29 (1960):57–107.

——. Reports in *Annuaire de l'École Pratique des Hautes Études: section des Sciences Religieuses.* Paris (1967–68):138–45; (1968–69):148–55; (1969–70):233–47.

——. *Terre Céleste et Corps de Resurrection.* Paris: Buchet-Chastel, 1961.

Curzon, George N. *Persia and the Persian Question.* 2 vols. London: Longmans, 1892.

Danish-Pujuh, Taqi. "Guftari az khaja tusi ba ravish-i batiniyyan" [An Essay by Tusi Written in the Style of the Ismailis]. *Majala-yi danishkada-yi adabiyyat-i danishgah-i tehran* (3 (1957):82–88.

Eliash, Joseph. "Ithna Ashari Shi'i Juristic Theory of Political and Legal Authority." *Studia Islamica* 29 (1969):17–30.

Gibb, Sir Hamilton A. R. *Modern Trends in Islam.* Chicago: University of Chicago Press, 1947.

Gobineau, Arthur de. *Religions et Philosophies dans l'Asie Centrale.* Paris: Didier, 1865.

——. *Trois Ans en Asie.* Paris: Leroux, 1905.

Hashimi Kirmani, Sayyid Muhammad. "Mazahib dar kirman" [Religions in Kirman]. *Mardum shinasi* 1 (1956):97–104 and 122–33.

——. "Nazari bi intikhabat-i kirman" [A Look on the Elections in Kirman]. *Ittihad-i Milli* 11 (1954–55).

——. "Taifa-yi shaikhiyya" [The Shaikhi School]. *Mardum shinasi* 2 (1958):238–54 and 348–61.

Hilli, Ibn al-Mutahhar Hasan b. Yusuf al-. *Al-bab'l hadi ashar: A Treatise on the Principles of the Shi'ite theology.* Translated by William M. Miller. London: Royal Asiatic Society, 1928.

Hodgson, Marshall G. S. "Batiniyya." *Encyclopedia of Islam,* 2nd. ed.

——. "How Did the Early Shi'i Become Sectarian?" *Journal of the American Oriental Society* 75 (1955):1–13.

———. "The Ismaili State." *The Cambridge History of Iran,* edited by J. A. Boyle. Cambridge: Cambridge University Press, 1968. Vol. 5.

———. *The Venture of Islam.* 3 vols. Chicago: University of Chicago Press, 1974.

Hourani, Albert. *Arabic Thought in the Liberal Age.* Oxford: Oxford University Press, 1962.

Ibrahimi, Abu al-Qasim. *Fihrist-i kutub-i marhum ahmad-i ahsai va sayir-i mashayikh-i azam* [A Bibliography of the Works of the Late Shaikh Ahmad Ahsai and of All the Great Shaikhs]. 2 vols. in 1. Kirman, 1957.

Ivanov, Mikhail. *Babidskie Vosstaniya Irane (1848–52) The Babi Uprisings of 1848– 52* (in Russian). Moscow: Trudy Instituta Vostokvedeniya 30 (1939).

Ivanow, W. *Brief Survey of the Evolution of Ismailism.* Bombay, 1952.

———. *Kalami Pir: A Treatise on Ismaili Doctrine.* Bombay, 1935.

———. *Studies in Early Persian Ismailism.* Leiden: Brill, 1948.

———. *Two Early Ismaili Treatises.* Bombay, 1933.

Jafri, Husain M. *The Origins and Early Development of Shi'a Islam.* London: Longmans, 1978.

Jamalzada, Muhammad Ali. "Tarjuma-yi hal-i sayyid jamal al-din vaiz" [A Biography of Sayyid Jamal al-Din Vaiz]. *Yaghma* 3 (1950–51):118–23, 163–70, 394–401.

Jani, Mirza. *Kitab nuqtat al-kaf* [The Book of the K Point]. Translated by E. G. Browne. Leiden: Brill, 1910.

Jolivet, Jean. *L'Intellect selon Kindi.* Leiden: Brill, 1971.

Katirai, M. *Framasunri dar iran* [Freemasonry in Iran]. Tehran, 1968.

Kazem Beg, Mirza Aleksandr. "Le Bab et les Babis ou le Soulèvement Politique et Religieux en Perse de 1845 à 1853." *Journal Asiatique* (Paris):7, 8 (1866):329–84 and 457–522; 196–252, 357–400 and 473–507.

Keddie, Nikki R. *Islamic Response to Imperialism: Political and Religious Writings of Sayyid Jamal al-Din "al-Afghani."* Berkeley: University of California Press, 1969.

———. "Religion and Irreligion in Early Iranian Nationalism." *Comparative Studies in Society and History* 4 (1962):265–95.

———. *Religion and Rebellion in Iran: The Tobacco Protest of 1891–92.* London: Frank Cass, 1966.

——. *Sayyid Jamal al-Din "al-Afghani": A Political Biography*. Berkeley: University of California Press, 1972.

Khansari, Muhammad Baqir. *Rauzat al-janat fi ahwal al-ulama wa al-Sadat* [The Gardens of Paradise]. 5 vols. Isfahan, 1962.

Kirmani, Mirza Aqa Khan. *Ayin-i skandari* [The Creed of Alexander]. Tehran, 1947.

——. *Hasht bihisht* [Eighth Paradise]. Tehran, 1958.

——. "Hikmat-i nazari" [Metaphysics]. Manuscript owned by Mr. Ali Muhammad Qasimi, Tehran.

——. "Kitab-i rihan" [The Book of Sweet Fragrance]. Manuscript owned by the late Professor Mujtaba Minuvi, Tehran.

——. "Kitab-i rizvan" [The Book of Paradise]. Manuscript owned by the late Professor Mujtaba Minuvi, Tehran.

——. *Qahva khana-yi surat ya haftad va dau millat* [The Coffehouse of Surat or Seventy-two Nations]. Tehran, 1969.

——. "Risala-yi insha allah masha allah" [Essay on "God Willing"]. Manuscript in the E. G. Browne Collection, Cambridge University Library, Cambridge, England.

——. "Sa maktub" [Three letters]. Manuscript owned by Professor Nikki R. Keddie, University of California at Los Angeles.

——. "Sad khitaba" [One Hundred Epistles]. Manuscript in the E. G. Browne Collection, Cambridge University Library, Cambridge, England.

——. *Salarnama* [Epic of the Leader]. Tehran, 1937.

——. "Takvin va tashri" [Book of Genesis and Revelations]. Manuscript owned by Mr. Ali Muhammad Qasimi, Tehran.

Kirmani, Muhammad Karim Khan. *Chahar fasl* [Four Essays]. Kirman, n.d.

——. *Hidayat al-subyan* [A Guide for Young Men]. Kirman, 1967.

——. *Hidayat al-talibin* [A Guide for Pupils]. Kirman, 1960.

——. *Irshad al-awwam* [A Guide for the Common People]. 4 vols. in 2. Kirman, 1934–36.

——. *Majma al-rasail-i farsi* [Collected Persian Essays]. 3 vols. in 1. Kirman, 1967–69.

——. *Rajum al-shayattin* [Killing the Devils]. Kirman, n.d.

——. *Rukn-i rabi* [The Fourth Pillar.]. Kirman, 1948.

——. *Si fasl* [Thirty Essays]. Kirman, 1949.

——. *Sultaniyya* [Royal Essay]. Kirman, 1963.

——. *Tir shahab dar radd-i bab khasran maab* [A Refutation of the Bab]. Kirman, n.d.

Kirmani, Shaikh Yahya Ahmad. *Farmandahan-i kirman* [The Governors of Kirman]. Tehran, n.d.

Lambton, Ann K. S. "Justice in the Medieval Persian Theory of Kingship." *Studia Islamica* 27 (1962):91–119.

——. "Quis Custodiet Custodes: Some Reflections on the Persian Theory of Government." *Studia Islamica* 5–6 (1955–56):125–48.

——. "The Secret Societies and the Persian Revolution of 1905–06." *St. Antony's Papers* 4 (1958):43–60.

——. "Some New Trends in Islamic Political Thought in Late Eighteenth–Early Nineteenth Century Persia." *Studia Islamica* 34 (1974):95–128.

——. *State and Government in Medieval Islam: An Introduction to the Study of Islamic Political Theory: The Jurists.* Oxford: Oxford University Press, 1981.

——. "The Theory of Kingship in the Nasihat al-Muluk of Ghazali." *Islamic Quarterly* 1 (1954):47–55.

Landau, Rom. *The Philosophy of Ibn Arabi.* London: Allen and Unwin, 1959.

MacEoin, Denis M. "From Shaykhism to Babism: A Study in Charismatic Renewal in Shi'i Islam." Ph.D. thesis, Cambridge University, 1979.

Madelung, W. "The Assumption of the Title of Shahanshah by the Buyids and the Reign of the Daylam." *Journal of Near Eastern Studies* 28 (1969):84–108.

——. "Ismailiyya." *Encyclopedia of Islam,* 2nd. ed.

——. "A Treatise of the Sharif al-Murtaza on the Legality of Working for the Government." *Bulletin of the School of Oriental and African Studies* (London) 43 (1980):18–31.

Mahdi, Muhsin. *Alfarabi's Philosophy of Plato and Aristotle.* New York: Free Press of Glencoe, 1962.

——. *Ibn Khaldun's Philosophy of History.* Chicago: University of Chicago Press, 1964.

——. "Islamic Philosophy in Contemporary Islamic Thought." In *God and Man in Contemporary Islamic Thought,* edited by Charles Malik. Beirut: American University of Beirut Press, 1972.

Majd al-Islam, Ahmad. *Tarikh-i inhilal-i majlis* [A History of the Fall of the National Assembly]. Isfahan, 1972.

Majlisi, Muhammad Baqir. *Haqq al-yaqin* [The Certain Truth]. Tehran, 1968.

Malikzada, Mihdi. *Tarikh-i inqilab-i mashrutiyyat-i iran* [A History of the Constitutional Revolution in Iran.]. 6 vols. Tehran, 1948–49.

——. *Zindigani-yi malik al-mutakallimin* [The Life of Malik al-Mutakallimin]. Tehran, n.d.

Malkum Khan, Mirza. *Kulliyat-i malkum khan* [The Complete Works of Malkum Khan]. Edited by H. Rabizada. Tehran, 1936.

————. *Majmua-yi athar-i mirza malkum khan* [Collected Works of Malkum Khan]. Edited by M. Tabatabai. Tehran, 1948.

————. "Usul-i taraqi" [The Principles of Progress]. Edited by Fikidun Adamiyat. *Sukhan* 16 (1966):70–73, 131–35, 250–54, 406–14, 481–89, 622–30.

Marquet, Yves. "Ikhwan al-Safa." *Encyclopedia of Islam*, 2nd. ed.

Mazzaoui, Michel. *The Origins of the Safavids*. Wiesbaden, 1972.

Minorski, Vladimir, trans. and ed. *Tadhkirat al-Muluk: A Manual of Safavid Administration*. London: Luzac, 1943.

Momen, Moojan, ed. *The Babi and Baha'i Religions, 1844–1944: Some Contemporary Western Accounts*. Oxford: George Ronald, 1981.

Morris, James Winston, trans. *The Wisdom of the Throne: An Introduction to the Philosophy of Mulla Sadra*. Princeton: Princeton University Press, 1981.

Mudarrisi Chahardihi, Murtiza. *Shaikhigari va babigari* [Shaikhism and Babism]. Tehran, 1972.

————, ed. *Sarguzasht va aqaid-i khaja tusi* [Life and Thought of Tusi]. Tehran, 1956.

————, ed. *Tahqiq dar bara-yi daura-yi ilkhanan-i iran* [A Research Study on the Period of the Ilkhans in Iran.] Tehran, 1963.

Nafisi, Said. *Tarikh-i ijtimai va siyasi-yi iran dar daura-yi muasir* [A Social and Political History of Iran in Modern Times]. 2 vols. Tehran, 1965.

Nasafi, Aziz al-Din. *Kitab al-insan al-kamil* [The Book of the Perfect Man]. Edited by M. Molé. Tehran, 1962.

Navai, Abdul Husain. *Fitna-yi bab* [The Revolt of the Bab]. Tehran, 1972.

————. "Hajj muhammad karim khan kirmani" [Hajj Muhammad Karim Khan Kirmani]. *Yadigar* 4, 5 (1949–50):62–73; 106–118.

Nazim al-Islam Kirmani. *Tarikh-i bidari-yi iraniyan* [The History of the Iranian Awakening]. 2 vols. Tehran, 1967.

Nicholson, Reynold A. *Studies in Islamic Mysticism*. Cambridge: Cambridge University Press, 1922.

Nicolas, A. L. M. *Essai sur le Sheikhisme*. 4 vols. Paris: Geuthner, 1910.

————. *Seyyed Ali Mohammad dit le Bab*. Paris: Geuthner, 1905.

————, trans. *Le Beyan Persan*. 2 vols. Paris: Leroux, 1911.

————, trans. *Le Livre des Sept Preuves*. Paris: Leroux, 1902.

Nurai, Firishta. *Tahqiq dar afkar-i mirza malkum khan nazim al-daula* [A Study on the Thought of Mirza Malkum Khan]. Tehran, 1973.

Pakdaman Natiq, Homa. *Az mast ka bar mast* [We Get What We Deserve]. Tehran, 1975.

——. *Djmal-ed-Din Assad Abadi dit Afghani*. Paris: Maisonneuve et Larose, 1969.

Rafati, Vahid. "The Development of Shaykhi Thought in Shi'i Islam." Ph.D. dissertation. University of California at Los Angeles, 1979.

Rahman, Fazlur. *The Philosophy of Mulla Sadra*. Albany: SUNY Press, 1975.

Rain, Ismail. *Faramushkhana va framasunri dar iran* [The House of Oblivion and Freemasonry in Iran]. Tehran, 1969.

——. *Mirza malkum khan* [Mirza Malkum Khan]. Tehran, 1971.

Rashti, Kazim. "Dalil al-mutahhayirin" [A Proof for the Confused]. Manuscript no. 5161, Tehran University Central Library.

——. "Risala-yi fiqhiyya" [An Essay on Jurisprudence]. Manuscript no. 3993, Tehran University Central Library.

——. "Usul al-din" [The Principles of Religion]. Manuscript no. 2693, Tehran University Central Library.

Sachedina, Abdulaziz. *Islamic Messianism: The Idea of the Mahdi in Twelver Shi'ism*. Albany: SUNY Press, 1981.

Sadra, Sadruddin Muhammad b. Ibrahim Shirazi known as Mulla. *Al-hikma al-muta'aliya fi'l-asfar al-aqliya al-arba'a* [The Transcendent Philosophy of the Four Journeys of the Intellect]. Edited by M. H. Tabatabai. Tehran, 1958.

——. *Kasr asnam al-jahiliyya* [The Destruction of the idols of Ignorance]. Edited by M. T. Danish-Pujuh. Tehran, 1961.

——. *Le Livre des Pénétrations Metaphysiques*. Edited and translated by Henri Corbin. Tehran, 1964.

——. *Sa fasl* [Three Essays]. Edited by H. Nasr. Tehran, 1961.

Safai, Ibrahim. *Asnad-i siyasi dauran-i qajariya* [Political Documents of the Qajar Period]. Tehran, 1967.

——. *Rahbaran-i mashruta* [The Leaders of the Constitutional Revolution]. Tehran, 1965.

Scarcia, Gianroberto. "Interno alle Controversie tra Ahbari e Usuli presso gli Imamiti di Persia." *Revista degli Studi Orientali* 33 (1958):211–50.

——. "Kerman 1905: la guerra tra seihi e balasari." *Annali del Instituto Universitario Orientale di Napoli* 13 (1963):186–203.

Shoghi Effendi, ed. and trans. *The Dawnbreakers: Nabil's Narrative of the Early Days of the Bahai Revelation.* Wilmette, Ill.: Bahai Publishing Trust, 1932.

Sipihr, Muhammad Taqi, known as Lisan al-Mulk. *Nasikh al-tawarikh* [The Abrogator of All Histories]. Tehran, 1965.

Subh-i Azal, Mirza Yahya Nuri, known as. "Tarikh-i badi" [History of the Novel (Revelation)]. Manuscript in the Babi Collection, Princeton University Library, Princeton, N.J.

Tabatabai, Muhammad Husain. "Sadr al-din muhammad b. ibrahim-i shirazi mujaddad-i islami dar qarn-i yazdah hijri" [Sadr al-Din Muhammad b. Ibrahim-i Shirazi: The Muslim Renewer of the Eleventh Islamic Century]. *Yadnama-yi mulla sadra.* Tehran, 1961.

Talibzada (Talibov), Abdul Rahim. *Idhahat* [Sacrifices]. Cairo, 1906.

——. *Kitab-i ahmad* [The Book of Ahmad]. Istanbul, 1893.

——. *Masail al-hayat* [Issues of Life]. Tiflis, 1906.

——. *Masalik al-muhsinin* [The Principles of the Beneficents]. Cairo, 1905.

"Tarikh-i babiyya" [History of Babism]. Manuscript in the Babi Collection, Princeton University Library, Princeton, N.J.

Tunkabuni, Muhammad b. Sulaiman. *Qisas al-ulama* [The History of the Ulama]. Tehran, 1887.

Tusi, Nasir al-Din. *Majmua-yi rasa'il* [Collected Essays]. Tehran, n.d.

——. *The Nasirean Ethics.* Translated by G. M. Wickens. London: Allen and Unwin, 1964.

——. *Tasawwurat ya rauzat al-taslim* [Imaginative conceptions or the Gardens of Submission]. Edited and translated by W. Ivanow. Leiden: Brill, 1950.

——. *Yadnama-yi khaja tusi* [Tusi Memorial Book]. Tehran, 1957.

Vasiqi, Sadr. *Sayyid jamal al-din husaini: payiguzar-i nihzatha-yi islami* [Sayyid Jamal al-Din Husaini: The Founder of the Islamic Movement]. Tehran, 1969.

Vaziri, Ahmad Ali Khan. *Tarikh-i kirman ya salariyya* [History of Kirman]. Tehran, n.d.

Watt, Montgomery, "The Reappraisal of Abbasid Shi'ism." In *Arabic and Islamic Studies in Honor of Sir Hamilton A. R. Gibb,* edited by F. Makdisi. Leiden: Brill, 1965.

——. "Shi'ism in the Umayyad Period." *Journal of the Royal Asiatic Society* (1960):158–72.

Index

MYSTICISM AND DISSENT

was composed in ten-point VIP Palatino and leaded two points,
with display type in Perpetua by Partners Composition;
printed by sheet-fed offset on 50-pound acid-free Glatfelter Antique Cream,
Smythe-sewn and bound over boards in Joanna Arrestox C,
by Maple-Vail Book Manufacturing Group, Inc.;
and published by

SYRACUSE UNIVERSITY PRESS

SYRACUSE, NEW YORK 13210